THE ULTIMATE

QUEEN

Also by Peter Lewry and Nigel Goodall

The Ultimate Cliff

THE ULTIMATE
QUEEN

PETER LEWRY
& NIGEL GOODALL

SIMON & SCHUSTER
A VIACOM COMPANY

First published in Great Britain by Simon & Schuster Ltd, 1998
A Viacom Company
Copyright © Nigel Goodall and Peter Lewry 1998

The right of Nigel Goodall and Peter Lewry to be identified as authors of this work
has been asserted by them in accordance with the Copyright, Designs and Patents
Act, 1988.

1 3 5 7 9 10 8 6 4 2

Simon & Schuster Ltd
West Garden Place
Kendal Street
London W2 2AQ

Simon & Schuster Australia
Sydney

A CIP catalogue record for this book is available from the British Library
ISBN 0-684-82149-4

Printed and bound in Great Britain by Lego Spa

DEDICATION

For my family and friends.
PL

For my son, Adam, and all those
who appreciate innovative rock music.
NG

CONTENTS

PART 4

COLLECTING QUEEN

PART 5

MISCELLANEA

PREFACE & ACKNOWLEDGEMENTS

Rock history was probably made the day Freddie Mercury, already singing with blues band Wreckage, was introduced to Roger Taylor and Brian May, the founder members of another band called Smile, who with Freddie joining them as their lead vocalist metamorphosed into Queen, and were later joined by fourth member, bassist John Deacon.

EMI Records promptly signed the band and in 1973 their debut album *Queen* was released and hailed as one of the most exciting developments ever in rock music.

Very soon Queen's popularity extended beyond the shores of the UK as they charted and triumphed around Europe, Japan, and the USA where in 1979 they topped the charts with 'Crazy Little Thing Called Love'.

Queen was always indisputedly run as a democratic organisation. All four members are each responsible for having penned number one singles for the band. This massive writing strength combined with spectacular lights, the faultless sound, a sprinkling of theatricality and Freddie's balletic movements made up Queen on stage and on film.

Through Freddie's ability to project himself and the band's music and image to the four corners of 70,000-seater venues, they became known as the prime developers of stadium rock, a reputation perpetuated by their pioneering tactics in South America where they performed to 231,000 fans in São Paulo, a world record at the time.

They also became known as the key innovators of pop videos as their catalogue of three minute clips became more and more adventurous in style, size and content.

Their phenomenal success continued around the globe throughout the eighties highlighted in 1985 by their unforgettable show-stealing performance on stage at Live Aid, and the Wembley Stadium a year later. It's unlikely that another band will ever excite audiences, be as innovative, or sell as many records – now estimated to be over 130 million – as Queen did during their twenty-five-year career. The sales of records and videos have never stopped.

Neither have the books, and although there have probably been more published on Queen than on any other artist or band, never before has any one book contained as much information as the one you are now holding in your hands.

And that was our goal in writing *The Ultimate Queen* – to provide a one-stop reference guide to the most celebrated rock band in the history of popular music. We hope to have acheved it, but of course, in a book of this nature, there is bound to be an occasional mistake or omission, despite our every effort to eliminate such problems with the help of certain people, who also made our task of putting it all together that much easier. We are especially grateful and indebted to Jim Jenkins for sharing his astute knowledge with us, and also to Jacky Smith at the Official International Queen Fan Club. We would also like to thank the many organisations and individuals that provided us with their help and support throughout the project including Queen's manager and lawyer Jim Beach, and the band's designer and photographic archivist Richard Gray for their kind permission to reproduce the numerous record sleeves. Thanks are also due to Queen's publicist, Phil Symes, for all his invaluable help; Tracy Finch at EMI UK; Jane Edwards at Parlophone Records; Kaylee Coxall at the BPI; the RIAA for their help with the Awards section; Andrew King at Omnibus Press; Robert Smith; Sue and Simon Jillett; Nicola Demott; Tony Durrant; Claire Green; Sarah and Steve Moulding for locating some of the more obscure illustrations; Carole Lewry for her endless support (as always); all those who maintain the Queen Internet sites for their often unsung research efforts, and finally our editor's Helen Gummer and Ingrid Connell and Aniz Damani in production.

We are also indebted to several books: *In Session Tonight*, Ken Garner (BBC Books, 1993); *The Guinness Book of Hit Singles*, Paul Gambaccini, Tim Rice, Jonathan Rice, (GRR Publications, 1997); *The Guinness Book of Hit Albums*, Paul Gambaccini, Tim Rice. Jonathan Rice (GRR Publications, 1997); *Rock Family Trees*, Pete Frame (Omnibus, 1993); *Record Collector Rare Record Price Guide 1997/98* (Diamond Publishing Group, 1997); *The Grammys For The Record*, Thomas O'Neil (Penguin Books, 1993); *Good Vibrations – A History Of Record Production*, Mark Cunningham (Castle Communications, 1996); *The Guinness Book Of Rock Stars*, Dafydd Ress & Luke Crampton (Guinness Publishing, 1994, 3rd edition); *The Complete Guide To The Music Of Queen*, Peter K Hogan (Omnibus, 1994); *Queen*, Mick St Michael (Carlton Books, 1995); *Queen In Their Own Words*, Mick St Michael (Omnibus, 1992); *Queen: The New Visual Documentary*, Ken Dean (Omnibus, 1991); *Queen Live: A Concert Documentary*, Greg Brooks (Omnibus, 1995).

We would also like to thank *Record Collector* for their excellent coverage of Queen over the years. All of the following issues we consulted during our research: *Rarities* (No. 69); *Solo & Discographies* (No. 102); *Top 100 Rarities* (No. 110); *Rare Picture Sleeves & Brian May Interview* (No. 114); *Live & Live Discography 1973–79* (No. 118); *On CD* (No. 123); *Live 1980's* (No. 133); *Update & Revised Discography* (No. 139); *Solo Update & Discographies* (No. 144); *Hollywood CD Remasters Review & Freddie Mercury Tribute* (No. 149); *On Video* (No. 154); *Smile, Larry Lurex & Cross & Discographies* (No. 160); *Bohemian Rhapsody* (No. 167); *Remastered* (No. 171); *Japanese Singles* (No. 178); *Collaborations Part 1* (No. 188); *Part 2* (No. 189); *Queen Before Queen Part 1: Brian May* (No. 195); *Part 2: Roger Taylor's Reaction* (No. 196); *Part 3: Smile* (No. 197); *Part 4: John Deacon* (No. 198); *Part 5: Freddie Mercury* (No. 199); *Freddie Mercury Photo Exhibition* (No. 208).

We sincerely thank you all.

(Ian Dickson/Redferns)

A rare studio publicity shot of Roger, Brian, Freddie and John (Richie Aaron/Redferns)

PART 1
INTRODUCING QUEEN

(Richie Aaron/Redferns)

QUOTES
FROM QUEEN

'Freddie was a friend of Tim Staffell's and came along to a lot of our gigs, and offered suggestions in a way that couldn't be refused! At that time, he hadn't really done any singing, and we didn't know he could – we thought he was just a theatrical rock musician.'

– Brian

'I was possibly the one person in the group who could look at it from the outside, because I came in as the fourth person in the band. I knew there was something but I wasn't convinced of it... until possibly the *Sheer Heart Attack* album.'

– John

'For the first two years nothing really happened. We were all studying, but progress in the band was nil. We had great ideas, though, and somehow I think we all felt we'd get through.'

– Roger

'We said okay, we're going to take the plunge into rock and we're really going to do a job at it, no half measures. We all had potentially good careers and we weren't prepared to settle for second best if we were going to abandon all the qualifications we had got in other fields.'

– Freddie

We don't especially go out and play heavy music or light music – it's just our kind of music.'

– Brian

'I'm just a musical prostitute, my dear!'

– Freddie

'We're not a singles group. We don't stake our reputation on singles and we never have done, but I think it's brought in a lot of younger people to our concerts.'

– Brian

'The concept of Queen is to be regal and majestic. Glamour is part of us, and we want to be dandy.'

– Freddie

'I had this idea ... I wanted the sound to sing and have the thickness but yet still have an edge so that it could articulate. So my dad and I designed the guitar ... the one that was made from an old fireplace.'

– Brian

'They wouldn't let us into Russia. They thought we'd corrupt the youth or something.'

– Freddie

'Criticism used to hurt me when I thought it could affect our careers. Nowadays it's all irrelevant. We know the opinions of the people that matter to us, and critics don't fall under that heading.'

– Brian

'It's rubbish to say we were hyped. We started playing the really small gigs and then we released an album. There was no big splash of publicity or anything.'

– Roger

'We'll be the Cecil B. De Mille of rock! Always wanting to do things bigger and better.'

– Freddie

'We're pretty proud of what we've done as a whole. We took chances. Some of the things we did set the world alight, and some didn't. But at least we made our own mistakes. We did what we wanted to do.'

– Brian

'Queen is like a huge rolling machine, and we're not working all the time. I am a musician by profession, that's my whole life, and I didn't want to waste it in easy retirement.'

– Roger

'People have been rumouring that Queen are going to split up for the last eight years at least. I've got some great cuttings at home from people saying "One thing is certain, Queen will no longer exist in a year's time". And that was in 1973.'

– Brian

'The reason we're successful, darling? My overall charisma, of course.'

– Freddie

'We were recording an album next door to The Sex Pistols. One day Sid Vicious stumbled in and yelled at Freddie, "'Ullo Fred, so you've really brought ballet to the masses then?" Freddie just turned round and said "Ah, Mr Ferocious. Well, we're trying our best dear!"'

– Roger

'We've always had our quiet periods and comebacks. I think Live Aid proved we didn't need backdrops or cover of darkness. Geldof called Live Aid a jukebox, so it seemed obvious to us to simply play the hits and get off.'

– Brian

'It was the one day [Live Aid] that I was proud to be involved with the music business. A lot of days you certainly don't feel that! But the day was fabulous, people forgot that element of competitiveness ... it was a good morale-booster for us too, because it showed us the strength of support we had in England, and it showed us what we had to offer as a band.'

– John

'We don't do enough shows these days, and I'd like to do more. I'll remember Live Aid till the day I die.'

– Brian

'I'm so powerful on stage that I seem to have created a monster. When I'm performing I'm an extrovert, yet inside I'm a completely different man.'

– Freddie

'Four weeks of rehearsals is more than we have ever done in our career. I think we are probably the best live band in the world at the moment and we are going to prove it – no one who comes to see us will be disappointed.'

– Roger

'Throughout our career we've been a very non-political group. We enjoy going to new places. We've toured America and Europe so many times that it's nice to go somewhere different. Everybody's been to South Africa, it's not as if we're setting a precedent. Elton John's been there. Rod Stewart, Cliff Richard. I know there can be a bit of a fuss, but apparently we're very popular down there. Basically, we want to play wherever the fans want to see us.'

– John

'I thought up the name Queen ... It's just a name, but it's very regal obviously, and it sounds splendid. It's a strong name, very universal and immediate. It had a lot of visual potential and was open to all sorts of interpretations. I was certainly aware of the gay connotations, but that was just one facet of it.'

– Freddie

'We still have the rock'n'roll gypsy mentality. Even after 12 years without a line-up change we still really enjoy the buzz from playing live and the fact that we have hit singles. Some bands in our position might take it all in their stride, but we're still like kids, we get very excited.'

– Roger

'We're pretty proud of what we've done as a whole. We still really enjoy the buzz from playing live and the fact that we have hit singles. Some bands in our position

(Richie Aaron/Redferns)

might take it all in their stride, but we're still like kids, we get very excited.'

– Roger

'We're pretty proud of what we've done as a whole. We took chances. Some of the things we did set the world alight, and some didn't. But at least we made our own mistakes. We did what we wanted to do.'

– Brian

QUOTES

ABOUT FREDDIE

'No one really knew Freddie. He was shy, gentle and kind. He wasn't the person he put over on stage.'

– Roger

'The first thing I remember about meeting him was that he seemed like a gypsy. He was nominally living with his parents, but stayed with whoever he wanted. He invited me round to his house where he had this little stereo and played some Hendrix. I said, "This guy really makes use of stereo", so we went from one speaker to the other, finding out how he produced those sounds.'

– Brian

'Freddie was one of the elite few who could really set a stadium alight. Along with millions of fans throughout the world, I will miss his exceptional performance and brilliant voice.'

– Francis Rossi

'If I hadn't had Freddie Mercury's lyrics to hold on to as a kid I don't know where I would be. It taught me about all forms of music ... it would open my mind. I never really had a bigger teacher in my whole life.'

– Axl Rose

'Definitely one of the greatest performers that ever lived. His ability to deliver a vocal was second to none.'

– Seal

'For me he represents an era when people were less afraid of living life to the full. This was in the seventies when rock's extravagance went beserk. Perhaps we're not living in that time any more. There's a glorious rebelliousness about it, of freedom attached to it, that represents that whole spirit of rock'n'roll.'

– Annie Lennox

'Quite simply, he was one of the most important figures in rock'n'roll in the past 20 years.'

– Elton John

'There's so few people behind the glamour who really make it as true performers. It's a very strange thoroughbred condition to be a successful musician and still be able to project it with confidence. Freddie had that, and there's not many people who had it.'

– Robert Plant

'Freddie to me was the ultimate performer although I grew up with their music, the thing to me about Freddie was that he was such an all-time great performer, and that's what I liked best about him.'

– Paul Young

'Freddie Mercury was such a big personality. Queen had records out throughout my whole life and it's part of us that everyone's lost.'

– Lisa Stansfield

'He brought operatic grandeur back to rock'n'roll and that encourages us to get symphonic and pretentious on our own.'

– Derek Smalls, Spinal Tap

'His contribution to the world will be everlasting.'

– Dave Clark

'The Freddie we knew wasn't wildly promiscuous or consumed by drugs. He had a responsible attitude to all the people he was close to.'

– Brian

'As far as we are concerned that is it. There is no point carrying on. It is impossible to replace Freddie.'

– John

BAND MEMBER BIOGRAPHIES

FREDDIE MERCURY
LEAD VOCALIST

Freddie in 1984 (Getty Images)

Freddie Mercury was born Faroukh Bulsara on 5 September 1946, in Zanzibar, an island that is now part of Tanzania, to parents Bomi and Jer. Despite his surname and birthplace, Freddie's parents were both British, and as a result Freddie attended boarding school in Panchgani, just outside Bombay in India until he was thirteen, at which time he returned to England. It was while at school that he began to be called Freddie, and where he began his piano lessons, reaching Grade Four in practical and theory. The family with the addition of younger sister, Kashmira, moved to England in 1963. On leaving Isleworth School in 1964 with three O levels and one A level in Art, Freddie entered Ealing College of Art to study Graphic Illustration, where his contemporaries included Peter Townsend of the Who, Ron Wood of The Faces and later, The Rolling Stones, and Roger Ruskin Spear of the Bonzo Dog Doo Dah Band. Freddie graduated in 1969 with a Diploma in Art and Design, equivalent to a degree, and joined his first serious band, Ibex, the same year. Along with his artistic sensibilities, and in common with most art school students of the period, Freddie became intrigued by the possibilities of pop music, and in early bands like Sour Milk Sea and Wreckage, he developed his songwriting, his stage persona, and changed his name to Mercury, reportedly after the Gods' mythological messenger.

Brian and Roger quickly became intrigued with Freddie's ideas, even though Brian was intent on continuing his studies. Freddie's plan was simple – combine the 'heaviness' of Led Zeppelin with a new kind of visual flair.

Outrageousness combined with pop sensibility was a formula that would eventually bring success. We must remember it was a time when David Bowie was still a folk singer with one 'fluke' pop hit, glam and glitter had not yet been invented, and the role model was Mick Jagger who had been camping it for years anyway. All that would change with the launch of Queen, with Freddie as lead vocalist.

'Art School teaches you to be more fashion conscious, to be always one step ahead,' Freddie told his new colleagues. Having attended some of the gigs Smile were playing, Freddie had asked, 'Why are you wasting your time doing this? You should do more original material. You should be more demonstrative in the way that you put the music across. If I was your singer that's what I would be doing!'

Brian and Roger had nevertheless been soured by their experiences with Smile. May had painstakingly built a guitar that was as good, if not better, than anything commercially available, and Freddie had some very definite ideas about presentation. All of them were intelligent and qualified individuals who could easily have found well-paid careers in the 'real world', but if they were to form a rock group, they seriously intended to make a success of it, and to do that, they would, throughout 1970, rehearse, write and hone their material, playing only at friends' parties.

BRIAN MAY
GUITARTIST

Brian Harold May was born on 19 July 1947 in Hampton, Middlesex, to parents Harold and Ruth. He started school in 1952 at Cardinal Road Infants, and later went to Hanworth Road Primary in Feltham, before winning a scholarship to enter Hampton Grammar School, where he discovered his interest in astronomy, and also became musically inspired by such names as Lonnie Donegan, The Shadows, The Ventures and Buddy Holly. He began playing guitar in various local bands from the age of fifteen, though most of the groups he was involved with never really made it past the stage of rehearsing in a garage. 'None of these groups really got anywhere because we never played any real gigs or took it that seriously', says May.

Among his contemporaries at Hampton Grammar, though, was a group called the Others, who released a version of 'Oh Yeah' in 1964, and because of Brian's reputation for jamming with anyone who would play, there were untrue rumours that he too was a member of the group. The Others enjoyed their brief moment of glory with one more single as the Sands, then disbanded soon after, just as

Brian live on stage (Mick Hutson/Redferns)

Brian started to build an electric guitar of his own design.

Unable to afford the Fender Stratocaster he coveted, Brian set about designing and building his own personal guitar with the aid of his father. Both were experienced in wood and metal work, and Brian himself was already a star physics student, so the task was probably not as difficult as it sounded, though the choice of materials did seem a little odd. The body of the guitar was solid mahogany, carved from the surround of a 200-year-old fireplace, and the springs of the tremelo unit were salvaged from an old motorbike! But despite being homemade, Brian's 'fireplace' guitar was eventually to make rock history as the one played on most of Queen's hit recordings, and is in fact the one Brian favours to play both on stage and in the studio to this day. A guitar that in material terms cost no more than eight pounds!

Brian left school in 1966 with eleven O levels and four A levels in Science, and a year later enrolled on a degree course in Physics at Imperial College in London where he eventually achieved a BSc Honours degree in Physics and Maths. Although he began work on a thesis to obtain a doctorate, having decided that he could combine his studies with music, he never completed it. He placed a hand-written note on the college noticeboard inviting other students and budding musicians to join him in forming a college band. The first to respond was bassist and vocalist Tim Staffell, and a drummer named Roger Taylor. 'We thought he was the best drummer we'd ever seen. I watched him tuning a snare – something I'd never seen done before – and I remember thinking how professional he looked.'

ROGER TAYLOR
DRUMMER

Roger Taylor was born Roger Meddows-Taylor on 26 July 1949 in Kings Lynn, Norfolk to parents Michael and Winnifred Meddows-Taylor. When Roger was eight, the family with younger sister Clare, moved to Truro in Cornwall and Roger was enrolled at Truro Cathedral School, where he joined the school choir and learnt to play the ukulele. He moved to Truro Public School three years later learning first the guitar and then, a year later, teaching himself the drums. His musical ambitions were frustrated by parental disapproval during his teenage years, though he did manage to join up and play with various local groups, first as a guitarist, then on drums and vocals.

Roger left school in 1967 with seven O levels and three A levels, and conceding to his family's wish that he pursue a serious career, moved to London to study as a dental student at the London Hospital Medical School and the Hospital Medical School in Whitechapel. A year later, he switched courses to study Biology at North London Polytechnic, leaving with a BSc.

In 1968 Roger joined Smile, the group that Brian and Tim Staffell had started at Imperial College, which quickly attracted a loyal following – the hardcore of which were undoubtedly fellow students at Imperial – on the London pub and college circuits. Despite their studies, the three young members of Smile were serious about developing their musical careers. But their inexperience of the music business resulted in signing a contract that was far from ideal. Mercury Records, at that time, was an American label with no real base in the UK other than a distribution arrangement, and they signed Smile on a one-off deal that took them into the recording studios with producer John Anthony. The resulting session was a single called 'Earth', a Tim Staffell song, backed with 'Step On Me', a May-Staffell collaboration. The disc did absolutely nothing, largely because it was released in the US with no group or record company support, and consequently, the lack of sales action in the States prevented the single from being released in the UK. Smile were quietly dropped from the label.

The disappointment of the poor sales performance and lack of release in Britain probably caused Tim Staffell to drift away from the others to pursue solo plans that for one reason or another never reached fruition. Reports indicate that although Smile's material was well suited to the time – some of which was to surface later on the first two Queen albums – Staffell's voice may not have adapted to the changing styles over the years in the way that his replacement's was able to do so well.

By the summer of 1969, Brian, feeling somewhat depressed, found employment teaching mathematics at a comprehensive school in London, uncertain whether to pursue his research studies. Tim Staffell, in the meantime, continued to pursue a music career forming a new band called Humpy Bong for which he became lead vocalist. Meanwhile, Staffell's flatmate, also a vocalist, joined Roger in running a second-hand clothes stall in Kensington Market. He was an ex-Art student with very definite ideas about how to run a pop group.

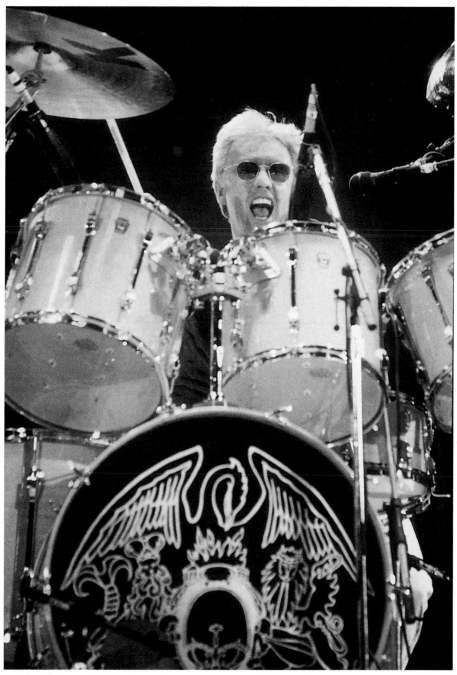

(Mick Hutson/Redferns)

JOHN DEACON
BASSIST

John Deacon was born in Oadby, Leicestershire on 19 August 1951 to parents Arthur Henry and Lilian. He attended Oadby Infants School from 1956, before moving onto Gartree High School, and later, Beauchamp Grammar. He did the usual round of teenage local groups before coming to London, where he was studying Electronics, and obtained his first class honours degree six months after joining Queen. His first musical instrument was the rhythm guitar before he learned to play bass and joined up with his first band called the Opposition. His first gig was at Enderby Youth Club in Leicester.

John left school in 1969 with eight O levels and three A levels to attend Chelsea College in London where he studied Electronics, eventually achieving two S levels in Physics and Maths, and a First Class Honours degree in Electronics, and despite being a few years younger, John quickly meshed with Brian, Roger and Freddie. 'We just knew he was the right one, even though he was so quiet. He hardly spoke to us at all,' Brian reflected later.

In the meantime, Freddie designed a logo for the group using their birth signs as inspiration, and with the addition of bassist John Deacon, the band became the quartet which the rock world would soon recognise as one of the industry's most durable rock bands. 'I was possibly the one person in the group who could look at it from the outside,' remarked John, 'because I came in as the fourth person in the band. I knew there was something there but I wasn't convinced of it ... until possibly the *Sheer Heart Attack* album.'

(Corbis)

BANDS BEFORE AND AFTER QUEEN

In this section we have listed all the bands that Queen members played in, before and after Queen.

Freddie

1959–1961:	The Hectics
1969–1969:	Ibex
1969–1969:	Wreckage
1970–1970:	Sour Milk Sea
1970–1991:	Queen

Brian

1964–1968:	1984
1968–1970:	Smile
1970–1991:	Queen
1992–to date:	The Brian May Band

Roger

1957–1957:	The Bubblingover Boys
1963–1964:	The Cousin Jacks
1964–1964:	Beat Unlimited
1964–1965:	The Falcons
1965–1965:	Johnny Quale & The Reactions
1965–1968:	The Reaction/Reaction
1968–1970:	Smile
1970–1991:	Queen
1987–1993:	The Cross
1994–to date:	The Roger Taylor Band

John

1965–1968:	The Opposition/The New Opposition
1968–1969:	Art
1970–1970:	Deacon
1971–1991:	Queen
1986–1986:	The Immortals

An early shot of Queen. Left to right: Roger, John, Freddie and Brian (S&G/Redferns)

THE BAND A–Z

A

Abbey, Peter – Dental student from Roger's college who became the manager of Brian and Roger's band Smile in 1968.

Ahwai, Robert – Founder member of John's band the Immortals.

Airy, Don – Played keyboard on 'Resurrection' and 'Nothing But Blue' (see also Other Musicians On Queen Records).

Andrews, Bernie – Produced the first live BBC radio sessions for Queen in 1973, and also the session in December of the same year.

Anthem Records – American-based record label that released Freddie's (as Larry Lurex) recording of the Beach Boys hit 'I Can Hear Music'.

Anthony, John – John first worked with Brian and Roger on the Smile recording sessions at Trident studios in June 1969, and later on the *Queen* album sessions in 1971 (see also Other Musicians On Queen Records).

Anvil – Engineered all the soundtrack recordings for the film *Flash Gordon*.

Aris, Brian – Photographer.

Armatrading, Joan – Vocalist who provided backing vocals on 'Don't Lose Your Head' (see also Other Musicians On Queen Records).

Aspel, Michael – TV presenter host of *This is Your Life* who presented Queen with their 25 Year Best Single award for 'Bohemian Rhapsody'.

Austin, Louie – Produced one track 'The Night Comes Down', for the *Queen* album in 1971.

Austin, Mary – Freddie's long time friend who inherited the majority of his estate after his death.

Air Apparent Inc. – US travel company who worked on Queen's Magic Tour in 1986.

B

Bailey, David – Photographer.

Baker, Roy Thomas – Producer and sound engineer who worked on numerous Queen album sessions including *Queen, Sheer Heart Attack, A Night At The Opera*, and *Jazz*.

Banks, Peter – Played synthesiser on 'In My Defence' (see also Other Musicians On Queen Records).

Barnett, Jimmy – Lighting engineer.

Bart, Pete – Later guitarist and vocalist with John's first group the Opposition. Had previously played with local band the Rapids Rave.

Battersby, Neil – Road manager for the Reaction, the group for which Roger was drummer.

Batty, Bob – Lighting technician.

Bawden, Peter John – Ex-guitarist with Cornish band the Staggerlees, and founder owner of PJs Discotheque in Truro who booked Brian and Roger's band Smile and billed them as Queen for the first time.

Beach, Jim – Queen's manager and lawyer since 1984, who also headed Queen Productions Ltd.

Begrand, Dominique Marie – Roger's wife whom he married in 1988 at Kensington Registry Office.

Beiriger, Mike – Second engineer on *The Works* album sessions.

Bell, Madeleine – Backing vocalist on 'The Golden Boy' (see also Other Musicians On Queen Records).

Benjamins, Steve – Drum technician and piano tuner.

Bennett, Roy – Lighting designer on Queen's Magic Tour in 1986.

Bishop, Debbie – Provided backing vocals on 'The Golden Boy' (see also Other Musicians On Queen Records).

Bloom, Amanda – Fan club secretary from 1978 to 1979.

Bowie, David – Rockstar, singer/songwriter who with Queen co-produced their duet together, 'Under Pressure', and also provided backing vocals on the unissued cut of 'Cool Cats' (see also Other Musicians On Queen Records). David also performed 'Under Pressure' with former Eurythmics vocalist Annie Lennox at the Freddie Mercury Concert staged at Wembley Stadium in April 1992.

Boxhall, Charlie – Keyboard and bass technician.

Bradfield, Andrew – One of the engineers who worked on *The Miracle* album sessions.

Bradley, Stuart – Bass player with the Roger Taylor Band.

Brainsby, Tony – Queen's publicist between 1973 and 1977.

Bray Studios – Former film studio that rented out one of their stages for rehearsals for the Freddie Mercury Tribute Concert.

Bridenthal, Bryn – Queen's US publicist since 1973.

Brokenshaw, Roger – Vocalist enlisted to replace Johnny Quale in the Reactions for whom Roger was drummer.

Brooks, Greg – Avid Queen collector for twenty years and known expert on the band who has contributed articles to *Record Collector* magazine, and author of the highly acclaimed *Queen Live – A Concert Documentary* (see also Books On Queen).

Brough, John – Sound engineer on numerous live recordings including those done for German radio in 1986, the Live At Wembley 86 concert for BBC Radio, the video taping of the 1987 Budapest concerts as well as the *Live Magic* set recorded at Knebworth. John was also one of the engineers on *The Miracle* album sessions.

Brown, Errol – Lead vocalist with Hot Chocolate who recorded a session with John in 1986.

Brown, Peter – Queen's personal assistant between 1975 and 1977.

Bullen, Nigel – Drummer with John's first band, the Opposition.

Burt, Jo – Played bass on 'Man Made Paradise' (also see Other Musicians On Queen Records).

Bush, Mel – Tour promoter who has been promoting concerts since 1960 working with such acts as the Eagles, the Beach Boys, Paul McCartney, Led Zeppelin, David Essex and Cliff Richard. He first worked with Queen in 1974, and continued to promote their tours in subsequent years.

C

Caballe, Montserrat – Spanish opera singer who recorded an album of duets with Freddie in 1987.

Cable, Robin Geoffrey – One of the producers on the second set of Queen's live radio sessions for the BBC in 1973. Was also staff engineer and producer at Trident studios who recorded Freddie's version of the Beach Boys hit 'I Can Hear Music', released as recorded by Larry Lurex.

Capitol Records – Queen's US record label between 1984 and 1989.

Castle, Barry – Played horns on 'Barcelona', Freddie's duet with Montserrat Caballe (see also Other Musicians On Queen Records).

Freddie with Montserrat Caballe (George Chin/Redferns)

Brian with girlfriend and former *Eastender's* actress, Anita Dobson (George Chin/Redferns)

Castledine, Clive – Schoolfriend and original bass player with John's first band, the Opposition.

Caswell, Mike – Guitarist with the Brian May Band.

Chant, Peter – Administrator of the Mercury-Phoenix Trust. Also Queen's accountant.

Chen, Phil – Bass player who worked on Brian's *Starfleet* sessions at LA's Record Plant in 1983 (see also Other Musicians On Queen Records).

Chester, Ron – Guitarist with John's first group the Opposition. Had previously played with the Outer Limits.

Chiasson, Roger – Illustrator.

Christie, John – Backing vocalist on 'Time' (also see Other Musicians On Queen Records).

Clair Brothers Audio – Tour sound.

Clair, Roy Barry – Sound technician.

Clark, Dave – Close friend of Freddie's, and former drummer with the Dave Clark Five, who went on to produce the West End musical 'Time' with Cliff Richard.

Freddie recorded three tracks for the original soundtrack album.

Coerten, Paul – Photographer.

Collins, John – Piano tuner and keyboard and bass technician.

Cooke, Simon - Merchandiser at Firstflame Ltd for Queen's Magic Tour in 1986.

Cooper, Angelique – One of the engineers who worked on *The Miracle* album sessions.

Cowan Symes & Associates – Public relations company who have worked for Queen since 1992.

Craven, Jim – Bass player with Johnny Quale and the Reactions. Roger was enlisted to join as their drummer in early 1965.

Cregan, Jim – Played guitar on 'Foreign Sand' and 'Final Destination' (see also Other Musicians On Queen Records).

Croft, Brian – Pre-production co-ordinator on Queen's Magic Tour in 1986.

Crossley, Michael – Keyboard player with the Roger Taylor Band (see also Other Musicians On Queen Records).

Cress, Curt – Drummer on Freddie's *Mr Bad Guy* album (see also Other Musicians On Queen Records).

D

Daltrey, Roger – Who vocalist who performed Queen's 'I Want It All' at the Freddie Mercury Tribute Concert on 20 April 1992 at Wembley Stadium.

Daniel, Geoff – Guitarist who replaced Graham Hankins in the Reactions while Roger was drummer.

Davidson, Alan – Photographer.

Devenney, Jim – Sound monitor on Queen's Magic Tour in 1986.

Dickinson, Bruce – Iron Maiden vocalist who collaborated with Brian on the track 'Smoke On The Water', released as a single and credited to Rock Aid Armenia.

Dilloway, Dave – Brian's schoolfriend, first musical collaborator, and founder member of Brian's first group, 1984.

Dobson, Anita – Former *EastEnders* actress who became romantically involved with Brian in 1986, and has remained his girlfriend ever since.

Dolezal, Rudi – Video director who co-produced and co-directed *The Queen Phenomenon* for Channel 4.

Dowding, David – Bass player with Roger's first instrumental trio Beat Unlimited, later renamed the Cousins Jack.

Dudley, Mike – Classmate and lead guitarist with Roger's first instrumental trio Beat Unlimited, later renamed the Cousins Jack, and who later joined Johnny Quale and the Reactions as the group's keyboard player and archivist.

Dugmore, Geoff – Drummer on 'Let Your Heart Rule' and 'Rolling Over' (see also Other Musicians On Queen Records).

E

Edmunds, Pete – Road manager for Brian and Roger's band Smile.

Edney, Spike – Keyboard player and Queen sideman who also played with the Brian May Band, and Roger's band the Cross.

Edwin Shirley Company – Trucking company used on tours.

Elektra Records – US record label that released Queen's singles and albums in America and Japan up to 1984.

Ellington, Lance – Backing vocalist on 'The Golden Boy' (see also Other Musicians On Queen Records).

EMI Records – UK record company that signed Queen to their label.

Espley, Alan – Lighting technician.

Etchells, John – Engineer who worked on the first and second live BBC radio sessions for Queen in 1973, and later on the *Live Killers* concert recordings in 1979.

Everett, Kenny – Close friend of Freddie's, disc jockey and television personality who was the first to play 'Bohemian Rhapsody' on radio. He died in 1995.

Everitt, Vicki – Fan club secretary from 1980 to 1982.

F

Fallon, Jason – Guitarist and vocalist with the Roger Taylor Band (see also Other Musicians On Queen Records).

Fannelli, Joe – Band assistant and co-ordinator.

Farnell, Christine – Mutual friend who introduced John to Brian and Roger at Maria Assumpta Teacher Training College in early 1971.

Firstflame Ltd – Merchandising company utilised for Queen's Magic Tour in 1986.

Fisher, Morgan – Keyboard player.

Foehlinger, Tom – Sound technician.

Forrester, Guy – Lighting technician.

Fowler, Simon – Photographer.

Franks, Mike – Producer who worked on the Queen live sessions for BBC Radio in December 1973.

Freestone, Peter – Administrative staff member at Queen Productions and band's personal assistant.

Fryer, Fritz – Produced the Smile tracks recorded at De Lane Lea studios in Wembley with the idea of completing an album for the American based Mercury record label.

G

Gallagher, Sally – Administrative staff member at Queen Productions Ltd who now runs Roger's management company.

Gamage, Chuck – Illustrator.

Garnham, John – Original bass player in Brian's first band, 1984.

Geldof, Bob – Boomtown Rats vocalist who organised the 'Live Aid' concert at Wembley Stadium in 1985

Gibb, Andy – Singer and younger brother of Bee Gees Maurice, Barry and Robin who provided vocals on the track 'Play The Game' in 1979 (see also Other Musicians On Queen Records).

Giddings, Terry – Security for Queen on tour.

Gillian, Ian – Deep Purple vocalist who collaborated with Brian on 'Smoke On The Water' single, released as Rock Aid Armenia in 1989.

Glover, Julie – Former secretary at Queen Productions, and later production manager with Brian.

Glover, Neil – Drum technician.

GLS Productions – Tour management company headed by Gerry Stickells and used by Queen.

Gore, Wally – Security for Queen on tour.

Griffin, Jeff – One of the producers for the second set of Queen's live sessions at the BBC in 1973.

Griffiths, Nick – Engineer who worked on the December 1973 live sessions for BBC Radio.

Grose, Johnny – Lead named vocalist with Johnny Quale and the Reactions. Roger was enlisted as the group's drummer in early 1965.

Groves, Martin – Studio equipment co-ordinator for the *Queen Rocks* album.

Goldsmith, Harvey – Tour promoter who first became involved with promoting Queen concerts from 1977 onwards as well as presenting the individual solo concerts by Freddie, Brian and Roger.

Gower, Bruce – Director of the innovative 'Bohemian Rhapsody' promotional video that introduced a new era in the music industry whereby videos would be used to promote records.

Gratzer, Alan – REO Speedwagon drummer who played on Brian's *Starfleet* Record Plant sessions in 1983 (see also Other Musicians On Queen Records).

Gray, Richard – Queen's designer and photographic archivist.

Gregory, Steve – Played saxophone on 'One Year Of Love' (see also Other Musicians On Queen Records).

Grosse, Mike – Temporary bass player with Queen in 1970.

Gunn, Jacky – Fan club secretary, now married as Jacky Smith, and co-author with Jim Jenkins of the official Queen biography *As It Began*.

H

Hale & Pace – Television comedy duo who recorded 'The Stonk' with Brian and Roger co-writing and co-producing.

Hammerton, Pete – Schoolfriend and guitarist/vocalist who played live with Brian in late 1965 at Shepperton Rowing Club.

Hankins, Graham – Guitarist with Johnny Quale and the Reactions.

Harris, Anoel – One of the engineers who worked on the *Innuendo* album sessions.

Hasebe, Koh – Photographer.

Hentschel, David – One of the engineers who worked on the *Queen* album sessions in 1971.

Hill, Dave – Vari-lites technician.

Hince, Peter – Keyboard and bass technician, and photographer.

Hodkinson, Mark – Author of the acclaimed book on Queen, *Early Years* (see also Books About Queen).

Hollywood Records – US record label owned by the Disney company who have released all of Queen's albums since *Innuendo*, and released the entire Queen back catalogue in the States, as well as Brian's and Roger's solo albums.

Holsten, Jack – Managing director of the US label Elektra who released all of Queen's singles and albums in America and Japan up to 1984.

Hopkins, Adrian – Merchandiser of official Queen memorabilia.

Howe, Steve – Played Spanish guitar on *Innuendo* (see also Other Musicians On Queen Records).

Humphries, Patrick – Wrote the text for Queen's Magic Tour brochure in 1986.

Hyland, Brendan – Security for Queen on tour.

J

Jackson, Laura – Author of two books, *Queen & I: The Brian May Story* and *Mercury – The King Of Queen* (see also Books About Queen).

Jarvis, Graham – Drummer on *In My Defence* (see also Other Musicians On Queen Records).

James, David – Photographer.

Jenkins, Jim – One of the most knowledgeable authorities on Queen, and also co-author with Jacky Gunn (now Jacky Smith) of the official Queen biography *As It Began* (see also Books About Queen).

John, Elton – Singer and songwriter who performed Queen's 'Bohemian Rhapsody' with Guns N' Roses vocalist Axl Rose at the Freddie Mercury Concert in April 1992 at Wembley Stadium.

Johnson, Magic – Founder of the Magic Johnson Foundation who received a cheque for $300,000 from Brian and Roger for AIDS Research at the MTV Awards in 1992.

Johnston, Deborah Ann – Played cello on the Freddie and Montserrat Caballe duet 'Barcelona' (see also Other Musicians On Queen Records).

Johnstone, Pat – Joint fan club secretary from 1974 to 1976.

Johnstone, Sue – Joint fan club secretary from 1974 to 1976.

K

Kanga, Homi – Violin player on the Freddie and Montserrat Caballe duet 'Barcelona' (see also Other Musicians On Queen Records).

Khalaf, James 'Trip' – Worked on various live recordings that included co-producing the live session for German radio in 1986, the Live At Wembley concert in 1986 for BBC Radio, and the Budapest concerts in 1987 as well as the *Live Magic* set.

Kimpton Walker Ltd – Set constructors for Queen's Magic Tour in 1986.

L

Leibman, Helen – Played cello on 'Baby It's Alright' and 'Life Changes' (see also Other Musicians On Queen Records).

Leigh-White, Rebecca – Provided backing vocals on 'Let Me Live' (see also Other Musicians On Queen Records).

Lennox, Annie – Former Eurythmics vocalist who performed 'Under Pressure' with David Bowie at the Freddie Mercury Tribute Concert at Wembley Stadium in April 1992.

Levine, Barry – Photographer.

Lewis, Laurie – Played violin on Freddie's and Montserrat Caballe's duet 'Barcelona' (see also Other Musicians On Queen Records).

Louthe, Bill – Sound technician.

Lycett, Chris – One of the producers on the second set of Queen's live radio sessions for the BBC in 1973.

Lyona, Gary – Second engineer who worked on *A Night At The Opera* album sessions in 1975.

M

Mack – Engineer and co-producer of numerous Queen albums including *The Game, Flash Gordon, Hot Space, The Works, A Kind Of Magic* and *Made In Heaven* (see also Other Musicians On Queen Records).

Macrae, Josh – Drummer with Roger's band the Cross. Also worked as one of the engineers on Queen's *Made In Heaven* album (see also Other Musicians On Queen Records).

Malandrone, Peter – Studio equipment co-ordinator for the *Queen Rocks* album released in 1997.

Mallet, David – Video director.

Mandel, Fred – Keyboard player who worked on Brian's *Starfleet* recording session at LA's Record Plant in 1983, as well as playing piano on Queen's 'Man On The Prowl', synths on 'I Want To Break Free', and 'Radio Ga Ga' (see also Other Musicians On Queen Records).

Manor Mobile Ltd – Live remote recording unit used on Queen's Magic Tour in 1986.

Marks, Michael – Photographer.

Martin, Arif – Played horns on 'Staying Power' for the *Hot Space* album (see also Other Musicians On Queen Records).

Martin, Gary – Provided backing vocals on 'Let Me Live' (see also Other Musicians On Queen Records).

Marvin, Hank – Shadows guitarist who recorded an instrumental version of Queen's 'We Are The Champions' with Brian in 1992.

Marx, Dick – Provided string arrangement on 'Foreign Sand' and 'Final Destination' (see also Other Musicians On Queen Records).

Mason, Andy – One of the engineers who worked on *The Miracle* album sessions.

Matthews, Neil – Photographer.

May, Harold – Brian's father who helped him construct the world's most famous home made guitar, the 'Red Special'.

McCall, Ross – Teen Freddie Mercury lookalike who was seen in *The Miracle* video and on *The Queen Phenomenon* on Channel 4.

Meade, Roxy – Queen's publicist from 1988 to 1992.

Menon, Bhaskar – Former president of Queen's UK and US record labels EMI and Capitol.

Menzies, Donal – Merchandiser at Firstflame Ltd for the Queen Magic Tour in 1986.

Mercury Records – The American-owned label who signed Brian and Roger's band Smile to their one and only record deal in 1969.

Metcalfe, Kevin – Mastering engineer of the *Queen Rocks* album released in 1997.

Meyer, Ann – Administrator for the Mercury Phoenix Trust.

Michael, George – Former Wham vocalist who performed 'These Are The Days Of Our Lives' with Lisa

(Suzi Gibbons/Redferns)

Stansfield, and 'Somebody To Love' with Queen at the Freddie Mercury Tribute Concert in April 1992 at Wembley Stadium. The performance with Queen was later released on the *Five Live* EP which gave rise to rumours that George Michael and Queen were coming together to form a new line-up with him as vocalist.

Minelli, Liza – Judy Garland's daughter and singer who performed 'We Are The Champions' at the Freddie Mercury Concert in April 1992 at Wembley Stadium.

Mitchell, Barry – Temporary bass player with Queen in 1970.

Moles, Steve – Lighting technician.

Moran, Mike – Played piano on 'All God's People' during the *Innuendo* album sessions (see also Other Musicians On Queen Records).

Morgan, Brett – Played drums on the album of Dave Clark's West End musical *Time* for which Freddie contributed three tracks (see also Musicians On Queen Records).

Moroder, Giorgio – Played keyboards on Freddie's 'Love Kills' (see also Other Musicians On Queen Records).

Moses, Jamie – Guitarist and vocalist with the Brian May Band.

Moss, Clayton – Lead guitarist and vocalist with Roger's band the Cross.

Mott, Gerry – Lighting technician.

Mullen, Chrissie – Brian's wife. They married at St Osmunds Church, Castelnau in Barnes on 29 May 1976.

Muller, Clare – Photographer.

Murray, Neil – Bass player with the Brian May Band (see also Other Musicians On Queen Records).

Myers, Mike – American actor who had a leading role in the movie *Wayne's World*, and who received a letter from Queen thanking him for using 'Bohemian Rhapsody' in the film.

N

Naiff, Lynton – Played strings on 'One Year Of Love' (see also Other Musicians On Queen Records).

Nail, Jimmy – Actor and singer whose hit single 'Love Don't Live Here Anymore' was produced by Roger.

Nelson, Jack – US A&R man who negotiated deal with EMI for Queen, and became co-manager of the band with Dave Thomas.

Noone, Peter – Bass player and backing vocalist with Roger's band the Cross. Not the same Peter Noone as the Herman's Hermit.

O

O'Brien, Rick – Production and stage manager with Queen on tour.

O'Donovan, Gill – Backing vocalist for Roger's band the Cross during their 1988 tour (see also Other Musicians On Queen Records).

O'List, Suzie – Backing vocalist on the *Shove It* album (see also Other Musicians On Queen Records).

O'Neil, Terry – Photographer.

O'Regan, Denis – Photographer.

Outer Limits – Merchandiser of *Queen Rocks* memorabilia.

P

Parfitt, Rick – Status Quo guitarist and vocalist who played guitar on 'It's An Illusion' (see also Other Musicians On Queen Records).

Parlophone Records – Queen's current UK record label that is owned by the EMI group.

Pask, Andy – Played bass on Queen's 'In My Defence' (see also Other Musicians On Queen Records).

Pavarotti, Luciano – Opera singer who organised a benefit concert in his Modena, Italy, horse stables for leukemia patients in 1992 with Brian among those performing to raise money.

Penrose, Ricky – Bass player who replaced Jim Craven in the Reactions while Roger was playing drums for them.

Perez, Lisa – Singer who was backed by Brian, Dave Dilloway, John Garnham, and Richard Thompson during a 'Battle Of The Bands' competition at the Top Rank Club in Croydon.

Phillips, Tim – Lighting technician.

Pickard, Therese – Fan club secretary from 1976 to 1978.

Picture Music International (PMI) – The video division of EMI Records which released most of Queen's commercial videos.

Plant, Robert – Led Zeppelin vocalist who collaborated with Brian on the 'Smoke On the Water' single, released as Rock Aid Armenia in 1989.

Planview Inc – Set designers who worked on Queen's Magic Tour in 1986.

Porter, Cathy – Backing vocalist with the Brian May Band. Also provided backing vocals on Queen's 'Let Me Live' (see also Other Musicians On Queen Records).

Powell, Cozy – Drummer with the Brian May Band (see also Other Musicians On Queen Records).

Prenter, Paul – Queen's manager between 1980 and 1984.

Preston, Shelley – Backing vocalist with the Brian May Band. Previously with Bucks Fizz as Jay Aston's replacement.

Preston, Neal – Photographer.

Pryce, Larry – Author of the first official biography published in 1976 (see also Books About Queen).

Pudifoot, Douglas – Photographer who took stills and also shot a three minute black-and-white 8mm home movie of Brian and Roger's band Smile at London's Royal Albert Hall in 1969.

Q

Quale, Johnny – Vocalist with Johnny Quale and the Reactions, a beat group Roger was enlisted into as drummer in 1966.

Queen Productions Ltd – Management company for the band headed by their manager and lawyer Jim Beach.

R

Reid, John – Elton John's manager who was signed as Queen's manager from 1975 to 1977.

Reizner, Lou – A&R man for the American-based Mercury record label who signed Brian and Roger's band Smile to a one-off single deal.

Rhodes, Zandra – Clothes designer for Queen between 1972 and 1975.

Richard, Cliff – Britain's longest lasting musical entertainer with hit singles scattered across five decades, who also appeared in Dave Clark's musical *Time*. Freddie contributed three tracks for the soundtrack album.

Richardson, Geoffrey – Played violin and viola on 'Baby It's Alright' and 'Life Changes' (see also Other Musicians On Queen Records).

Ricotti, Frank – Played percussion on the Freddie and Montserrat Caballe duet 'Barcelona' (see also Other Musicians On Queen Records).

Richards, David – Second engineer who worked on the 1979 *Live Killers* set and as co-producer on *A Kind Of Magic*, *The Miracle*, *Innuendo*, and *Made In Heaven* albums (see also Other Musicians On Queen Records).

Rider, Claude – One of the engineers who worked on *The Miracle* album sessions.

Rochford, Damien – Illustrator for the *Queen Rocks* album released in 1997.

Rock, Mick – Photographer and author of *A Photographic Record 1969-1980* published in 1985 (see also Books On Queen).

Rock It Cargo – Freight forwarders on Queen's Magic Tour in 1986.

Roger, Susan – Remixed 'Body Language' for the Hollywood Records reissue.

Rohsler, Peter – Photographer.

Rondo Promotions – Agency to which Brian and Roger's band Smile were signed.

Rose, Axl – Guns N' Roses vocalist who performed 'Bohemian Rhapsody' with Elton John at the Freddie Mercury Tribute Concert in April 1992 at Wembley Stadium.

Ross, Jonathan – TV presenter who presented Queen with ITV's 'Top Band Of The Eighties' Award on Cilla Black's *Goodbye To The Eighties* TV show in 1989.

Rossacher, Hannes – Video director.

Rue, Harold – US tour promoter.

Russell, Ray – Played guitar on 'Time' (see also Other Musicians On Queen Records).

Ryder, Maggie – Backing vocalist with the Brian May Band (see also Other Musicians On Queen Records).

S

Seal – Singer who performed Queen's 'Who Wants To Live Forever' at the Freddie Mercury Concert on 20 April 1992 at Wembley Stadium.

Seymour, Jane – Actress who appeared with Freddie at the Fashion Aid Charity Show in 1985.

Sharpe, Ted – One of the engineers who worked on the *Queen* album sessions at Trident studios in 1971.

Sheffield, Barry – Former co-owner of Trident Audio Productions and Studios where Queen made their first recordings.

Sheffield, Norman – Former co-owner of Trident Audio Productions and Studios where Queen made their first recordings.

Shirley-Smith, Justin – One of the engineers who worked on *The Miracle*, *Innuendo*, and *Made In Heaven* album sessions.

Smith, Chris – Keyboard player with Brian and Roger's band Smile for a brief period.

Smith, Mike – Illustrator who worked on Queen's Magic Tour brochure in 1986.

Snell, John 'Acker' – Acker Bilk devotee and saxophone player with Johnny Quale and the Reactions.

Spalding, Phil – Played bass on 'Revelation', 'The Key' and 'Old Friends' (see also Other Musicians On Queen Records).

Staffell, Tim – Harmonica player and vocalist with Brian's first band, 1984, before forming Smile with Brian in 1968 in which he was the bass player and vocalist.

Stansfield, Lisa – Singer who performed Queen's 'These Are The Days Of Our Lives' with George Michael at the Freddie Mercury Tribute Concert on 20 April 1992 at Wembley Stadium.

Stevens, Shakin' – Britain's most successful recording artist of the eighties whose hit single 'Radio' featured Roger on drums.

Stickells, Gerry – Queen's tour manager since 1976 as well as being tour manager on solo tours by Freddie, Brian and Roger.

Stockley, Miriam – Backing vocalist with the Brian May Band. Also provided the backing vocals on Queen's 'Let Me Live' (see also Other Musicians On Queen Records).

Stoddart, Peter – Flatmate and guitarist who formed the R&B quartet 'Deacon' with John in 1971 for a 'one-only' gig at Chelsea College.

Stone, Mike – Engineer who worked on numerous album sessions including *Queen*, *Queen II*, *Sheer Heart Attack*, *A Night At The Opera*, *A Day At The Races*, and *News Of The World*. Mike also provided backing vocals

on the track 'Good Old Fashioned Lover Boy' (see also Other Musicians On Queen Records).

Straker, Peter – Backing vocalist on 'Time' and 'The Golden Boy' (see also Other Musicians On Queen Records).

T

Taylor, Chris – Queen's tour co-ordinator.

Taylor, Elizabeth – Actress who appeared at the Freddie Mercury Tribute Concert in April 1992 at Wembley Stadium to give a moving speech about AIDS Awareness.

Testi, Ken – Manager of Freddie's pre-Queen group Ibex, and Queen's first manager from 1970 to 1972.

Tetslaff, Veronica – John's wife whom he married at the Carmelite Church in Kensington Church Street on 18 January 1975.

Thomas, Dave – Queen's former co-manager between 1971 and 1975.

Thompson, Chris – Provided vocals and backing vocals on 'Rollin' Over'. Was also backing vocalist on early Brian May gigs (see also Other Musicians On Queen Records).

Thompson, Richard – Founder member of Brian's first group, 1984.

Thorning, Rick – Bass player who replaced Ricky Penrose in the Reaction, the group for which Roger was drummer.

Tibbs, Gary – Bass player on 'Back To The Light', 'Let Your Heart Rule Your Head', and 'Rolling Over' (see also Other Musicians On Queen Records).

Toad In The Hole – Tour caterers.

Tomkins, Derek – Engineered three demo tracks by John's second group, Art, at Beck's studio in Northamptonshire.

Trax – London soul group who recorded a session of material at Trident studios with Freddie, Roger and Brian.

Trident Audio Productions – Studio that signed Queen to a production, publishing and management deal, and where the band recorded their debut album *Queen*.

Trinifold Travel Ltd – Tour travel company that worked on Queen's Magic Tour in 1986.

Tutchener, Simon – Lighting director.

V

Van Halen, Eddie – Van Halen guitarist who played on Brian's *Starfleet* sessions at LA's Record Plant studios in 1983 (see also Other Musicians On Queen Records).
Vincent, Paul – Played guitar on 'Mr Bad Guy' and 'In My Defence' (see also Other Musicians On Queen Records).

W

Weisman, Mike – Keyboard and bass technician.
Wells, John – Tour security.
Williams, David – Guitarist and vocalist with John's first group the Opposition. Had previously played with the Outer Limits.
Williams, Tony – Tour wardrobe.
Williamson, Mark – Backing vocalist on 'The Golden Boy' (see also Other Musicians On Queen Records).
Wissnet, Stephen – Played bass on the *Mr Bad Guy* album (see also Other Musicians On Queen Records).
Witter, Simon – Journalist who wrote the narration for *The Queen Phenomenon* on Channel 4.
Woodlark Productions – Early merchandising company of official Queen memorabilia.
Woods, Carol – Provided backing vocals on Freddie's 'The Golden Boy' (see also Other Musicians On Queen Records).

Workman, Geoff – Engineer who worked on the *Jazz* album sessions in 1978.

Y

Yates, Candy – Provided backing vocals on 'Baby It's Alright' and 'The Also Rans' (see also Other Musicians On Queen Records).
Yates, Clare – Provided backing vocals on 'Baby It's Alright' and 'The Also Rans' (see also Other Musicians On Queen Records).
Yoshiki – Provided drum programming on 'Foreign Sand' and 'Final Destination' (see also Other Musicians On Queen Records).
Young, Richard – Original guitarist and vocalist with John's first group the Opposition, he later became their keyboard player and group archivist, keeping a diary of each gig played, the equipment used, and amounts of money earned.

Z

Zakatek, Lenny – Founder member of John's band The Immortals.
Zellis, Brian – Guitar technician.
Zenith Lighting – Lighting company.

CHRONOLOGY
OF MAJOR EVENTS
1946–1998

In this section we have recorded a diary of major events between 1946 and 1998 relating to Queen's amazing career: from the birth dates of Freddie, Brian, Roger, and John through their school years, early bands, and onto the formation and development of Queen as the world's best-loved band, as well as their individual projects as solo artists. As with most categories for Queen this is considerable and whereas we do not promise that every single event is recorded, we have attempted to list the most important ones to provide a month by month diary of the dates that have shaped their lives and careers.

(Jim Jenkins)

5 September 1946 – Faroukh Bulsara (Freddie Mercury) born on the small island of Zanzibar, now part of Tanzania.

19 July 1947 – Brian May born in Hampton Hill, Twickenham, London.

26 July 1949 – Roger Meddows-Taylor (Roger Taylor) born in Kings Lynn, Norfolk.

19 August 1951 – John Deacon born in Leicester.

September 1951 – Freddie is enrolled at the Zanzibar Missionary School.

September 1952 – Brian is enrolled at Cardinal Road Infants School.

September 1954 – Brian is enrolled at Hanworth Road Primary School and Roger at Kings Lynn Gaywood Primary School.

September 1956 – John is enrolled at Evington Lindon Junior where he remains until moving to Oadby Langmoor Junior School two years later.

March 1957 – Roger's family move from Norfolk to Cornwall where Roger is enrolled at the Bosvigo School in Truro where he forms his first group, a skiffle outfit called the Bubblingover Boys.

September 1957 – Roger is enrolled at the Truro Cathedral School for three years before moving to Truro Public School in September 1960, where he forms an instrumental trio called Beat Unlimited, that later changed its name to the Cousin Jacks.

September 1958 – Brian is enrolled at Hampton Grammar School in Middlesex where he meets Tim Staffell.

September 1962 – John is enrolled at the Gartree High School in Leicester where he remains until July 1966 before starting at Leicester's Beauchamp Grammar School in the September of that year.

April 1963 – Freddie moves from St Peter's Boarding School in Panchgani which he had been attending since February 1955, to St Josephs Convent School in Zanzibar where he remains until January 1964.

August 1963–March 1965 – With help from his father Harold May, an electronics engineer, Brian constructs the world's most famous home-made guitar, the 'Red Special' by hand-carving the instrument from a nineteenth century fireplace.

January 1964 – Freddie's family moves from Zanzibar to Feltham in Middlesex, England, and now lives less than 100 yards from Brian's home.

September 1964 – Freddie enrolls at the Isleworth Polytechnic where he remains until July 1966 before transferring to Ealing Technical College the following September.

Summer 1964 – Roger and Mike Dudley abandon their trio Beat Unlimited/Cousin Jacks.

October 1964 – Roger is enlisted to the Falcons, and remains with the group until the following February.

28 October 1964 – Brian and friends – Dave Dilloway, John 'Jag' Garnham, Richard Thompson and Tim Staffell, calling themselves 1984 after the futuristic novel by George Orwell – appear at St Mary's Church Hall in Twickenham.

12 March 1965 – Roger now enlisted to Johnny Quale and the Reactions appears at the Princess Pavilion at Falmouth supported by Blues By Four.

15 March 1965 – Johnny Quale and the Reactions enter the fifth annual Rock and Rhythm Championships of Cornwall – a sixteen act competition organised by the Truro Round Table.

August 1965 – John forms his first band calling themselves the Opposition, with a line-up of Richard Young, Clive Castledine, and Nigel Bullon. The personnel will change considerably over the next six years.

October 1965 – Brian enrolls at London's Imperial College to read Physics and Infa-red Astronomy after leaving school with ten O level and three A level examination passes.

15/29 January 1966 – Brian's band 1984 appear at the Thames Rowing Club in Putney. Their set includes rock'n'roll standards from the catalogues of Litle Richard, Chuck Berry, Muddy Waters, the Coasters, and the Beatles among others.

29 April 1966 – John's band change their name to the New Opposition due to another group calling themselves The Opposition.

23 October 1966 – The New Opposition win all the heats in the 'Midland Beat Contest', gaining a place in the finals that are eventually cancelled and abandoned.

13 May 1967 – Brian's band 1984 supports Jimi Hendrix at a gig staged at London's Imperial College.

28 June 1967 – Brian and Dave Dilloway play on a recording session at Abbey Road Studios in London for a folk-rock band called Left Handed Marriage and record two songs 'I Need Time' and 'Appointment'.

31 July 1967 – Brian's second recording session with Left Handed Marriage at Regent Sound Studios in London. The group records new versions of 'I Need Time' and a new track titled 'She Was Once My Friend'.

9 September 1967 – 1984 win the local heats of a 'Battle of the Bands' competition at the Top Rank Club in Croydon, and are consequently invited to participate in an all-night gala event for one of the key gigs of the London underground scene.

October 1967 – Roger enrolls at the London Hospital Medical College in Whitechapel to study denistry before moving on to North London Polytechnic in October 1971 and remaining there until the following summer.

23 December 1967 – Brian's band 1984 play a 30-minute set at London's Olympia Theatre supporting

headliners Jimi Hendrix, Traffic, Pink Floyd, the Herd, and Tyrannosaurus Rex.

16 March 1968 – For a gig at Gartree School, John's group the Opposition change their name to Art.

October 1968 – Roger is auditioned by Brian and Tim Staffell at Tim's Shepherds Bush flat in response to Brian's ad for a 'Ginger Baker type' drummer and is immediately enlisted to their group, Smile.

26 October 1968 – Smile make their debut appearance as one of two support bands to Pink Floyd at London's Imperial College.

Late October 1968 – Peter Abbey, a dental student from Roger's college, becomes Smile's manager.

1 March 1969 – Freddie, Brian, Roger and Tim attend Led Zeppelin's gig at London's Fishmonger's Hall.

March 1969 – Freddie becomes friend and supporter to Smile offering his advice whenever it was needed (and sometimes when it wasn't), even though he has not yet performed with the group publicly.

May 1969 – Freddie graduates from Ealing College of Art in London with a diploma in Graphic Art and Design, and sets up a fashion stall in London's Kensington Market with Roger.

May 1969 – Smile are signed to their first and only record deal with the American-owned Mercury Records.

June 1969 – Smile's first recording session at Trident Studios. They record Tim Staffell's 'Earth', and 'Step On Me' penned by Brian and Tim.

September 1969 – Although performing with Ibex, Freddie still attends gigs with Smile whenever he can. He also moves into the flat shared by Brian, Roger and Tim in Ferry Road, Barnes in South West London.

October 1969 – John enrolls at Chelsea College where he remains until June 1972.

13 December 1969 – Smile play London's Marquee Club in Wardour Street as support band to Nick Lowe's Kippington Lodge showcase.

April 1970 – Tim Staffell leaves Smile to join ex-Bee Gee Colin Petersen's group, Humpy Bong, but persuades flat mate Freddie to join Brian and Roger's group to replace him. He jumps at the opportunity after his own outfits – Ibex, Wreckage, and Sour Milk Sea had all disbanded.

April 1970 – Queen is formed with the first line-up of Brian, Roger and Freddie, and temporary bass players Mike Grose and Barry Mitchell.

27 June 1970 – Billed as Smile for the last time, the group play a gig at Truro City Hall.

12 July 1970 – Queen make their London debut at Imperial College.

25 July 1970 – Smile appear under their new name of Queen at PJ's Discotheque in Truro, Cornwall.

31 July 1970 – The ad for Queen's appearance at Truro City Hall is billed as the 'fantastic band formerly known as Smile'.

14 November 1970 – Queen play a gig at Ballspark College in Hertford.

21 November 1970 – John forms an R&B quartet with guitarist Peter Stoddart, and perform their only gig at Chelsea College simply billed as 'Deacon'.

5 December 1970 – Queen play Shoreditch College in Egham.

Late February 1971 – John Deacon is enlisted into Queen as the band's permanent bass player replacing temporary bass players Grose and Mitchell.

19 February 1971 – Queen play a gig at Hornsey Town Hall for Hornsey's College of Estate Management.

20 February 1971 – Freddie's microphone 'packs up' during the band's set at Kingston Polytechnic which results in Freddie having to use Roger's affixed drum mike.

July–September 1971 – On tour – South West England.

6 October 1971 – Queen play a concert at London's Imperial College.

31 December 1971 – Queen make an appearance at a New Year's dance at the Twickenham Rugby Club in London.

July 1972 – Queen are invited to showcase new recording hardware at De Lane Lea Studios. Recording a demo tape, studio engineers Roy Thomas Baker and John Anthony suggest to their employers, Trident Audio Productions, that Queen should be signed.

November 1972 – After Trident executives attend a Queen concert, the company signs the band to a production, publishing and management deal. Engineers Baker and Anthony commence work on a debut album at Trident Studios, recording in vacant time. Meanwhile US A&R man Jack Nelson negotiates a record deal with EMI, who sign the group for their new, but never launched, label.

5 February 1973 – Queen's first recording session for BBC Radio One. The first song put on tape was 'Keep Yourself Alive'.

9 April 1973 – EMI launch Queen with a gig at London's Marquee Club in Wardour Street.

29 June 1973 – A revival version of the Beach Boys hit 'I Can Hear Music' by Larry Lurex (Freddie Mercury) is released.

6 July 1973 – EMI 2036 'Keep Yourself Alive'/'Son and Daughter' is released as Queen's debut single, but receives virtually no radio airplay and consequently fails to reach the charts.

13 July 1973 – EMI issues Queen's first album, appropiately titled, *Queen* which spends seventeen weeks on the UK album chart peaking at No. 24.

August 1973 – The album *Queen II* is recorded at Trident Studios, and is produced by Roy Thomas Baker and Queen.

13 September 1973 – Queen play a gig at the Golders Green Hippodrome which is recorded by Radio Luxembourg for broadcast the following month.

20 October 1973 – Queen play a gig at the Paris Theatre in London which is recorded by BBC Radio One for a later 'In Concert' broadcast.

12 November–28 December 1973 – Queen's first tour of the UK as support band to Mott The Hoople.

February 1974 – Queen appear at the open-air Sunbury Music Festival in Melbourne, Australia.

1 March 1974 – Queen's first headlining British tour opens at Blackpool's Winter Gardens.

2-31 March 1974 – On tour in the UK.

16 April–12 May 1974 – On tour in the US.

6 April 1974 – The second album *Queen II* peaks at No. 5 in the UK album charts during a 29-week run.

13 April 1974 – EMI 2121 'Seven Seas of Rhye', a re-working of a track from the *Queen* album reaches No. 10 on the UK singles chart. The band also make their debut on *Top Of The Pops* replacing a 'last minute' unavailable David Bowie promo film.

16 May 1974 – Queen abandon their US tour in New York, as Brian collapses with hepatitis, which eventually develops into a duodenal ulcer.

July–September 1974 – Queen record tracks for their album *Sheer Heart Attack* at Trident, Rockfield, and Air Studios.

11 October 1974 – EMI 2229 'Killer Queen'/'Flick Of The Wrist' is released spending eleven weeks on the UK singles chart, reaching No. 2 and earning the band a silver disc.

30 October 1974 – Queen's third album *Sheer Heart Attack* charts at No. 2 during a 42-week run as the band open their UK tour at Manchester's Palace Theatre.

20 November 1974 – UK tour closes at the Rainbow Theatre in London.

23 November –10 December 1974 – On tour in Europe.

17 January 1975 – EMI release Queen's new single 'Now I'm Here'/'Lily Of The Valley'.

18 January 1975 – John marries Veronica Agnes Mary Tetslaff at Carmelite Church in Kensington Church Street, London.

5 February 1975 – Queen's US tour opens in Columbus, Ohio.

15 February 1975 – EMI 2256 'Now I'm Here' peaks at No. 11 in the UK singles chart as Queen is voted 'Band of the Year' in Britain's *Melody Maker*.

7 April 1975 – Queen's final US concert is cancelled due to Freddie's throat problems. The band leave for a ten day vacation in Hawaii.

19 April–1 May 1975 – On tour in Japan

May 1975 - 'Killer Queen' and parent album *Sheer Heart Attack* both reach No. 12 in the US singles and album charts respectively.

June–July 1975 – Queen rehearse material for the album *A Night At The Opera*.

3 July 1975 – Queen open their own Mountain Studios in Montreux, Switzerland.

August 1975 – Freddie, Brian and Roger record a session with London soul group Trax at Trident Studios. No material from this session is ever released.

August–November 1975 – Queen record tracks for their album *A Night At The Opera* at Sarm, Roundhouse, Olympic, Rockfield, Scorpio and Lansdowne Studios in England.

19 September 1975 – Queen splits with Trident and sign with Elton John's manager, John Reid.

31 October 1975 – Although initially reluctant, EMI issue 'Bohemian Rhapsody' as a single after a copy of the track is leaked to Kenny Everett at London's Capital Radio.

14 November–16 December 1975 – On tour in the UK.

29 November 1975 – EMI 2375 'Bohemian Rhapsody' – now edited from 7 minutes down to 5 minutes 52 seconds – tops the UK singles chart for the first of nine weeks, the longest run at No. 1 since Paul Anka's 'Diana' in 1957. Bruce Gowers's innovative promotional video film also boosts the single's sales performance to platinum status throughout the world, and heralds a new era in the music industry of utilising videos to promote records.

3 December 1975 – EMI issue the new album *A Night At The Opera*.

24 December 1975 – Queen's Hammersmith Odeon concert in London is simultaneously broadcast live on BBC Television and Radio One for a special edition of BBC 2's *The Old Grey Whistle Test*.

27 December 1975 – The album *A Night At The Opera* hits the No. 1 spot in the UK for a chart run of almost a year, and reaches No. 4 in the US.

27 January 1976 – Queen open a four-month tour of the US, Japan and Australia at the Palace Theatre, Waterbury, Connecticut.

7 February 1976 – The debut album *Queen* reaches No. 24 on the UK album chart more than two years after its original release.

April 1976 – 'Bohemian Rhapsody' reaches No. 9 in the US as the *Queen At The Rainbow* film is released to UK cinemas as support feature to *The Hustle* starring Burt Reynolds.

24 May 1976 – 'Bohemian Rhapsody' wins the 'Best Selling British Record' category in the 21st Annual Ivor Novello Awards staged at London's Dorchester Hotel.

29 May 1976 – Brian marries Chrissie Mullen at St Osmunds Church, Castelnau in Barnes.

July 1976 – EMI 2494 'You're My Best Friend'/ '39' is released and eventually reaches No. 16 in the US and No. 7 in the UK where it spends eight weeks on the chart and is awarded a silver disc.

July–November 1976 – Queen record tracks for their album *A Day At The Races* at the Manor and Sarm East Studios.

18 September 1976 – Queen perform a free concert in London's Hyde Park before an estimated crowd of 150,000. Kiki Dee, Supercharge and Steve Hillage are the support acts. The concert is broadcast live by London's Capital Radio.

12 November 1976 – EMI release the new Queen single 'Somebody To Love'/'White Man'.

1 December 1976 – Queen pull out of a scheduled television appearance on the *Today* show at the last minute and are replaced by new EMI signing The Sex Pistols.

11 December 1976 – EMI 2565 'Somebody To Love' spends eight weeks on the UK singles chart peaking at No. 2 and earning itself silver disc sales status.

28 December 1976 – BBC TV repeats *The Old Grey Whistle Test* Queen concert first screened live the previous Christmas.

8 January 1977 – The album *A Day At The Races* tops the UK album chart and eventually hits No. 5 in the US.

13 January 1977 – Queen open their US tour at the Milwaukee Auditorium.

2 April 1977 – EMI 2593 'Tie Your Mother Down' reaches No. 31 on the UK chart, and reaches No. 49 in the US the following week.

May 1977 – As the band tours Europe, their first EP, with lead track 'Good Old Fashioned Lover Boy' reaches No. 17 and spends ten weeks on the UK singles chart.

17 June 1977 – Queen announce they are to become tax exiles.

July–September 1977 – Queen record tracks for their album *News Of The World* at Basing Street and Wessex Studios.

26 August 1977 – Roger Taylor becomes the first member of Queen to cut a solo disc and releases 'I Wanna Testify'/'Turn On The TV'.

October 1977–December 1977 – Queen on tour in the US.

7 October 1977 – EMI issue the new Queen single 'We Are The Champions'/'We Will Rock You' as a double A-side.

18 October 1977 – 'Bohemian Rhapsody' ties with Procol Harum's 'A Whiter Shade of Pale' as the 'Best British Pop Single 1952–1977' at the British Record Industry Britannia Awards at Wembley Conference Centre honouring the Queen's Silver Jubilee and the centenary of recorded sound.

November 1977 – 'We Are The Champions'/'We Will Rock You' reaches No. 2 and spends a total of ten weeks on the UK singles chart, while in the US the single becomes the most successful record to date reaching No. 4 and achieving platinum sales status.

11 November–22 December 1977 – On tour in the US.

28 November 1977 – EMI issue the new album *News Of The World* which eventually spends nineteen weeks on the chart peaking at the No. 4 position and achieving gold sales status.

10 February 1978 – EMI release 'Spread Your Wings'/'Sheer Heart Attack' as the new single which eventually reaches No. 39 in the UK chart.

12 April –3 May 1978 – On tour in Europe

6-12 May 1978 – On tour in the UK culminating with two shows at the Empire Pool, Wembley.

July–September 1978 – Queen cut tracks for the *Jazz* album at Mountain Studios in Montreux and Super Bear Studios in Nice.

13 October 1978 – EMI issue another double A-side single in Britain. 'Fat Bottomed Girls'/'Bicycle Race' eventually reaches No. 11, spending eleven weeks on the chart and achieving silver disc award status.

28 October 1978 – Queen open their US tour at the Mid-South Coliseum in Memphis.

10 November 1978 – EMI release the album *Jazz* which eventually reaches No. 2 in the UK, spends twenty-six weeks on the chart, and achieves gold disc status.

18–20 December 1978 – US tour closes with concerts at the Los Angeles Forum.

17 January–6 May 1979 – On tour in Europe and the Far East.

26 January 1979 – EMI 2910 'Don't Stop Me Now'/'In Only Seven Days' is released as the new UK single. In the US Elektra release the track with 'More Of That Jazz' as the B-side.

March 1979 – 'Don't Stop Me Now' reaches No. 9 on the UK singles chart, but stops at No. 86 in the US.

June 1979 – Queen start recording *The Game* at Musicland Studios in Munich.

22 June 1979 – EMI releases the live performance double album *Live Killers* recorded at various venues on the European tour between January and March. The album reaches No. 3 in the UK and spends twenty-eight weeks on the chart.

29 June 1979 – 'Love Of My Life' (Live)/'Now I'm Here' (Live) is released as the new single and reaches No. 63 on the UK singles chart.

August 1979 – The double album *Live Killers* reaches No. 16 in the US album chart.

5 October 1979 – EMI 5001 'Crazy Little Thing Called Love'/'We Will Rock You' (Live) is released and eventually spends thirteen weeks on the UK chart peaking at No. 2 and achieving gold sales status. The single represents a diversion for Queen with a new sound, new image (short hair) and a fun video that even the critics liked. The track also marks Freddie's debut as rhythm guitarist.

24 November 1979–22 December 1979 – On tour in the UK.

December 1979 – Elektra finally release 'Crazy Little Thing Called Love' in the US after radio stations begin playing imported copies.

26 December 1979 – Queen end their current UK tour with a charity concert in aid of the people of Kampuchea at London's Hammersmith Odeon. Queen's entire set is recorded, but only one track 'Now I'm Here' is released.

25 January 1980 – EMI 5022 'Save Me'/'Let Me Entertain You' (Live) is released and reaches No. 11 spending seven weeks on the UK singles chart.

February–May 1980 – Recording sessions on *The Game* resume at Musicland Studios in Munich.

23 February 1980 – 'Crazy Little Thing Called Love' tops the US singles chart.

30 May 1980 – EMI issue 'Play The Game'/'A Human Body' as the new single. It eventually reaches No. 14 in the UK and No. 42 in the US.

30 June 1980 – EMI release *The Game* which spends eighteen weeks on the UK album chart and reaching the pinnacle position just as the band open their US tour at the PNE Coliseum in Vancouver, Canada.

1 July–30 September 1980 – On tour in the US which ends with three concerts at Madison Square Garden in New York.

22 August 1980 – 'Another One Bites The Dust'/'Dragon Attack' becomes the third single to be released from the album *The Game* and reaches No. 7 in the UK spending nine weeks on the singles chart. In the US the single is released with 'Don't Try Suicide' as the B-side.

20 September 1980 – *The Game* begins a five-week run on top of the US album chart.

October–November 1980 – Final recording sessions for the *Flash Gordon* original film soundtrack takes place at Anvil Studios in England.

4 October 1980 – 'Another One Bites The Dust' tops the US singles chart for three weeks. Several R&B/Urban radio stations in the US unexpectedly support the single contributing to its No. 2 position on the R&B charts.

23 November–1 December 1980 – On tour in Europe.

24 November 1980 – EMI 5126 'Flash'/'Football Fight' is released which spends twelve weeks on the chart peaking at No. 10 and achieving silver sales status.

8 December 1980 – EMI release *Flash Gordon*, Queen's original soundtrack album for the futurist film of the same name. It spends fourteen weeks on the UK chart peaking at No. 10 and winning a gold disc award. The band also become the first to be included in *The Guinness Book of Records* as being among Britain's highest paid executives.

8–10 December 1980 – The British leg of Queen's current European tour culminates with three concerts at London's Wembley Arena.

12–18 December 1980 – On tour in Europe.

30 January 1981 – 'Another One Bites The Dust' wins the Favourite Single in the Pop/Rock category at the eighth annual American Music Awards staged at the ABC-TV Studios in Hollywood.

12–18 February 1981 – On tour in Japan.

28 February – 21 March 1981 – On tour in South America.

30 March 1981 – Roger Taylor's second solo single 'Future Management' from his upcoming solo album *Fun In Space* – recorded in six weeks in Switzerland – is released.

6 April 1981 – Roger Taylor's first solo album *Fun In Space* is released.

25 September–17 October 1981 – On tour – Venezuela and Mexico.

26 October 1981 – EMI 5250 'Under Pressure' by Queen and David Bowie is released as the new single eventually reaching the No. 1 position and spending ten weeks on the UK singles chart. In the US, the single reaches No. 29.

2 November 1981 – *Queen's Greatest Hits* is released and eventually tops the UK bestseller lists spending 165 weeks on the album chart. In the US, the compilation reaches No. 14.

24–25 November 1981 – Queen play concerts in Montreal, Canada.

December 1981 – Queen continue recording tracks for the *Hot Space* album at Mountain Studios in Montreux and Musicland in Munich.

8 December 1981 – The Royal Philharmonic Orchestra perform an evening of Queen compositions at a charity concert to aid leukaemia research.

9 April–21 May 1982 – On tour in Europe.

19 April 1982 – EMI 5293 'Body Language'/'Life Is Real' is released which peaks at No. 25 in the UK, and No. 11 in the US.

23 April 1982 – EMI release the new album *Hot Space* which eventually spends nineteen weeks on the UK chart peaking at No. 4, and No. 22 in the US.

5 June 1982 – Queen play a concert at Milton Keynes Bowl which is filmed by Channel 4 Television for later broadcast.

19 July 1982 – Elektra issue 'Calling All Girls'/'Put Out The Fire' as the new single in the US which eventually peaks at No. 60.

21 July–15 September 1982 – On tour in the US.

9 August 1982 – EMI release 'Back Chat' (remix)/'Staying Power' as the new single in the UK.

19 October–3 November 1982 – On tour in Japan.

7 January 1983 – Film of the 5 June 1982 concert at Milton Keynes broadcast by Channel 4.

21–22 April 1983 – Brian collects a group of friends together for a session at Record Plant Studios in Los Angeles that include Eddie Van Halen on guitar, Fred Mandel on keyboards, Phil Chen on bass, and REO Speedwagon drummer Alan Gratzer.

24 October 1983 – EMI issue Brian's 'Starfleet'/'Son Of Starfleet' from the star-session in Los Angeles. The track is based on a Japanese children's puppet sci-fi series theme, and peaks at No. 65 on the UK singles chart.

31 October 1983 – EMI releases Brian's mini-album *Starfleet Project* which peaks at No. 35 on the UK chart.

23 January 1984 – 'Radio Ga Ga'/'I Go Crazy' is released by EMI and eventually enters the UK singles lists at No. 4 and climbs to No. 2 just behind Frankie Goes To Hollywood's 'Relax'. 'Radio Ga Ga' spent a total of nine weeks on the chart and the video includes footage from Fritz Lang's *Metropolis*.

27 February 1984 – EMI release the new album *The Works* which eventually peaks at No. 2 in the UK and remains on the chart for forty-eight weeks. In the US, the album reaches No. 23.

2 April 1984 – EMI issue 'I Want To Break Free'/'Machines' which eventually reaches No. 3 and is subsequently adopted by Shell for TV commercials. In the US, 'Radio Ga Ga' peaks at No. 16 in the singles chart.

12 May 1984 – Queen make an appearance at the Golden Rose Festival in Montreux, Switzerland.

28 June 1984 – Queen is honoured with the Silver Clef Award at the Annual Nordoff-Robbins Music Therapy Centre Lunch in London.

16 July 1984 – EMI release 'It's A Hard Life'/'Is This The World We Created' which spends nine weeks on the UK chart peaking at No. 6.

July 1984 – Rehearsals of over twelve hours a day for the forthcoming tour are held in Munich.

24 August 1984 – Queen opened their European tour in Belgium.

28–29 August 1984 – Queen play two concerts in Dublin.

31 August–8 September 1984 – The British leg of the European tour includes three nights at the NEC Birmingham, and four nights at London's Wembley Arena.

10 September 1984 – EMI issues the new single 'Hammer To Fall'/'Tear It Up' which spends thirteen weeks on the UK chart peaking at No. 8, while Peppermint Video Music releases 'We Will Rock You', and Freddie releases his first solo single 'Love Kills', a song written for the soundtrack of *Metropolis*.

12–30 September 1984 – On tour in Europe.

5–20 October 1984 – Queen play eight shows at the Sun City Super Bowl in South Africa placing them on the United Nations cultural blacklist.

19 November 1984 – PMI releases a four-track video compilation EP *The Works*.

26 November 1984 – 'Thank God It's Christmas'/'Man On The Prowl'/'Keep Passing The Open Windows' is released and eventually reaches No. 21 on the UK singles chart.

11–18 January 1985 – Queen make an appearance at the 'Rock In Rio' Festival in Rio de Janeiro as local clergy issue a statement that the band's show will corrupt the nation's youth.

9 April 1985 - Freddie's second solo single 'I Was Born To Love You'/'Stop All The Fighting' is released eventually reaching No. 11 in the UK, and No. 76 in the US.

13–29 April 1985 – On tour in Australia.
29 April 1985 – CBS release Freddie's first solo album *Mr Bad Guy* which peaks at No. 10 on the UK chart.

8–15 May 1985 – On tour in Japan.

1 July 1985 – 'Made In Heaven'/'She Blows Hot & Cold', the second single from Freddie's *Mr Bad Guy* album is released.

13 July 1985 – Queen make an appearance for the Live Aid concert at Wembley Stadium which is regarded by many as the highlight of the UK end of the benefit spectacular.

4 November 1985 – EMI issue 'One Vision' from the soundtrack of the film *Iron Eagle* as the new single. It eventually reaches No. 7 on the UK singles chart.

5 December 1985 – EMI release *The Complete Works*, a limited-edition boxed set of all Queen albums to date (excluding *Greatest Hits*) with an additional album *Complete Vision* comprising singles and B sides that escaped inclusion elsewhere up to and including 'One Vision'/'Blurred Vision'. All fourteen albums are digitally remastered and packaged in plain white sleeves (the original artwork is reproduced in one of two booklets that are included in the package).

February 1986 – John records a song with Hot Chocolate singer Errol Brown.

17 March 1986 – EMI release the new single 'A Kind Of Magic'/'A Dozen Red Roses For My Darling' which eventually peaks at No. 3 on the UK chart.

April 1986 – Freddie contributes three tracks to the cast recording of Dave Clark's stage musical *Time*.

25–27 April 1986 – Queen's first ever Fan Club Convention is staged at Great Yarmouth in Norfolk.

May 1986 – John forms the Immortals with Robert Ahwai and Lenny Zakatek to record his first solo single released on MCA, 'No Turning Back', for the soundtrack of the film *Biggles*.

6 May 1986 – EMI 5559 is Freddie's rendition of the title theme of Dave Clark's musical *Time* which eventually enters the chart and reaches No. 24 as Brian becomes romantically linked with actress Anita Dobson.

21 May 1986 – EMI issue the new album *A Kind Of Magic* which eventually spends sixty-two weeks on the UK chart and peaks at the No. 1 position.

7–29 June 1986 – On tour in Europe.

9 June 1986 – EMI release 'Friends Will Be Friends'/'Seven Seas of Rhye' from the album *A Kind Of Magic*. It spends eight weeks on the chart and reaches No. 14 in the UK.

June 1986 – MCA issues the soundtrack album from *Biggles* credited to John Deacon's band the Immortals.

1 July–4 August 1986 – On tour in Europe with UK dates including two shows at Wembley Stadium, the second of which is taped for simultaneous broadcast on Independent television and radio.

21 July 1986 – PMI release Freddie's first video EP featuring four recent singles.

9 August 1986 - Queen play their biggest-ever concert in the UK and unknowingly at the time, their last ever, at Knebworth Park. Besides a six thousand square foot stage, Queen used 180 Clare Brothers S4 speaker cabinets, 8.6 miles of cable, 5 power generators providing 5000 amps, an immense sound system powered by half a million watts and special delay towers to take account of the size of the venue. Above the stage was a 20 x 30 foot Starvision screen, the extreme weight of which was counterbalanced by a huge water reservoir at the rear.

15 September 1986 – EMI issue 'Who Wants To Live Forever'/'Killer Queen' which eventually spends five weeks on the UK singles chart peaking at No. 24.

25 October 1986 – *Real Magic* is broadcast live by satellite on UK Independent television and radio simultaneously, the first such achievement.

1 December 1986 – EMI release *Live Magic* recorded on the European tour at various venues in July and August. It spends forty-four weeks on the UK album chart peaking at No. 3 and achieving platinum award status.

1 January 1987 – EMI issue *Live Magic* on compact disc a month after its vinyl counterpart and the last non-simultaneous Queen release. The CD is marginally longer than the LP.

16 February 1987 – PMI release Queen's *Live In Budapest* video recorded at the Nepstadion in Budapest the previous July during the band's European tour.

23 February 1987 – EMI 6151 'The Great Pretender'/'Exercises In Free Love' is released as Freddie's new single, and becomes his highest-charting solo disc to date reaching No. 4 in the UK and spending nine weeks on the chart. An accompanying video single is also issued.

15 April 1987 – Queen is honoured with the Outstanding Contribution To British Music trophy at the 32nd Annual Ivor Novello Awards staged at London's Grosvenor House Hotel.

June 1987 – Freddie participates in the TV special *Ibiza 92*, at the Ku Club in Ibiza.

12 September 1987 – 'Bohemian Rhapsody'/'Life With Brian' by *Young Ones* spin-off group Bad News and produced by Brian, enters the singles chart and reaches No. 44 in a five-week stay in the UK.

21 September 1987 – Roger playing guitar rather than drums has formed the Cross with Clayton Moss on guitar, Spike Edney on keyboards, Peter Noone (not the Herman's Hermit) on bass, and Josh Macrae on drums. Signed to the Virgin label, their debut single 'Cowboys And Indians' is released, eventually reaching No. 74 in the UK bestselling singles chart where it remains for one week.

10 October 1987 – Polydor releases *Barcelona*, an album of duets between Freddie and Montserrat Caballe which eventually reaches No. 15 in the UK and spends eight weeks on the chart.

24 October 1987 – The Cross make their first live television performance on the ITV channel.

26 October 1987 – 'Barcelona'/'Exercises In Free Love', a duet between Freddie and Spanish opera singer Montserrat Caballe is released, reaching No. 8 on the UK singles chart.

30 November 1987 – PMI issues a three-volumed video compilation appropriately titled *The Magic Years* which chronicles Queen's extensive recording and visual career. Each video is also made available individually.

25 January 1988 – Roger marries Dominique Marie Begrand at Kensington Registry Office, Old Town Hall in London's Kings Road on the same day that Virgin release *Shove It!*, the debut album by Roger's band the Cross, which eventually peaks at No. 58 in the UK.

February 1988 – The Music & Media label releases an interview picture disc.

19 February 1988 – Roger's band, the Cross, open their first concert tour of the UK at Leeds University.

8 October 1988 – Freddie and Caballe highlight a star-studded show to launch Barcelona's successful bid for the 1992 Olympic Games at the Avinguda De Maria Cristina stadium.

13 May 1989 – 'I Want It All', the first single taken from the forthcoming album *The Miracle* enters the chart at No. 3 in the UK for a seven-week stay.

3 June 1989 – *The Miracle*, Queen's first studio album for three years, enters the chart at No. 1.

17 June 1989 – 'I Want It All' reaches No. 50 in the US as *The Miracle* goes to No. 24 on their album chart.

8 July 1989 – 'Breakthru' reaches No. 7 in the UK singles chart.

26 August 1989 – 'The Invisible Man' reaches No. 12 on the UK singles chart.

28 October 1989 – 'Scandal' climbs to No. 25 on the UK singles chart.

9 December 1989 – Brian collaborates with Ian Gillan, Robert Plant, and Bruce Dickinson as Rock Aid Armenia with a remake of 'Smoke On The Water' which reaches No. 39 on the UK bestselling lists with all profits from the record going to the victims of the Armenian earthquake disaster.

16 December 1989 – The album *Queen At The Beeb*, collecting together all the highlights of Queen's BBC radio sessions, peaks at No. 67 in the UK.

18 February 1990 – Queen collects the BPI Award for Outstanding Contribution to British Music at the ninth annual *BRIT* Awards at the Dominion Theatre in London.

November 1990 – Brian composes the score for the Red & Gold Theatre Company's production of *Macbeth*.

26 January 1991 – 'Innuendo' tops the UK singles chart in its week of release. At 6 minutes, 32 seconds, the track is the third longest UK No. 1 of all time, behind the Beatles' 'Hey Jude' and Simple Minds' 'Belfast Child'.

16 February 1991 – The new album *Innuendo* enters the UK chart at No. 1, and also begins a rapid US chart rise.

March 1991 – Brian co-produces, co-writes and performs on the UK Comic Relief 1991 charity single, 'The Stonk' recorded by Hale & Pace & The Stonkers.

23 March 1991 – 'I'm Going Slightly Mad' peaks at No. 22 in the UK singles chart.

1 June 1991 – 'Headlong' reaches No. 14 in the UK singles chart.

19 October 1991 – Brian takes part in the closing night of the 'Guitar Legends' series in Seville, Spain performing 'Now I'm Here, Tie Your Mother Down', and 'Driven By You'.

2 November 1991 – 'The Show Must Go On' reaches No. 16 on the UK singles chart.

9 November 1991 – The compilation album *Greatest Hits II* enters the UK chart at No. 1.

24 November 1991 – Freddie dies of complications from AIDS at his Holland Park home in London. A statement is issued by the band and Jim Beach: *'We have lost the greatest and most beloved member of our family. We feel overwhelming grief that he has gone, sadness that he should be cut down at the height of his creativity, but above all great pride in the courageous way he lived and died. It has been a privilege for us to have shared such magical times. As soon as we are able we would like to celebrate his life in the style to which he was accustomed.'* The group's publicist, Roxy Meade, requested that donations be sent to the Terence Higgins Trust.

7 December 1991 – *Live Magic, A Kind Of Magic*, and *Innuendo* all re-chart at No. 51, No. 66, and No. 34 respectively in the UK.

14 December 1991 – Brian's 'Driven By You' as used in a Ford car commercial reaches No. 6 in the UK singles chart.

21 December 1991 – 'Bohemian Rhapsody'/'These Are The Days of Our Lives' re-enters the UK chart at No. 1 making it the biggest selling single since Band Aid's 1984 chart topper. *Greatest Hits* reaches No. 8 on the UK album chart.

2 February 1992 – 'Bohemian Rhapsody' wins Best British Single at the 11th annual BRIT Awards at London's Hammersmith Odeon presented by Simon Mayo, and Freddie is posthumously honoured with the 'Outstanding Contribution to British Music' Special Award.

15 April 1992 – 'Bohemian Rhapsody' is named 'Best Selling A-Side', and Brian's 'Driven By You' as 'Best Theme From A TV/Radio Commercial' at the annual Ivor Novello Awards at London's Grosvenor House. The band donates $1.76 million to the Terrence Higgins Trust from the profits of the reissued 'Bohemian Rhapsody'.

20 April 1992 - Brian, John and Roger stage 'A Concert For Life' before a crowd of 70,000 at Wembley Stadium as a tribute to Freddie and a fundraiser for AIDS Awareness. Broadcast to an unprecedented seventy countries worldwide, the event features a plea by Elizabeth Taylor and performances by Metallica, Extreme, Bob Geldof, Spinal Tap, Def Leppard, Guns N' Roses and U2 (via satellite from Sacramento), a first-ever live concert link with South Africa, and versions of Queen-backed songs by George Michael, Lisa Stansfield, the London Community Gospel Choir, David Bowie, Annie Lennox, Elton John and Axl Rose. Liza Minnelli leads the all-star choral finale of 'We Are The Champions', and Brian closes an emotional night providing the guitar part of 'God Save The Queen' with vocals supplied by the audience. Spinal Tap introduced their performance, resplendent in regal outfits, declaring that they will cut short their set by 35 songs 'because we know Freddie would have wanted it this way'.

9 May 1992 – 'Bohemian Rhapsody' already extensively featured in the hit movie *Wayne's World*, reaches No. 2 in the US singles chart as the compilation *Classic Queen* peaks at No. 4 in the US album lists. All profits from the sale of the single go to the Magic Johnson AIDS Foundation.

23 May 1992 – In a statement released by attorneys, Freddie Mercury has bequeathed the majority of his estate (approximately £10 million) to long-time friend Mary Austin.

26 May 1992 – *Queen Live At Wembley* is released on video.

6 June 1992 – The album *Live at Wembley '86* debuts at its UK No. 2 peak behind Lionel Richie's *Back To Front*.

20 June 1992 – The album *Live At Wembley* bows at its US No. 53 pinnacle.

8 August 1992 – 'We Will Rock You'/'We Are The Champions' reaches No. 52 on the US singles chart.

15 August 1992 – After the song is used as the theme for the Olympic Games on BBC Television, Freddie and Montserrat Caballe's reissued 'Barcelona' single peaks at No. 2 in the UK chart, and the reissued parent album reaches No. 15 a week later.

9 September 1992 – Brian and Roger present a cheque for $300,000 to Magic Johnson for his Magic Johnson Foundation for AIDS Research at the ninth annual MTV Awards, at the Pauley Pavilion, Los Angeles at which 'Bohemian Rhapsody' wins the 'Best Video From A Film' category.

19 September 1992 – Brian's 'Too Much Love Will Kill You' peaks at No. 5 on the UK singles chart.

27 September 1992 – Brian performs at a benefit for leukemia patients in Luciano Pavarotti's horse stables in Modena, Italy, with Sting, Suzanne Vega, Aaron Neville & the Neville Brothers, Mike Oldfield, Luciano Pavarotti, Bob Geldof, Gipsy Kings, Ute Lemper and Zucchero.

10 October 1992 – Brian's 'Back To The Light' reaches No. 6 on the UK singles chart as Queen's *Greatest Hits* album reaches No. 11 in the US.

17 October 1992 – Hank Marvin's 'We Are The Champions' featuring Brian May charts for one week at No. 66 in the UK.

9 November 1992 – *Queen: Days Of Our Lives* airs on MTV Europe.

13 November 1992 – Roger and Jim Beach open the first Freddie Mercury Building for AIDS Research in Holland.

28 November 1992 – Brian's *Back To The Light* reaches No. 19 in the UK as Freddie's *The Freddie Mercury Album* debuts at its UK No. 4 peak.

19 December 1992 – Freddie's 'In My Defense' reaches No. 8 in the UK singles chart.

9 January 1993 – *Greatest Hits* and *Greatest Hits II* reach the UK album chart at No. 33 and No. 25 respectively.

16 January 1993 – The compilation album *Classic Queen* reaches No. 94 in the US.

6 February 1993 – Freddie's reissued 'The Great Pretender' – featured in the movie *Night In The City* – bows at its No. 29 peak in the UK.

23 February 1993 – Brian's band comprising Cozy Powell on drums, Neil Murray on bass, Spike Edney on keyboards, Mike Caswell on guitar, Chris Thompson, Maggie Ryder, and Miriam Stookloy on vocals opens for the Guns N' Roses concert in Austin, Texas.

23 March 1993 – The Paul Rodgers-assembled *Tribute To Muddy Waters* featuring Brian is released by Victory Music.

1 May 1993 – Queen and George Michael's EP *Five Live* from 1992's 'A Concert For Life' enters the UK chart at No. 1 where it stays for three weeks.

8 May 1993 – *Five Live* is issued as an album in the US, and debuts at its No. 46 peak.

29 May 1993 – Extracted 'Somebody To Love' with George Michael reaches No. 30 in the US.

4 June 1993 – Following US dates supporting Guns N' Roses, the Brian May Band embarks on a ten-date 'Back To The Light' UK tour at the Playhouse Theatre in Edinburgh.

26 June 1993 – Brian's 'Resurrection' with Cozy Powell reaches No. 23 on the UK singles chart.

14 August 1993 – Freddie's 'Living On My Own' tops the UK singles chart.

17 December 1993 – Freddie's personal stamp collection together with other Queen memorabilia is sold under auction at Sotheby's in London raising over £8,000 for the Mercury Phoenix Trust.

18 December 1993 – Brian's 'Last Horizon' debuts at its UK No. 51 peak.

30 May 1994 – 'Bohemian Rhapsody' tops the BBC Radio One 'All Time Top 100' with 'The Show Must Go On' placed at No. 44, 'These Are The Days Of Our Lives' at No. 49, and 'Innuendo' at No. 78.

1 August 1994 – PMI issues Queen's first video-CD format release with *Greatest Flix I* and *Greatest Flix II*.

19 November–4 December 1994 – Roger takes his band on tour in the UK.

21 August 1995 – Brian, Roger and John provide funds to several young British film directors in association with the British Film Institute to help finance short film production in connection with Queen's *Made In Heaven* album.

6 November 1995 – EMI release the new Queen album *Made In Heaven* featuring Freddie's last vocal work which enters the chart at No. 1.

25 June 1996 – BBC Radio One bans Queen's single 'Let Me Live' from their playlist on the grounds of being 'too old fashioned'.

22 November 1996 – The Freddie Mercury Photographic Exhibition is launched at the Royal Albert Hall in London.

17 January 1997 – Brian, Roger and John performed with Elton John in a ballet conceived and choreographed in tribute to Freddie's 'The Show Must Go On' at the National Theatre De Chailiot in Paris, and receive an award from the French Minister of Culture to recognise their continuing contribution to AIDS charities.

27 May 1997 – Queen receive an Ivor Novello award for 'Too Much Love Will Kill You' as the 'Best Song – Musically and Lyrically'.

15 August 1997 – Queen receive the 'Lifetime Achievement' award for their contribution to music at the Comets Awards staged in Cologne, Germany.

3 November 1997 – EMI release a new compilation album of Queen's best rock tracks appropriately titled *Queen Rocks*.

March 1998 – Electronic Arts release *Queen – The Eye*, a unique interactive CD Rom game inspired by the music and art of Queen

Freddie live on stage at the Rainbow, 31 March 1974 (© Jill Furmanovsky)

PART 2
THE MUSIC

(Fin Costello/Redferns)

(Mick Hutson/Redferns)

SONGS A–Z

UK ISSUES AND US SINGLES

The following section details all Queen and solo recordings giving information on composer and where each track appeared. Singles are listed for all formats followed by albums and videos.

(Ian Dickson/Redferns)

'39

(May)

Singles:

You're My Best Friend/'39

Albums:

A Night At The Opera

Live Killers

The Complete Works

The Ultimate Queen

Live At The Brixton Academy

Videos:

Live At The Brixton Academy

A

A DOZEN RED ROSES FOR MY DARLING

(Taylor)

Singles:

A Kind Of Magic/A DOZEN RED ROSES FOR MY DARLING

A Kind Of Magic (extended)/A DOZEN RED ROSES FOR MY DARLING (12" single)

A Kind Of Magic (extended)/A DOZEN RED ROSES FOR MY DARLING (12" picture disc)

A Kind Of Magic/A DOZEN RED ROSES FOR MY DARLING/One Vision (3" CD single)

Princes Of The Universe/A DOZEN RED ROSES FOR MY DARLING (US single)

A HUMAN BODY

(Taylor)

Singles:

Play The Game/A HUMAN BODY

Albums:

The Complete Works

A KIND OF MAGIC

(Taylor)

Singles:

A KIND OF MAGIC/A Dozen Red

Roses For My Darling

A KIND OF MAGIC (extended)/A Dozen Red Roses For My Darling (12" single)

A KIND OF MAGIC (extended)/A Dozen Red Roses For My Darling (12" picture disc)

A KIND OF MAGIC/A Dozen Red Roses For My Darling/One Vision (3" CD single)

Who Wants To Live Forever/A KIND OF MAGIC/Killer Queen

A KIND OF MAGIC (extended remix)/Gimme The Prize (US single)

Albums:

A Kind Of Magic

Live Magic

Greatest Hits II

Live At Wembley

The Ultimate Queen

The 12" Collection

Videos:

Who Wants To Live Forever/A KIND OF MAGIC

Live In Budapest

Live At Wembley

Greatest Flix II

Box Of Flix

Classic Queen

Now That's What I Call Music #7

Highlander II

A SOUL BROTHER

(Taylor)

Albums:

The Complete Works

A WINTER'S TALE

(Queen)

Singles:

A WINTER'S TALE/Thank God It's Christmas/Rock In Rio Blues (CD single)

A WINTER'S TALE/Now I'm

Here/You're My Best Friend/Somebody To Love (CD single)

Albums:

Made In Heaven

The Ultimate Queen

Videos:

Queen The Films (Made In Heaven)

ABANDON FIRE

(Taylor/Richards)

Albums:

Strange Frontier

ACTION THIS DAY

(Taylor)

Albums:

Hot Space

The Complete Works

The Ultimate Queen

AIRHEADS

(Taylor)

Albums:

Fun In Space

ALL DEAD, ALL DEAD

(May)

Albums:

News Of The World

The Complete Works

The Ultimate Queen

ALL GOD'S PEOPLE

(Queen/Moran)

Singles:

Headlong/ALL GOD'S PEOPLE

Headlong/ALL GOD'S PEOPLE/Mad The Swine (12" single)

Albums:

Innuendo

The Ultimate Queen

ANOTHER ONE BITES THE DUST

(Deacon)

Singles:

  ANOTHER ONE BITES THE
    DUST/Dragon Attack

  ANOTHER ONE BITES THE
    DUST/ Dragon Attack/Las
    Palabras de Amor (3" CD
    single)

  ANOTHER ONE BITES THE
    DUST/Don't Try Suicide (US
    single)

Albums:

  The Game

  Greatest Hits

  Live Magic

  Live At Wembley

  The Ultimate Queen

Videos:

  We Will Rock You

  Greatest Flix I

  Rare Live

  Live At Wembley

  Box Of Flix

  Hell's Bells-The Dangers Of
    Rock 'N' Roll

  Biggles

APRIL LADY

(unknown)

Albums:

  Gettin' Smile

ARBORIA (PLANET OF THE TREE MEN)

(Deacon)

Albums:

  Flash Gordon

  The Complete Works

  The Ultimate Queen

B

BACK TO THE LIGHT

(May)

Singles:

  BACK TO THE LIGHT/Nothin' But
    Blue

  BACK TO THE LIGHT/Nothin' But
    Blue (guitar version)/Starfleet
    (12" single)

  BACK TO THE LIGHT/Nothin' But
    Blue (guitar version)/Blues
    Breaker (CD single)

  BACK TO THE LIGHT (radio
    version)/BACK TO THE LIGHT
    (album version)/Nothin' But
    Blue (guitar version) (CD
    single)

Albums:

  Back To The Light

  Live At The Brixton Academy

Videos:

  Live At The Brixton Academy

BACKCHAT

(Deacon)

Singles:

  BACKCHAT/Staying Power

  BACKCHAT (extended
    remix)/Staying Power (12"
    single)

  Staying Power/BACKCHAT (US
    single)

Albums:

  Hot Space

  The Complete Works

  The Ultimate Queen

BARCELONA

(Mercury/Moran)

Singles:

  BARCELONA/Exercises In Free
    Love (with Montserrat Caballe)

  BARCELONA/Exercises In Free
    Love (with Montserrat

Caballe)/BARCELONA
    (extended) (12" single)

  BARCELONA/Exercises In Free
    Love (with Montserrat
    Caballe)/BARCELONA
    (extended) (CD single)

Albums:

  Barcelona

  The Freddie Mercury Album

Videos:

  Now That's What I Call Music #10

  Now You Can See The Music

  The Barcelona EP

BATTLE THEME

(May)

Albums:

  Flash Gordon

  The Complete Works

  The Ultimate Queen

BEAUTIFUL DREAMS

(Taylor)

Albums:

  Strange Frontier

BETTER THINGS

(Moss)

Albums:

  Mad, Bad And Dangerous To
    Know

BICYCLE RACE

(Mercury)

Singles:

  BICYCLE RACE/Fat Bottomed
    Girls

Albums:

  Jazz

  Live Killers

  Greatest Hits

  The Complete Works

  The Ultimate Queen

  Jazz (1991 remix) (US CD)

Videos:

    Greatest Flix I

    Box Of Flix

BIG SPENDER

(Coleman & Fields)

Albums:

    Live At Wembley

    Videos:

        Rare Live

BIJOU

(Queen)

Singles:

    Innuendo/BIJOU

    Innuendo/BIJOU (12" single)

    Innuendo/Under Pressure/BIJOU

        (12" picture disc)

    Innuendo (explosive version)/

        Under Pressure/BIJOU (CD

        single)

    These Are The Days Of Our

        Lives/BIJOU (US single)

Albums:

    Innuendo

    The Ultimate Queen

BLAG

(unknown)

Albums:

    Gettin' Smile

BLUES BREAKER

(May)

Singles:

    Back To The Light/Nothin' But

        Blue (guitar version)/BLUES

        BREAKER (CD single)

Albums:

    Starfleet

BLURRED VISION

(Queen)

Singles:

    One Vision/BLURRED VISION

One Vision (extended)/BLURRED

    VISION (12" single)

Albums:

    The Complete Works

BODY LANGUAGE

(Mercury)

Singles:

    BODY LANGUAGE/Life Is Real

    Under Pressure/Soul Brother/

        BODY LANGUAGE (3" CD single)

    The Show Must Go On/Keep

        Yourself Alive/Queen

        Talks/BODY LANGUAGE (CD

        single)

Albums:

    Hot Space

    The Complete Works

    The Ultimate Queen

    Hot Space (remix) (US CD)

Videos:

    Sexy Shorts

BOHEMIAN RHAPSODY

(Mercury)

Singles:

    BOHEMIAN RHAPSODY/I'm In

        Love With My Car

    BOHEMIAN RHAPSODY/I'm In

        Love With My Car (limited

        edition blue vinyl)

    BOHEMIAN RHAPSODY/I'm In

        Love With My Car (limited

        edition blue vinyl with card

        sleeve)

    BOHEMIAN RHAPSODY/I'm In

        Love With My Car (limited

        edition blue vinyl with extras)

    BOHEMIAN RHAPSODY/You're

        My Best Friend/I'm In Love With

        My Car (3" CD Single)

    BOHEMIAN RHAPSODY/I'm In

        Love With My Car (CD Single)

    BOHEMIAN RHAPSODY/These

        Are The Days Of Our Lives

BOHEMIAN RHAPSODY/The

    Show Must Go On (US Single)

Albums:

    A Night At The Opera

    Live Killers

    Greatest Hits

    Live Magic

    Live At Wembley

    The Ultimate Queen

    The 12" Collection

Videos:

    BOHEMIAN RHAPSODY/Crazy

        Little Thing Called Love

    We Will Rock You

    Greatest Flix I

    Live In Japan

    Live In Rio

    Live In Budapest

    Live At Wembley

    Box Of Flix

    Classic Queen

    Wayne's World

BREAKDOWN

(Noone)

Albums:

    Mad, Bad And Dangerous To

        Know

BREAKTHRU

(Queen)

Singles:

    BREAKTHRU/Stealin'

    BREAKTHRU (7" mix)/Stealin'

        (12" single)

    BREAKTHRU/Stealin' (shaped

        picture disc)

    BREAKTHRU (extended)/

        Stealin'/BREAKTHRU (CD

        single)

    BREAKTHRU/I Want It All (US

        single)

Albums:

    The Miracle

    Greatest Hits II

The Ultimate Queen
The 12" Collection
Videos:
The Miracle Video EP
Greatest Flix II
Box Of Flix

BRIGHTON ROCK
(May)
Singles:
Killer Queen/Flick Of The Wrist/
BRIGHTON ROCK (3" CD single)
Albums:
Queen II
Live Killers
Live At Wembley
The Ultimate Queen
Videos:
Live In Rio
Live At Wembley

BRING BACK THAT LEROY BROWN
(Mercury)
Albums:
Queen II
The Complete Works
The Ultimate Queen
Videos:
Live At The Rainbow

C

CALLING ALL GIRLS
(Taylor)
Singles:
CALLING ALL THE GIRLS/
Put Out The Fire (US single)
Albums:
Hot Space
The Complete Works
The Ultimate Queen

CHINESE TORTURE
(Queen)

Albums:
The Miracle (US CD)

CLOSER TO YOU
(Edney)
Albums:
Mad, Bad And Dangerous To Know

COMING SOON
(Taylor)
Albums:
The Game
The Complete Works
The Ultimate Queen

CONTACT
(Taylor)
Singles:
Heaven For Everyone/Love On A
Tightrope (Like An
Animal)/CONTACT (12" single)

COOL CAT
(Mercury/Deacon)
Singles:
Las Palabras De Amor/COOL
CAT
Albums:
Hot Space
The Complete Works
The Ultimate Queen

COWBOYS AND INDIANS
(Taylor)
Singles:
COWBOYS AND INDIANS/Loves
Lies Bleeding
COWBOYS AND INDIANS (full
length version)/Loves Lies
Bleeding (12" single)
Shove It/COWBOYS AND
INDIANS/Shove It (extended
version) (CD single)
Albums:
Shove It

CRASH DIVE ON MINGO CITY
(May)
Albums:
Flash Gordon
The Complete Works
The Ultimate Queen

CRAZY LITTLE THING CALLED LOVE
(Mercury)
Singles:
CRAZY LITTLE THING CALLED
LOVE/Spread Your Wings (live)
CRAZY LITTLE THING CALLED
LOVE/Spread Your Wings/Flash
(3" CD single)
Albums:
The Game
Greatest Hits
Live At Wembley
The Ultimate Queen
Videos:
Bohemian Rhapsody/CRAZY
LITTLE THING CALLED LOVE
We Will Rock You
Greatest Flix I
Live In Japan
Rare Live
Live In Budapest
Live At Wembley
Box Of Flix

D

DANCER
(May)
Albums:
Hot Space

THE DARK
(May)
Albums:
Back To The Light

DEAD ON TIME

(May)

Albums:

Jazz

The Complete Works

The Ultimate Queen

DEAR FRIENDS

(May)

Albums:

Queen II

The Complete Works

The Ultimate Queen

DEAR MR MURDOCH

(Taylor)

Singles:

Happiness/DEAR MR
MURDOCH/Everybody Hurts
Sometime (live)/Old Friends
(12" single)

Albums:

Happiness

DEATH ON TWO LEGS

(Mercury)

Singles:

Queen's First EP

Albums:

A Night At The Opera

Live Killers

The Complete Works

The Ultimate Queen

DELILAH

(Queen)

Albums:

Innuendo

The Ultimate Queen

DOING ALL RIGHT (Queen Version)

(May/Staffell)

Singles:

Liar/DOING ALRIGHT (US single)

Albums:

Queen

Queen At The Beeb

The Complete Works

The Ultimate Queen

DOIN' ALL RIGHT (Smile Version)

(May/Staffell)

Albums:

Gettin' Smile

DON'T LOSE YOUR HEAD

(Taylor)

Singles:

Pain Is So Close To Pleasure
(remix)/DON'T LOSE YOUR
HEAD (US single)

Albums:

A Kind Of Magic

The Ultimate Queen

DON'T STOP ME NOW

(Mercury)

Singles:

DON'T STOP ME NOW/In Only 7
Days

DON'T STOP ME NOW/More Of
That Jazz (US single)

Albums:

Jazz

Live Killers

Greatest Hits

The Complete Works

The Ultimate Queen

Videos:

Greatest Flix I

Box Of Flix

DON'T TRY SUICIDE

(Mercury)

Singles:

Another One Bites The
Dust/DON'T TRY SUICIDE (US
single)

Albums:

The Game

The Complete Works

The Ultimate Queen

DON'T TRY TOO HARD

(Queen)

Albums:

Innuendo

The Ultimate Queen

DRAGON ATTACK

(May)

Singles:

Another One Bites The
Dust/DRAGON ATTACK

Another One Bites The Dust/
DRAGON ATTACK/Las Palabras
De Amor (3" CD single)

Albums:

The Game

The Complete Works

The Ultimate Queen

The Game (1991 remix) (US CD)

Videos:

We Will Rock You

Live In Japan

DREAMER'S BALL

(May)

Albums:

Jazz

Live Killers

The Complete Works

The Ultimate Queen

DRIVEN BY YOU

(May)

Singles:

DRIVEN BY YOU/Just One Life

DRIVEN BY YOU (single version)/
DRIVEN BY YOU (Ford advert
version)/Just One Life (album
version)/Just One Life
(guitar version) (12" single)

DRIVEN BY YOU (single version)/
DRIVEN BY YOU (Ford advert
version)/Just One Life (album
version)/Just One Life (guitar
version) (CD single)
Too Much Love Will Kill You
(album version)/I'm Scared
(single version)/Too Much Love
Will Kill You (guitar version)/
DRIVEN BY YOU (new
version) (CD single)
Albums:
Back To The Light
Live At The Brixton Academy
Videos:
Live At The Brixton Academy

DROWSE

(Taylor)
Singles:
Tie Your Mother Down/DROWSE
(US single)
Albums:
A Day At The Races
The Complete Works
The Ultimate Queen

E

EARTH

(Staffell)
Singles:
EARTH/Step On Me
Albums:
Gettin' Smile

ENSUENO

(Caballe/Mercury/Moran)
Albums:
Barcelona

ESCAPE FROM THE SWAMP

(Taylor)
Albums:
Flash Gordon

The Complete Works
The Ultimate Queen

EVERYBODY HURTS SOMETIME

(Taylor)
Singles:
Happiness/Dear Mr
Murdoch/EVERYBODY HURTS
SOMETIME (live)/Old Friends
(12" single)
Albums:
Happiness

EXECUTION OF FLASH

(Deacon)
Albums:
Flash Gordon
The Complete Works
The Ultimate Queen

EXERCISES IN FREE LOVE
(Freddie Vocal)

(Mercury/Moran)
Singles:
The Great Pretender/EXERCISES
IN FREE LOVE
The Great Pretender (extended)/
The Great Pretender (7"
version)/EXERCISES IN FREE
LOVE (12" single)
Albums:
The Freddie Mercury Album

EXERCISES IN FREE LOVE
(Montserrat Vocal)

(Mercury/Moran)
Singles:
Barcelona/EXERCISES IN FREE
LOVE (with Montserrat Caballe)
Barcelona/EXERCISES IN FREE
LOVE (with Montserrat Caballe)/
Barcelona (extended) (12"
single)
Barcelona/EXERCISES IN FREE
LOVE (with Montserrat Caballe)/

Barcelona (extended) (CD
single)

F

THE FAIRY FELLERS
MASTERSTROKE

(Mercury)
Albums:
Queen II
The Complete Works
The Ultimate Queen

THE FALLEN PRIEST

(Mercury/Moran/Rice)
Singles:
The Golden Boy/THE FALLEN
PRIEST
The Golden Boy/THE FALLEN
PRIEST/The Golden Boy
(instrumental) (12" single)
The Golden Boy/THE FALLEN
PRIEST/The Golden Boy
(instrumental) (CD single)
Albums:
Barcelona

FAT BOTTOMED GIRLS

(May)
Singles:
Bicycle Race/FAT BOTTOMED
GIRLS
We Are The Champions/We Will
Rock You/FAT BOTTOMED
GIRLS (3" CD single)
Albums:
Jazz
Greatest Hits
The Complete Works
The Ultimate Queen
Jazz (1991 remix) (US CD)
Queen Rocks
Videos:
Greatest Flix I
Box Of Flix

FATHER TO SON

(May)

Albums:

Queen II

The Complete Works

The Ultimate Queen

Videos:

Live At The Rainbow

FIGHT FROM THE INSIDE

(Taylor)

Albums:

News Of The World

The Complete Works

The Ultimate Queen

FINAL DESTINATION (Cross Version)

(Taylor)

Albums:

Mad, Bad And Dangerous To Know

FINAL DESTINATION (Roger Version)

(Taylor)

Singles:

Foreign Sand (single version)/
Foreign Sand (album version)/
You Had To Be There/FINAL
DESTINATION (12" single)

FLASH (aka Flash's Theme)

(May)

Singles:

FLASH/Football Fight

Crazy Little Thing Called
Love/Spread Your Wings/
FLASH (3" CD single)

Albums:

Flash Gordon

Greatest Hits

The Complete Works

The Ultimate Queen

Flash Gordon (1991 remix) (US
CD)

Videos:

Greatest Flix I

Live In Japan

Box Of Flix

FLASH TO THE RESCUE

(May)

Albums:

Flash Gordon

The Complete Works

The Ultimate Queen

FLASH'S THEME REPRISE

(May)

Albums:

Flash Gordon

The Complete Works

The Ultimate Queen

FLICK OF THE WRIST

(Mercury)

Singles:

Killer Queen/FLICK OF THE
WRIST

Killer Queen/FLICK OF THE
WRIST/Brighton Rock (3" CD
single)

Albums:

Queen II

The Complete Works

The Ultimate Queen

FOOLIN' AROUND

(Mercury)

Albums:

Mr Bad Guy

The Freddie Mercury Album

Teachers

Videos:

Teachers

FOOTBALL FIGHT

(Mercury)

Singles:

Flash/FOOTBALL FIGHT

Albums:

Flash Gordon

The Complete Works

The Ultimate Queen

FOREIGN SAND

(Taylor)

Singles:

FOREIGN SAND/You Had To Be
There

FOREIGN SAND (single
version)/FOREIGN SAND (album
version)/You Had To Be
There/Final Destination (12"
single)

Albums:

Happiness

FOREVER

(May)

Singles:

Who Wants To Live Forever (7"
version)/Who Wants To Live
Forever (album version)/Killer
Queen/FOREVER (12"
single)

Albums:

A Kind Of Magic (US CD)

FOXY LADY

(Hendrix)

Albums:

Mad, Bad And Dangerous To
Know (CD issue)

FREEDOM TRAIN

(Taylor)

Albums:

Happiness

FRIENDS WILL BE FRIENDS

(Mercury/Deacon)

Singles:

FRIENDS WILL BE
FRIENDS/Seven Seas Of Rhye

FRIENDS WILL BE
FRIENDS/Seven Seas Of Rhye
(7" picture disc)
FRIENDS WILL BE FRIENDS (12"
mix)/FRIENDS WILL BE
FRIENDS (7" mix)/Seven Seas
Of Rhye (12" single)
Albums:
A Kind Of Magic
Live Magic
Greatest Hits II
Live At Wembley
The Ultimate Queen
Videos:
Live In Budapest
Live At Wembley
Greatest Flix II
Box Of Flix

FUN IN SPACE
(Taylor)
Singles:
My Country/FUN IN SPACE
Albums:
Fun In Space

FUN IT
(Taylor)
Singles:
Jealousy/FUN IT (US single)
Albums:
Jazz
The Complete Works
The Ultimate Queen

FUNNY HOW LOVE IS
(Mercury)
Singles:
Seven Seas Of Rhye/See What A
Fool I've Been/FUNNY HOW
LOVE IS (3" CD single)
Albums:
Queen II
The Complete Works
The Ultimate Queen

FUTURE MANAGEMENT
(Taylor)
Singles:
FUTURE MANAGEMENT/Laugh
Or Cry
Albums:
Fun In Space

G

GET DOWN, MAKE LOVE
(Mercury)
Albums:
News Of The World
Live Killers
The Complete Works
The Ultimate Queen
Videos:
We Will Rock You

GIMME SOME LOVIN'
(Winwood, Winwood & Davis)
Albums:
Live At Wembley
The Ultimate Queen

**GIMME THE PRIZE (KURGAN'S
THEME)**
(May)
Singles:
A Kind Of Magic (extended
remix)/GIMME THE PRIZE (US
single)
Albums:
A Kind Of Magic
The Ultimate Queen

GOD SAVE THE QUEEN
(Arranged: May)
Albums:
A Night At The Opera
Live Killers
Live Magic
Live At Wembley
The Ultimate Queen

Videos:
We Will Rock You
Live In Rio
Live In Budapest
Live At Wembley
Live At The Rainbow

THE GOLDEN BOY
(Mercury/Moran/Rice)
Singles:
THE GOLDEN BOY/The Fallen
Priest
THE GOLDEN BOY/The Fallen
Priest/THE GOLDEN BOY
(instrumental) (12" single)
THE GOLDEN BOY/The Fallen
Priest/THE GOLDEN BOY
(instrumental) (CD single)
Albums:
Barcelona
Videos:
The Barcelona EP

GOING BACK
(Goffin/King)
Singles:
I Can Hear Music/GOING BACK

GOOD COMPANY
(May)
Albums:
A Night At The Opera
The Complete Works
The Ultimate Queen

**GOOD OLD FASHIONED LOVER
BOY**
(Mercury)
Singles:
Queen's First EP
Albums:
A Day At The Races
Greatest Hits
The Complete Works
The Ultimate Queen

GOOD TIMES ARE NOW

(Taylor)

Albums:

Fun In Space

GREAT KING RAT

(Mercury)

Albums:

Queen

Queen At The Beeb

The Complete Works

The Ultimate Queen

THE GREAT PRETENDER

(Ram)

Singles:

THE GREAT PRETENDER
(extended)/THE GREAT
PRETENDER (7" version)/
Exercises In Free Love (12"
single)

THE GREAT PRETENDER/
Exercises In Free Love (12"
single)

THE GREAT PRETENDER/Stop All
The Fighting

Albums:

The Freddie Mercury Album

Videos:

The Great Pretender

Now That's What I Call Music #9

GUIDE ME HOME

(Mercury/Moran)

Singles:

How Can I Go On/GUIDE ME
HOME/Overture Piccante (12"
single)

How Can I Go On/GUIDE ME
HOME/Overture Piccante (CD
single)

Albums:

Barcelona

H

HAMMER TO FALL

(May)

Singles:

HAMMER TO FALL/Tear It Up

HAMMER TO FALL (headbangers
mix)/Tear It Up (12" single)

Radio Ga Ga/I Go Crazy/
HAMMER TO FALL (edit) (3" CD
Single)

Albums:

The Works

Live Magic

Greatest Hits II

Live At Wembley

The Ultimate Queen

The 12" Collection

Live At The Brixton Academy

Queen Rocks

Videos:

Live In Rio

Rare Live

The Works Video EP

Live In Budapest

Live At Wembley

Greatest Flix II

Box Of Flix

Classic Queen

Live At The Brixton Academy

HANG ON IN THERE

(Queen)

Singles:

I Want It All/HANG ON IN THERE

I Want It All (album version)/I
Want It All (edit)/HANG ON IN
THERE (12" single)

I Want It All (album version)/
HANG ON IN THERE/I Want It
All (edit) (CD single)

Albums:

The Miracle (US CD)

HAPPINESS

(Taylor)

Singles:

HAPPINESS/Ride The Wild
Wind

HAPPINESS/Dear Mr Murdoch/
Everybody Hurts Sometime
(live)/Old Friends (12" single)

Albums:

Happiness

HEADLONG

(Queen)

Singles:

HEADLONG/All God's People

HEADLONG/All God's
People/Mad The Swine (12"
single)

HEADLONG (edit)/Under
Pressure (US single)

Albums:

Innuendo

Greatest Hits II

The Ultimate Queen

Live At The Brixton Academy

Queen Rocks

Videos:

Greatest Flix II

Box Of Flix

Classic Queen

Live At The Brixton Academy

HEAVEN FOR EVERYONE
(Cross Version)

(Taylor)

Singles:

HEAVEN FOR EVERYONE/Love
On A Tightrope (Like An Animal)

HEAVEN FOR EVERYONE/Love
On A Tightrope (Like An
Animal)/Contact (12" single)

Albums:

Shove It

HEAVEN FOR EVERYONE
(Queen Version)
(Taylor)
Singles:
 HEAVEN FOR EVERYONE (single
  version)/It's A Beautiful
  Day/HEAVEN FOR EVERYONE
  (album version) (CD single)
 HEAVEN FOR EVERYONE (single
  version)/Keep Yourself Alive/

Seven Seas Of Rhye/Killer
 Queen (CD single)
Albums:
 Made In Heaven
 The Ultimate Queen
Videos:
 Queen The Films (Made In Heaven)

HELLO MARY LOU
(Pitney)

Albums:
 Live At Wembley
 The Ultimate Queen

THE HERO
(May)
Albums:
 Flash Gordon
 The Complete Works
 The Ultimate Queen

(David Redfern/Redferns)

HIJACK MY HEART

(Queen)

Singles:

The Invisible Man/HIJACK MY
HEART

The Invisible Man/HIJACK
MY HEART (7" clear vinyl)

The Invisible Man (single version)/
HIJACK MY HEART (12"
single)

The Invisible Man/HIJACK MY
HEART/The Invisible Man (12"
clear vinyl)

The Invisible Man (extended)/
HIJACK MY HEART/The Invisible
Man (CD single)

THE HITMAN

(Queen)

Singles:

I'm Going Slightly Mad/THE
HITMAN

I'm Going Slightly Mad/THE
HITMAN/Lost Opportunity (12"
single)

Albums:

Innuendo

The Ultimate Queen

HOW CAN I GO ON

(Mercury/Moran)

Singles:

HOW CAN I GO ON/Overture
Piccante

HOW CAN I GO ON/Guide Me
Home/Overture Piccante (12"
single)

HOW CAN I GO ON/Guide Me
Home/Overture Piccante (CD
single)

Albums:

Barcelona

Videos:

The Barcelona EP

I

I CAN HEAR MUSIC

(Spector/Greenwich/Barry)

Singles:

I CAN HEAR MUSIC/Goin' Back

I CAN'T LIVE WITH YOU

(Queen)

Albums:

Innuendo

The Ultimate Queen

Queen Rocks

**I CRY FOR YOU (LOVE, HOPE
AND CONFUSION)**

(Taylor)

Singles:

Strange Frontier/I CRY FOR
YOU Strange Frontier
(extended)/I CRY FOR YOU/
Two Sharp Pencils (12"
single)

Albums:

Strange Frontier

I GO CRAZY

(May)

Singles:

Radio Ga Ga/I GO CRAZY

Radio Ga Ga (extended)/Radio
Ga Ga (dub)/I GO CRAZY (12"
single)

Radio Ga Ga/I GO
CRAZY/Hammer To Fall (edit)
(3" CD single)

Albums:

The Complete Works

The Works (12" mix) (US CD)

I WANNA TESTIFY

(Taylor/Clinton/Taylor)

Singles:

I WANNA TESTIFY/Turn On The
TV

I WANT IT ALL

(Queen)

Singles:

I WANT IT ALL/Hang On In There

I WANT IT ALL (album version)/I
WANT IT ALL (edit)/Hang On In
There (12" single)

I WANT IT ALL (album version)/
Hang On In There/I WANT IT
ALL (edit) (CD single)

Breakthru/I WANT IT ALL (US
single)

Albums:

The Miracle

Greatest Hits II

The Ultimate Queen

Queen Rocks

Videos:

Rare Live

The Miracle Video EP

Greatest Flix II

Box Of Flix

Now That's What I Call Music
#15

Classic Queen

I WANT TO BREAK FREE

(Deacon)

Singles:

I WANT TO BREAK
FREE/Machines (or Back To
Humans)

I WANT TO BREAK FREE
(extended remix)/Machines (or
Back To Humans) (12" single)

I WANT TO BREAK FREE
(remix)/Machines (or Back To
Humans)/It's A Hard Life (3"
CD single)

Albums:

The Works

Live Magic

Greatest Hits II

Live At Wembley

The Ultimate Queen

The Works (12" mix) (US CD)
The 12" Collection
Videos:
  Live In Rio
  The Works Video EP
  Live In Budapest
  Live At Wembley
  Greatest Flix II
  Box Of Flix

I WAS BORN TO LOVE YOU
(Freddie Version)
(Mercury)
Singles:
  I WAS BORN TO LOVE YOU/Stop
    All The Fighting
  I WAS BORN TO LOVE YOU
    (extended)/Stop All The
    Fighting (12" single)
Albums:
  Mr Bad Guy
Videos:
  Freddie Mercury: The Video EP

I WAS BORN TO LOVE YOU
(Queen Version)
(Mercury)
Albums:
  Made In Heaven
Videos:
  Queen The Films (Made In Heaven)

I'M GOING SLIGHTLY MAD
(Queen)
Singles:
  I'M GOING SLIGHTLY MAD/The
    Hitman
  I'M GOING SLIGHTLY MAD/The
    Hitman/Lost Opportunity (12"
    single)
Albums:
  Innuendo
  Greatest Hits II
  The Ultimate Queen
Videos:

Greatest Flix II
Box Of Flix
Classic Queen

I'M IN LOVE WITH MY CAR
(Taylor)
Singles:
  Bohemian Rhapsody/I'M IN LOVE
    WITH MY CAR
  Bohemian Rhapsody/I'M IN LOVE
    WITH MY CAR (limited edition
    blue vinyl)
  Bohemian Rhapsody/I'M IN LOVE
    WITH MY CAR (limited edition
    blue vinyl with card sleeve)
  Bohemian Rhapsody/I'M IN LOVE
    WITH MY CAR (limited edition
    blue vinyl with extras)
  Bohemian Rhapsody/You're My
    Best Friend/I'M IN LOVE WITH
    MY CAR (3" CD single)
  Bohemian Rhapsody/I'M IN LOVE
    WITH MY CAR (CD single)
Albums:
  A Night At The Opera
  Live Killers
  The Complete Works
  The Ultimate Queen
  A Night At The Opera (1991
    remix) (US CD)
  Queen Rocks
Videos:
  We Will Rock You

I'M SCARED
(May)
Singles:
  Too Much Love Will Kill You/I'M
    SCARED
  Too Much Love Will Kill You
    (album version)/I'M SCARED
    (single version)/Too Much
    Love Will Kill You (guitar
    version)/Driven By You
    (new version) (CD single)

Albums:
  Back To The Light

THE INVISIBLE MAN
(Queen)
Singles:
  THE INVISIBLE MAN/Hijack My
    Heart
  THE INVISIBLE MAN/Hijack My
    Heart (7" clear vinyl)
  THE INVISIBLE MAN (single
    version)/Hijack My Heart (12"
    single)
  THE INVISIBLE MAN
    (extended)/Hijack My Heart/
    THE INVISIBLE MAN (12"
    clear vinyl)
  THE INVISIBLE MAN
    (extended)/Hijack My Heart/
    THE INVISIBLE MAN (CD
    single)
Albums:
  The Miracle
  Greatest Hits II
  The Ultimate Queen
  The 12" Collection
Videos:
  The Miracle Video EP
  Greatest Flix II
  Box Of Flix

IF YOU CAN'T BEAT THEM
(Deacon)
Albums:
  Jazz
  The Complete Works
  The Ultimate Queen

IN MY DEFENCE
(Clark/Soames/Daniels)
Singles:
  IN MY DEFENCE/Love Kills
Albums:
  The Freddie Mercury Album

Queen on tour during the Eighties (David Redfern/Redferns)

IN ONLY SEVEN DAYS

(Deacon)

Singles:

Don't Stop Me Now/IN ONLY
SEVEN DAYS

Albums:

Jazz

The Complete Works

The Ultimate Queen

IN THE DEATH CELL

(Taylor)

Albums:

Flash Gordon

The Complete Works

The Ultimate Queen

IN THE LAP OF THE GODS

(Mercury)

Albums:

Sheer Heart Attack

Live At Wembley

The Ultimate Queen

Videos:

Live At The Rainbow

**IN THE LAP OF THE
GODS...REVISITED**

(Mercury)

Albums:

Sheer Heart Attack

The Complete Works

The Ultimate Queen

Videos:

Live In Budapest

Live At Wembley

Live At The Rainbow

IN THE SPACE CAPSULE

(Taylor)

Albums:

Flash Gordon

The Complete Works

The Ultimate Queen

INNUENDO

(Queen)

Singles:

INNUENDO/Bijou

INNUENDO/Bijou (12" single)

INNUENDO (explosive
version)/Under Pressure/Bijou
(12" picture disc)

INNUENDO (explosive version)/
Under Pressure/Bijou (CD
single)

Albums:

Innuendo

Greatest Hits II

The Ultimate Queen

Videos:

Greatest Flix II

Box Of Flix

The Awards 1992

**INTERLUDE IN
CONSTANTINOPLE**

(Taylor)

Albums:

Fun In Space

**IS THIS THE WORLD WE
CREATED...?**

(Mercury/May)

Singles:

It's A Hard Life/IS THIS THE
WORLD WE CREATED...?

It's A Hard Life (extended
remix)/It's A Hard Life/IS THIS
THE WORLD WE CREATED...?
(12" single)

It's A Hard Life/IS THIS THE
WORLD WE CREATED...? (12"
picture disc)

Albums:

The Works

Live Magic

Live At Wembley

The Ultimate Queen

Videos:

Live In Rio

Live In Budapest

Live At Wembley

Greenpeace Non-Toxic Video Hits

IT'S A BEAUTIFUL DAY

(Queen)

Singles:

Heaven For Everyone (single
version)/IT'S A BEAUTIFUL
DAY/Heaven For Everyone
(album version) (CD single)

Albums:

Made In Heaven

The Ultimate Queen

IT'S A HARD LIFE

(Mercury)

Singles:

IT'S A HARD LIFE/Is This The
World We Created...?

IT'S A HARD LIFE (extended
remix)/IT'S A HARD LIFE/Is This
The World We Created...? (12"
single)

IT'S A HARD LIFE/Is This The
World We Created...? (12"
picture disc)

I Want To Break Free (remix)/
Machines (or Back To
Humans)/IT'S A HARD LIFE (3"
CD single)

Albums:

The Works

Greatest Hits II

The Complete Works

The Ultimate Queen

The 12" Collection

Videos:

Live In Rio

The Works Video EP

Greatest Flix II

Box Of Flix

Now That's What I Call
Music #4

IT'S AN ILLUSION

(Taylor/Parfitt)

Albums:

Strange Frontier

IT'S LATE

(May)

Singles:

IT'S LATE/Sheer Heart Attack
(US Single)

Albums:

News Of The World

The Complete Works

The Ultimate Queen

Queen Rocks

J

JAILHOUSE ROCK

(Leiber/Stoller)

Videos:

Live At The Rainbow

Rare Live

JEALOUSY

(Mercury)

Singles:

JEALOUSY/Fun It (US Single)

Albums:

Jazz

The Complete Works

The Ultimate Queen

JESUS

(Mercury)

Albums:

Queen

The Complete Works

The Ultimate Queen

JUST ONE LIFE

(May)

Singles:

Driven By You/JUST ONE LIFE

Driven By You (single version)/

Driven By You (Ford advert
version)/JUST ONE LIFE
(album version)/JUST ONE
LIFE (guitar version) (12"
single)

Driven By You (single version)/
Driven By You (Ford advert
version)/JUST ONE LIFE
(album version)/JUST ONE
LIFE (guitar version) (CD
single)

Albums:

Back To The Light

K

**KEEP PASSING THE OPEN
WINDOWS**

(Mercury)

Singles:

Thank God It's Christmas/Man
On The Prowl/KEEP PASSING
THE OPEN WINDOWS

Thank God It's Christmas/Man
On The Prowl (extended
remix)/KEEP PASSING THE
OPEN WINDOWS (extended)
(12" single)

Albums:

The Works

The Complete Works

The Ultimate Queen

KEEP YOURSELF ALIVE

(May)

Singles:

KEEP YOURSELF ALIVE/Son And
Daughter

The Show Must Go On/KEEP
YOURSELF ALIVE

The Show Must Go On/KEEP
YOURSELF ALIVE/Queen Talks
(12" single)

The Show Must Go On/KEEP
YOURSELF ALIVE/Queen

Talks/Body Language (CD
single)

Heaven For Everyone (single
version)/KEEP YOURSELF
ALIVE/Seven Seas Of
Rhye/Killer Queen (CD single)

KEEP YOURSELF ALIVE/Lily Of
The Valley (US single)

Albums:

Queen

Live Killers

The Old Grey Whistle Test

Queen At The Beeb

The Complete Works

The Ultimate Queen

Queen (remake) (US CD)

Queen Rocks

Videos:

We Will Rock You

Live In Rio

Rare Live

Live At The Rainbow

Box Of Flix

Classic Queen

KHASHOGGI'S SHIP

(Queen)

Albums:

The Miracle

The Ultimate Queen

KILLER QUEEN

(Mercury)

Singles:

KILLER QUEEN/Flick Of The Wrist

KILLER QUEEN/Flick Of The
Wrist/Brighton Rock (3" CD
single)

Who Wants To Live Forever/A
Kind Of Magic/KILLER QUEEN

Who Wants To Live Forever (7"
version)/Who Wants To Live
Forever (album version)/
KILLER QUEEN/Forever (12"
single)

Heaven For Everyone (single
version)/Keep Yourself Alive/
Seven Seas Of Rhye/KILLER
QUEEN (CD single)
Albums:
Queen II
Live Killers
Greatest Hits
The Ultimate Queen
Videos:
We Will Rock You
Greatest Flix I
Rare Live
Live At The Rainbow
Box Of Flix
Rock Idols
Sexy Shorts

KILLING TIME

(Taylor)
Singles:
Man On Fire/KILLING TIME
Man On Fire (extended)/KILLING
TIME
Albums:
Strange Frontier

THE KISS

(Mercury)
Albums:
Flash Gordon
The Complete Works
The Ultimate Queen

L

LA JAPONAISE

(Mercury/Moran)
Albums:
Barcelona

**LAS PALABRAS DE AMOR (THE
WORDS OF LOVE)**

(May)
Singles:

Freddie in thoughtful mood (S&G/Redferns)

LAS PALABRAS DE AMOR/Cool
Cat
Another One Bites The Dust/
Dragon Attack/LAS
PALABRAS DE AMOR (3" CD
single)
Albums:
Hot Space
The Complete Works
The Ultimate Queen

LAST HORIZON

(May)
Singles:
LAST HORIZON/ '39 (live)/Let
Your Heart Rule Your Head
LAST HORIZON (radio
version)/LAST HORIZON (live
version)/LAST HORIZON
(album version)/We Will Rock
You (live slow version)/We
Will Rock You (live fast
version) (CD single)
Albums:
Back To The Light
Live At The Brixton Academy
Videos:
Live At The Brixton Academy

LAUGH OR CRY

(Taylor)
Singles:
Future Management/LAUGH OR
CRY
Albums:
Fun In Space

'God save our Queen . . . ' (Corbis)

LAZING ON A SUNDAY AFTERNOON

(Mercury)

Albums:

A Night At The Opera

The Complete Works

The Ultimate Queen

LEAVING HOME AIN'T EASY

(May)

Albums:

Jazz

The Complete Works

The Ultimate Queen

LET ME ENTERTAIN YOU

(Mercury)

Singles:

We Will Rock You (live)/LET ME ENTERTAIN YOU (live) (US single)

Albums:

Jazz

Live Killers

The Complete Works

The Ultimate Queen

Videos:

We Will Rock You

LET ME LIVE

(Queen)

Singles:

LET ME LIVE/Bicycle Race/Fat Bottomed Girls/Don't Stop Me Now (CD single)

LET ME LIVE/Fairy King/Doin' Alright/Liar (CD single)

Albums:

Made In Heaven

The Ultimate Queen

Videos:

Queen The Films (Made In Heaven)

LET ME OUT

(May)

Albums:

Starfleet

LET YOUR HEART RULE YOUR HEAD

(May)

Albums:

Back To The Light

Live At The Brixton Academy

Videos:

Live At The Brixton Academy

LET'S GET CRAZY

(Taylor)

Albums:

Fun In Space

LET'S TURN IT ON

(Mercury)

Singles:

Love Me Like There's No Tomorrow/LET'S TURN IT ON

Love Me Like There's No Tomorrow (extended)/LET'S TURN IT ON (extended) (12" single)

Albums:

Mr Bad Guy

The Freddie Mercury Album

LIAR (Queen)

(Mercury)

Singles:

LIAR/Doing All Right (US single)

Albums:

Queen

Queen At The Beeb

The Complete Works

The Ultimate Queen

Queen (1991 remix) (US CD)

Videos:

Live In Rio

Rare Live

Live At The Rainbow

Box Of Flix

LIAR (Cross)

(Noone)

Albums:

Mad, Bad And Dangerous To Know

LIFE IS REAL (Song for Lennon)

(Mercury)

Singles:

Body Language/LIFE IS REAL

Albums:

Hot Space

The Complete Works

The Ultimate Queen

LILY OF THE VALLEY

(Mercury)

Singles:

Now I'm Here/LILY OF THE VALLEY

Keep Yourself Alive/LILY OF THE VALLEY (US single)

Albums:

Queen II

The Complete Works

The Ultimate Queen

LIVING ON MY OWN

(Mercury)

Singles:

LIVING ON MY OWN/My Love Is Dangerous

LIVING ON MY OWN (extended)/ My Love Is Dangerous (extended) (12" single)

LIVING ON MY OWN (extended version)/LIVING ON MY OWN (club version)/LIVING ON MY OWN (dub version)/LIVING ON MY OWN (L.A. version) (12" single)

LIVING ON MY OWN (radio

mix)/LIVING ON MY OWN
(extended mix)/LIVING ON MY
OWN (club version)/LIVING
ON MY OWN (album mix)
(CD single)
Albums:
Mr Bad Guy
The Freddie Mercury Album
Videos:
Freddie Mercury: The Video EP

LONELINESS
(Taylor)
Albums:
Happiness

LONG AWAY
(May)
Singles:
LONG AWAY/You And I (US single)
Albums:
A Day At The Races
The Complete Works
The Ultimate Queen

THE LOSER IN THE END
(Taylor)
Albums:
Queen II
The Complete Works
The Ultimate Queen

LOST OPPORTUNITY
(Queen)
Singles:
I'm Going Slightly Mad/The
Hitman/LOST OPPORTUNITY
(12" single)

LOVE KILLS
(Mercury/Moroder)
Singles:
LOVE KILLS/Rotwangs Party
LOVE KILLS (extended)/
Rotwangs Party (12" single)

In My Defence/LOVE KILLS
Albums:
The Freddie Mercury Album
Videos:
Metropolis

LOVE LIES BLEEDING
(Taylor)
Singles:
Cowboys And Indians/LOVES
LIES BLEEDING
Cowboys And Indians (full length
version)/LOVES LIES BLEEDING
(12" single)
Albums:
Shove It

**LOVE ME LIKE THERE'S NO
TOMORROW**
(Mercury)
Singles:
LOVE ME LIKE THERE'S NO
TOMORROW/Let's Turn It On
LOVE ME LIKE THERE'S NO
TOMORROW (extended)/Let's
Turn It On (extended) (12"
single)
Albums:
Mr Bad Guy

LOVE OF MY LIFE
(Mercury)
Singles:
LOVE OF MY LIFE (live)/Now I'm
Here (live)
Albums:
A Night At The Opera
Live Killers
Live At Wembley
The Ultimate Queen
Live At The Brixton Academy
Videos:
We Will Rock You
Greatest Flix I
Live In Japan

Live In Rio
Live In Budapest
Rare Live
Box Of Flix
Live At The Brixton Academy

**LOVE ON A TIGHTROPE (LIKE
AN ANIMAL)**
(Taylor)
Singles:
Heaven For Everyone/LOVE ON A
TIGHTROPE (LIKE AN ANIMAL)
Heaven For Everyone/LOVE ON A
TIGHTROPE (LIKE AN ANIMAL)/
Contact (12" single)
Albums:
Shove It

LOVE TOKEN
(May)
Singles:
Resurrection/LOVE TOKEN/Too
Much Love Will Kill You (live)
(12" single)
Resurrection/LOVE TOKEN/Too
Much Love Will Kill You (live)
(CD single)
Albums:
Back To The Light
Live At The Brixton Academy
Videos:
Live At The Brixton Academy

M

**MACHINES (or Back To
Humans)**
(May/Taylor)
Singles:
I Want To Break Free/MACHINES
(or BACK TO HUMANS)
I Want To Break Free (extended
remix)/MACHINES (or BACK TO
HUMANS) (12" single)
I Want To Break Free (remix)/

MACHINES (or BACK TO
HUMANS)/It's A Hard Life (3"
CD single)
Albums:
The Works
The Complete Works
The Ultimate Queen
The 12" Collection

MAD THE SWINE
(Mercury)
Singles:
Headlong/All God's People/MAD
THE SWINE (12" single)
Albums:
Queen (US CD)

**MADE IN HEAVEN (Freddie
Version)**
(Mercury)
Singles:
MADE IN HEAVEN/She Blows Hot
And Cold
MADE IN HEAVEN (extended
remix)/MADE IN HEAVEN
(remix)/She Blows Hot And
Cold (extended) (12" single)
Albums:
Mr Bad Guy
Videos:
Freddie Mercury: The Video EP

**MADE IN HEAVEN (Queen
Version)**
(Mercury)
Albums:
Made In Heaven
The Ultimate Queen
Videos:
Queen The Films (Made In Heaven)

MAGIC IS LOOSE
(Taylor)
Albums:
Fun In Space

MAN MADE PARADISE
(Mercury)
Albums:
Mr Bad Guy

MAN ON FIRE
(Taylor)
Singles:
MAN ON FIRE/Killing Time
MAN ON FIRE (extended)/Killing
Time
Albums:
Strange Frontier

MAN ON THE PROWL
(Mercury)
Singles:
Thank God It's Christmas/MAN
ON THE PROWL/Keep Passing
The Open Windows
Thank God It's Christmas/
MAN ON THE PROWL
(extended remix)/Keep
Passing The Open
Windows (extended) (12"
single)
Albums:
The 12" Collection

MANIPULATOR
(Taylor/Strange)
Singles:
MANIPULATOR (extended
mix)/Stand Up For Love/
MANIPULATOR (12"
single)

MARCH OF THE BLACK QUEEN
(Mercury)
Albums:
Queen II
The Complete Works
The Ultimate Queen
Videos:
Live At The Rainbow

MARRIAGE OF DALE AND MING
(May/Taylor)
Albums:
Flash Gordon
The Complete Works
The Ultimate Queen

MASTERS OF WAR
(Dylan)
Albums:
Strange Frontier

THE MILLIONAIRE WALTZ
(Mercury)
Albums:
A Day At The Races
The Complete Works
The Ultimate Queen

MING'S THEME
(Mercury)
Albums:
Flash Gordon
The Complete Works
The Ultimate Queen

THE MIRACLE
(Queen)
Singles:
THE MIRACLE/Stone Cold Crazy
(live)
THE MIRACLE/Stone Cold Crazy
(live)/My Melancholy Blues (live)
(12" single)
THE MIRACLE/Stone Cold Crazy
(live)/My Melancholy Blues (live)
(CD single)
Albums:
The Miracle
Greatest Hits II
The Ultimate Queen
Videos:
Greatest Flix II
Box Of Flix
Classic Queen

(Patrick Ford/Redferns)

MISFIRE

(Deacon)

Albums:

Queen II

The Complete Works

The Ultimate Queen

MODERN TIMES ROCK 'N' ROLL

(Taylor)

Albums:

Queen

Queen At The Beeb

The Complete Works

The Ultimate Queen

MORE OF THAT JAZZ

(Taylor)

Singles:

Don't Stop Me Now/MORE OF
THAT JAZZ (US single)

Albums:

Jazz

The Complete Works

The Ultimate Queen

MOTHER LOVE

(May/Mercury)

Albums:

Made In Heaven

The Ultimate Queen

Videos:

Queen The Films (Made In
Heaven)

MR BAD GUY

(Mercury)

Albums:

Mr Bad Guy

The Freddie Mercury Album

MUSTAPHA

(Mercury)

Albums:

Jazz

Live Killers

The Complete Works

The Ultimate Queen

MY BABY DOES ME

(Queen)

Albums:

The Miracle

The Ultimate Queen

MY COUNTRY I & II

(Taylor)

Singles:

MY COUNTRY/Fun In Space

Albums:

Fun In Space

MY FAIRY KING

(Mercury)

Albums:

Queen

Queen At The Beeb

The Complete Works

The Ultimate Queen

MY LIFE HAS BEEN SAVED

(Queen)

Singles:

Scandal/MY LIFE HAS BEEN
SAVED

Scandal (7" mix)/MY LIFE HAS
BEEN SAVED (12" single)

Scandal (extended)/MY LIFE HAS
BEEN SAVED/Scandal (CD single)

Albums:

Made In Heaven

The Ultimate Queen

Videos:

Queen The Films (Made In
Heaven)

MY LOVE IS DANGEROUS

(Mercury)

Singles:

Living On My Own/MY LOVE IS
DANGEROUS

Living On My Own (extended)/MY
LOVE IS DANGEROUS
(extended) (12" single)

Albums:

Mr Bad Guy

MY MELANCHOLY BLUES

(Mercury)

Singles:

The Miracle/Stone Cold Crazy
(live)/MY MELANCHOLY BLUES
(live) (12" single)

The Miracle/Stone Cold Crazy
(live)/MY MELANCHOLY BLUES
(live) (CD single)

Albums:

News Of The World

The Ultimate Queen

Videos:

Rare Live

<u>N</u>

NAZIS 1994

(Taylor)

Singles:

NAZIS 1994/NAZIS 1994

NAZIS 1994/NAZIS 1994 (radio
mix)/NAZIS 1994 (Makita mix
extended)/NAZIS 1994 (big
science mix) (12" single)

NAZIS 1994/NAZIS 1994 (radio
mix)/NAZIS 1994 (kick mix)/
NAZIS 1994 (Schindler's mix)/
NAZIS 1994 (Makita mix
extended)/NAZIS 1994 (big
science mix) (CD single)

Albums:

Happiness

NEED YOUR LOVING TONIGHT

(Deacon)

Singles:

NEED YOUR LOVING TONIGHT/
Rock It (US single)

Albums:
  The Game
  The Complete Works
  The Ultimate Queen

NEVERMORE
(Mercury)
Albums:
  Queen II
  The Complete Works
  The Ultimate Queen

THE NIGHT COMES DOWN
(May)
Albums:
  Queen
  The Complete Works
  The Ultimate Queen

NO TURNING BACK
(Deacon/Ahwai)
Singles:
  NO TURNING BACK/NO TURNING
    BACK (chocs away mix)
Albums:
  Biggles
Videos:
  Biggles

NO VIOLINS
(Taylor)
Albums:
  Fun In Space

NOTHIN' BUT BLUE
(May/Powell/Nicholls/Makin)
Singles:
  Back To The Light/NOTHIN' BUT
BLUE (guitar version)/Starfleet (12"
single)
  Back To The Light/NOTHIN' BUT
    BLUE (guitar version)/Blues
    Breaker (CD single)
  Back To The Light (radio version)/
    Back To The Light (album

version)/NOTHIN' BUT BLUE
  (guitar version) (CD single)
Albums:
  Back To The Light

NOW I'M HERE
(May)
Singles:
  NOW I'M HERE/Lily Of The Valley
  Love Of My Life (live)/NOW I'M
    HERE (live)
  A Winter's Tale/NOW I'M
    HERE/You're My Best Friend/
    Somebody To Love (CD single)
Albums:
  Queen II
  Live Killers
  Concert For The People Of
    Kampuchea
  Greatest Hits
  Live At Wembley
  The Ultimate Queen
  Live At The Brixton Academy
  Queen Rocks
Videos:
  We Will Rock You
  Live In Japan
  Live In Rio
  Live In Budapest
  Live At The Rainbow
  Box Of Flix
  Live At The Brixton Academy

O

OGRE BATTLE
(Mercury)
Albums:
  Queen II
  Queen At The Beeb
  The Complete Works
  The Ultimate Queen
  Queen II (1991 remix) (US CD)
Videos:
  Live At The Rainbow

OLD FRIENDS
(Taylor)
Singles:
  Happiness/Dear Mr Murdoch/
    Everybody Hurts Sometime (live)/
    OLD FRIENDS (12" single)
Albums:
  Happiness

OLD MEN (LAY DOWN)
(Taylor)
Albums:
  Mad, Bad And Dangerous To Know

ON TOP OF THE WORLD MA
(The Cross)
Albums:
  Mad, Bad And Dangerous To
    Know

ONE VISION
(Queen)
Singles:
  ONE VISION/Blurred Vision
  ONE VISION (extended)/Blurred
    Vision (12" single)
  A Kind Of Magic/A Dozen Red
    Roses For My Darling/ONE
    VISION (3" CD single)
Albums:
  A Kind Of Magic
  Live Magic
  Greatest Hits II
  Live At Wembley
  A Kind Of Magic (US CD)
  Queen Rocks
Videos:
  Live In Budapest
  Live At Wembley
  Greatest Flix II
  Box Of Flix
  Classic Queen
  Now That's What I Call
    Music #6
  Iron Eagle

ONE YEAR OF LOVE

(Deacon)

Albums:

A Kind Of Magic

The Ultimate Queen

Videos:

Classic Queen

OVERTURE PICCANTE

(Mercury/Moran)

Singles:

How Can I Go On/OVERTURE
PICCANTE

How Can I Go On/Guide Me
Home/OVERTURE PICCANTE
(12" single)

How Can I Go On/Guide Me
Home/OVERTURE PICCANTE
(CD single)

Albums:

Barcelona

P

PAIN IS SO CLOSE TO PLEASURE

(Mercury/Deacon)

Singles:

PAIN IS SO CLOSE TO
PLEASURE (remix)/Don't Lose
Your Head (US single)

Albums:

A Kind Of Magic

The Ultimate Queen

The 12" Collection

PARTY

(Queen)

Albums:

The Miracle

The Ultimate Queen

PASSION FOR TRASH

(Macrae)

Singles:

Power To Love/PASSION FOR
TRASH

Power To Love (extended
version)/PASSION FOR
TRASH/Power To Love (12"
single)

Power To Love (extended
version)/PASSION FOR TRASH/
Power To Love (CD single)

Albums:

Mad, Bad And Dangerous To
Know

PENETRATION GURU

(Moss)

Albums:

Mad, Bad And Dangerous To
Know

PLAY THE GAME

(Mercury)

Singles:

PLAY THE GAME/A Human Body

Albums:

The Game

Greatest Hits

The Complete Works

The Ultimate Queen

Videos:

We Will Rock You

Greatest Flix I

Box Of Flix

POLAR BEAR

(unknown)

Albums:

Gettin' Smile

POWER TO LOVE

(Macrae/Noone/Moss)

Singles:

POWER TO LOVE/Passion For
Trash

POWER TO LOVE (extended
version)/Passion For Trash/

POWER TO LOVE (12" single)

POWER TO LOVE (extended
version)/Passion For Trash/

POWER TO LOVE (CD single)

Albums:

Mad, Bad And Dangerous To Know

PRINCES OF THE UNIVERSE

(Mercury)

Singles:

PRINCES OF THE UNIVERSE/A
Dozen Red Roses For My
Darling (US single)

Albums:

A Kind Of Magic

The Ultimate Queen

PROCESSION

(May)

Albums:

Queen II

The Complete Works

The Ultimate Queen

Videos:

Live At The Rainbow

THE PROPHET'S SONG

(May)

Albums:

A Night At The Opera

The Complete Works

The Ultimate Queen

PUT OUT THE FIRE

(May)

Singles:

Calling All The Girls/PUT OUT
THE FIRE (US single)

Albums:

Hot Space

The Complete Works

The Ultimate Queen

Queen Rocks

Videos:

Live In Japan

(Andrew Putler/Redferns)

R

RACING IN THE STREET
(Springsteen)
Albums:
   Strange Frontier

RADIO GA GA
(Taylor)
Singles:
   RADIO GA GA/I Go Crazy
   RADIO GA GA (extended)/RADIO
      GA GA (dub)/I Go Crazy (12"
      single)
   RADIO GA GA/I Go Crazy/
      Hammer To Fall (edit) (3" CD
      single)
Albums:
   The Works
   Live Magic
   Greatest Hits II
   Live At Wembley
   The Ultimate Queen
   The Works (12" mix) (US CD)
   The 12" Collection
Videos:
   Live In Rio
   Rare Live
   The Works Video EP
   Live In Budapest
   Live At Wembley
   Greatest Flix II
   Box Of Flix
   Classic Queen

RAIN MUST FALL
(Queen)
Albums:
   The Miracle
   The Ultimate Queen

RESURRECTION
(May/Page)
Singles:
   RESURRECTION/Love Token/Too

Much Love Will Kill You (live)
   (12" single)
RESURRECTION/Love Token/Too
   Much Love Will Kill You (live)
   (CD single)
Albums:
   Back To The Light
   Live At The Brixton Academy
Videos:
   Live At The Brixton Academy

REVELATION
(Taylor)
Albums:
   Happiness

RIDE THE WILD WIND
(Queen)
Singles:
   Happiness/RIDE THE WILD WIND
Albums:
   Innuendo
   The Ultimate Queen

THE RING
(Mercury)
Albums:
   Flash Gordon
   The Complete Works
   The Ultimate Queen

ROCK IN RIO BLUES
(Queen)
Singles:
   A Winter's Tale/Thank God It's
      Christmas/ROCK IN RIO BLUES
      (CD single)

ROCK IT
(Taylor)
Singles:
   Need Your Loving Tonight/ROCK
      IT (US Single)
Albums:
   The Game

The Complete Works
The Ultimate Queen

ROLLIN' OVER
(Marriott/Lane)
Albums:
   Back To The Light

ROTWANGS PARTY
(Marriott/Lane)
Singles:
   Love Kills/ROTWANGS PARTY
   Love Kills (extended)/
      ROTWANGS PARTY (12"
      single)

ROUGH JUSTICE
(Taylor)
Singles:
   Shove It/ROUGH JUSTICE
   Shove It/Shove It
      (metropolix)/ROUGH JUSTICE
      (12" single)
Albums:
   Shove It

S

SAIL AWAY SWEET SISTER
(May)
Albums:
   The Game
   The Complete Works
   The Ultimate Queen

SAVE ME
(May)
Singles:
   SAVE ME/Let Me Entertain You
      (live)
Albums:
   The Game
   Greatest Hits
   The Complete Works
   The Ultimate Queen

Videos:
  We Will Rock You
  Greatest Flix I
  Live In Japan
  Box Of Flix

SCANDAL

(Queen)
Singles:
  SCANDAL/My Life Has Been Saved
  SCANDAL (7" mix)/My Life Has
    Been Saved (12" single)
  SCANDAL (extended)/My Life
    Has Been Saved/SCANDAL (CD
    singles)
Albums:
  The Miracle
  The Ultimate Queen
  The Miracle (12" mix) (US CD)
Videos:
  The Miracle Video EP

SEASIDE RENDEZVOUS

(Mercury)
Albums:
  A Night At The Opera
  The Complete Works
  The Ultimate Queen

THE 2ND SHELF MIX

(Taylor)
Albums:
  Shove It (CD issue)

SEE WHAT A FOOL I'VE BEEN

(May)
Singles:
  SEE WHAT A FOOL I'VE BEEN/
    Seven Seas Of Rhye
  Seven Seas Of Rhye/SEE WHAT
    A FOOL I'VE BEEN/Funny How
    Love Is (3" CD single)
Albums:
  The Complete Works
  Queen II (US CD)

SEVEN SEAS OF RHYE

(Mercury)
Singles:
  SEVEN SEAS OF RHYE/See What
    A Fool I've Been
  Friends Will Be Friends/SEVEN
    SEAS OF RHYE
  Friends Will Be Friends/SEVEN
    SEAS OF RHYE (7" picture
    disc)
  Friends Will Be Friends (12"
    mix)/Friends Will Be Friends (7"
    mix)/SEVEN SEAS OF RHYE
    (12" single)
  SEVEN SEAS OF RHYE/See What
    A Fool I've Been/Funny How
    Love Is (3" CD single)
  Heaven For Everyone (single
    version)/Keep Yourself Alive/
    SEVEN SEAS OF RHYE/Killer
    Queen (CD single)
Albums:
  Queen
  Queen II
  Greatest Hits
  Live Magic
  Live At Wembley
  The Ultimate Queen
  Queen II (1991 remix) (US CD)
  Queen Rocks
Videos:
  Live In Rio
  Live In Budapest
  Live At Wembley

SHE BLOWS HOT AND COLD

(Mercury)
Singles:
  Made In Heaven/SHE BLOWS
    HOT AND COLD
  Made In Heaven (extended
    remix)/Made In Heaven
    (remix)/SHE BLOWS HOT AND
    COLD (extended) (12"
    single)

SHE MAKES ME (STORMTROOPER IN STILETTOES)

(May)
Albums:
  Queen II
  The Complete Works
  The Ultimate Queen

SHEER HEART ATTACK

(Taylor)
Singles:
  SHEER HEART ATTACK/Spread
    Your Wings
  It's Late/SHEER HEART ATTACK
    (US Single)
Albums:
  News Of The World
  Live Killers
  The Complete Works
  The Ultimate Queen
  Queen Rocks
Videos:
  Rare Live

SHOVE IT

(Taylor)
Singles:
  SHOVE IT/Rough Justice
  SHOVE IT/SHOVE IT
    (metropolix)/Rough Justice (12"
    single)
  SHOVE IT/Cowboys And
    Indians/SHOVE IT
    (extended version) (CD
    single)
Albums:
  Shove It

THE SHOW MUST GO ON

(Queen)
Singles:
  THE SHOW MUST GO ON/Keep
    Yourself Alive
  THE SHOW MUST GO ON/Keep

Yourself Alive/Queen Talks (12"
single)
THE SHOW MUST GO ON/Keep
Yourself Alive/Queen Talks/
Body Language (CD single)
Bohemian Rhapsody/THE SHOW
MUST GO ON (US single)
Albums:
Innuendo
Greatest Hits II
The Ultimate Queen
The 12" Collection
Videos:
Greatest Flix II
Box Of Flix
Classic Queen

SINCE YOU BEEN GONE
(Unknown)
Albums:
Live At The Brixton Academy
Videos:
Live At The Brixton Academy

SISTER BLUE
(Noone)
Albums:
Mad, Bad And Dangerous To Know

SLEEPING ON THE SIDEWALK
(May)
Albums:
News Of The World
The Complete Works
The Ultimate Queen

SOME DAY ONE DAY
(May)
Albums:
Queen II
The Complete Works
The Ultimate Queen

SOMEBODY TO LOVE
(Mercury)

Singles:
SOMEBODY TO LOVE/White Man
SOMEBODY TO LOVE/White
Man/Tie Your Mother Down (3"
CD single)
A Winter's Tale/Now I'm Here/
You're My Best Friend/
SOMEBODY TO LOVE (CD
single)
Albums:
A Day At The Races
Greatest Hits
The Complete Works
The Ultimate Queen
A Day At The Races (remix) (US
CD)
Videos:
We Will Rock You
Greatest Flix I
Rare Live
Box Of Flix

SON AND DAUGHTER
(May)
Singles:
Keep Yourself Alive/SON AND
DAUGHTER
Albums:
Queen
Queen At The Beeb
The Complete Works
The Ultimate Queen
Videos:
Live At The Rainbow

SON OF STARFLEET
(May)
Singles:
Starfleet/SON OF STARFLEET

SOUL BROTHER
(Queen)
Singles:
Under Pressure/SOUL BROTHER
Under Pressure/SOUL

BROTHER/Body Language (3"
CD single)

SPREAD YOUR WINGS
(Deacon)
Singles:
SPREAD YOUR WINGS/Sheer
Heart Attack
Crazy Little Thing Called
Love/SPREAD YOUR WINGS
(live)
Crazy Little Thing Called
Love/SPREAD YOUR
WINGS/Flash (3" CD single)
Too Much Love Will Kill You/
SPREAD YOUR WINGS/We Will
Rock You/We Are The
Champions (CD single)
Albums:
News Of The World
Live Killers
The Complete Works
The Ultimate Queen
Videos:
Greatest Flix I
Box Of Flix

STAND UP FOR LOVE
(Taylor)
Singles:
Manipulator (extended
mix)/STAND UP FOR LOVE/
Manipulator (12" single)
Albums:
Shove It

STARFLEET
(Bliss)
Singles:
STARFLEET/Son Of Starfleet
Back To The Light/Nothin' But
Blue (guitar version)/
STARFLEET (12" single)
Albums:
Starfleet

STAYING POWER

(Mercury)

Singles:

Backchat/STAYING POWER

Backchat (extended
remix)/STAYING POWER (12"
single)

STAYING POWER/Backchat (US
single)

Albums:

Hot Space

The Complete Works

The Ultimate Queen

STEALIN'

(Queen)

Singles:

Breakthru/STEALIN'

Breakthru (7" mix)/STEALIN' (12"
single)

Breakthru/STEALIN' (shaped
picture disc)

Breakthru (extended)/
STEALIN'/Breakthru (CD
single)

STEP ON ME

(May/Staffell)

Singles:

Earth/STEP ON ME

Albums:

Gettin' Smile

STONE COLD CRAZY

(Queen)

Singles:

The Miracle/STONE COLD
CRAZY (live)

The Miracle/STONE COLD
CRAZY (live)/My
Melancholy Blues (live) (12"
single)

The Miracle/STONE COLD
CRAZY (live)/My Melancholy
Blues (live) (CD single)

Albums:

Queen II

The Ultimate Queen

Sheer Heart Attack (1991 remix)
(US CD)

Queen Rocks

Videos:

Rare Live

Live At The Rainbow

Classic Queen

STOP ALL THE FIGHTING

(Mercury)

Singles:

I Was Born To Love You/STOP
ALL THE FIGHTING

I Was Born To Love You/STOP
ALL THE FIGHTING (12"
single)

The Great Pretender/STOP ALL
THE FIGHTING

STRANGE FRONTIER

(Taylor)

Singles:

STRANGE FRONTIER/I Cry For
You

STRANGE FRONTIER (extended)/I
Cry For You/Two Sharp Pencils
(12" single)

Albums:

Strange Frontier

STUPID CUPID

(Sedaka & Greenfield)

Videos:

Rare Live

SWEET LADY

(May)

Albums:

A Night At The Opera

The Complete Works

The Ultimate Queen

T

TAVASZI SZEL VIZET ARASZT

(-)

Videos:

Live In Budapest

TEAR IT UP

(May)

Singles:

Hammer To Fall/TEAR IT UP

Hammer To Fall (headbangers
mix)/TEAR IT UP (12" single)

Albums:

The Works

Live At Wembley

The Ultimate Queen

Queen Rocks

Videos:

Live In Budapest

TENEMENT FUNSTER

(Taylor)

Singles:

Queen's First EP

Albums:

Queen II

The Complete Works

The Ultimate Queen

TEO TORRIATTE (LET US CLING TOGETHER)

(May)

Albums:

A Day At The Races

The Complete Works

The Ultimate Queen

Videos:

Live In Japan

THANK GOD IT'S CHRISTMAS

(May/Taylor)

Singles:

THANK GOD IT'S CHRISTMAS/
Man On The Prowl/Keep

Passing The Open Windows
THANK GOD IT'S CHRISTMAS/
Man On The Prowl (extended
remix)/Keep Passing The
Open Windows (extended)
(12" single)
A Winter's Tale/THANK GOD IT'S
CHRISTMAS/Rock In Rio Blues
(CD single)
Albums:
The Complete Works

THERE MUST BE MORE TO LIFE THAN THIS

(Mercury)
Albums:
Mr Bad Guy

THESE ARE THE DAYS OF OUR LIVES

(Queen)
Singles:
Bohemian Rhapsody/THESE ARE
THE DAYS OF OUR LIVES
THESE ARE THE DAYS OF OUR
LIVES/Bijou (US single)
Albums:
Innuendo
The Ultimate Queen
Videos:
Classic Queen

TIE YOUR MOTHER DOWN

(May)
Singles:
TIE YOUR MOTHER DOWN/You
And I
Somebody To Love/White
Man/TIE YOUR MOTHER DOWN
(3" CD single)
TIE YOUR MOTHER DOWN/
Drowse (US single)
Albums:
A Day At The Races
Live Killers

Live Magic
Live At Wembley
The Ultimate Queen
A Day At The Races (remix) (US
CD)
Live At The Brixton Academy
Queen Rocks
Videos:
We Will Rock You
Greatest Flix I
Live In Rio
Live In Japan
Rare Live
Live In Budapest
Live At Wembley
Box Of Flix
Classic Queen
Live At The Brixton Academy

TIME

(Clark/Christie)
Singles:
TIME/TIME (instrumental)
TIME (extended version)/TIME (7"
version)/TIME (instrumental)
(12" single)
Albums:
The Freddie Mercury Album
Time
Videos:
Freddie Mercury: The Video EP

TOO MUCH LOVE WILL KILL YOU (Brian Version)

(May/Musker/Lamers)
Singles:
TOO MUCH LOVE WILL KILL
YOU/I'm Scared
TOO MUCH LOVE WILL KILL YOU
(album version)/I'm Scared
(single version)/TOO MUCH
LOVE WILL KILL YOU (guitar
version)/Driven By You
(new version) (CD single)
Resurrection/Love Token/TOO

MUCH LOVE WILL KILL YOU
(live) (12" single)
Resurrection/Love Token/TOO
MUCH LOVE WILL KILL YOU
(live) (CD single)
Albums:
Back To The Light
Live At The Brixton Academy
Video:
Live At The Brixton Academy

TOO MUCH LOVE WILL KILL YOU (Queen Version)

(May/Musker/Lamers)
Singles:
TOO MUCH LOVE WILL KILL
YOU/Spread Your Wings/We
Will Rock You/We Are The
Champions (CD single)
Albums:
Made In Heaven
The Ultimate Queen
Videos:
Queen The Films (Made In
Heaven)

TOUCH THE SKY

(Taylor)
Albums:
Happiness

TURN ON THE TV

(Taylor)
Singles:
I Wanna Testify/TURN ON THE
TV

TUTTI FRUTTI

(Penniman)
Albums:
Live At Wembley
The Ultimate Queen
Videos:
Live In Budapest
Live At Wembley

TWO SHARP PENCILS

(Taylor)

Singles:

> Strange Frontier (extended)/I Cry
> For You/TWO SHARP PENCILS
> (12" single)

UNDER PRESSURE

(Queen/Bowie)

Singles:

> UNDER PRESSURE/Soul Brother
> Innuendo/UNDER PRESSURE/
> Bijou (12" picture disc)
> UNDER PRESSURE/Soul
> Brother/Body Language (3" CD
> single)
> Innuendo (explosive version)/
> UNDER PRESSURE/Bijou (CD
> single)
> Headlong (edit)/UNDER
> PRESSURE (US single)

Albums:

> Hot Space
> Live Magic
> Greatest Hits II
> Live At Wembley
> The Ultimate Queen

Videos:

> We Will Rock You
> Live In Japan
> Live In Budapest
> Live At Wembley
> Greatest Flix II
> Box Of Flix
> Classic Queen
> Smash Hits-Now That's What I
> Call Music

VULTAN'S THEME

(Mercury)

Albums:

> Flash Gordon
> The Complete Works
> The Ultimate Queen

WAS IT ALL WORTH IT

(Queen)

Albums:

> The Miracle
> The Ultimate Queen

WE ARE THE CHAMPIONS

(Mercury)

Singles:

> WE ARE THE CHAMPIONS/We
> Will Rock You
> WE ARE THE CHAMPIONS/We
> Will Rock You/Fat Bottomed
> Girls (3" CD single)
> Too Much Love Will Kill You/
> Spread Your Wings/We Will
> Rock You/WE ARE THE
> CHAMPIONS (CD single)

Albums:

> News Of The World
> Live Killers
> Greatest Hits
> Live Magic
> Live At Wembley
> The Ultimate Queen

Videos:

> We Will Rock You
> Greatest Flix I
> Live In Rio
> Live In Japan
> Real Live
> Live In Budapest
> Live At Wembley
> Box Of Flix

THE WEDDING MARCH

(May)

Albums:

> Flash Gordon

The Complete Works
The Ultimate Queen

WE WILL ROCK YOU

(May)

Singles:

> We Are The Champions/WE WILL
> ROCK YOU
> We Are The Champions/WE WILL
> ROCK YOU/Fat Bottomed Girls
> (3" CD single)
> WE WILL ROCK YOU (live)/Let Me
> Entertain You (live) (US single)
> Too Much Love Will Kill You/
> Spread Your Wings/WE WILL
> ROCK YOU/We Are The
> Champions (CD single)

Albums:

> News Of The World
> Live Killers
> Greatest Hits
> Live Magic
> Live At Wembley
> The Ultimate Queen
> News Of The World (remix) (US
> CD)
> Live At The Brixton Academy
> Queen Rocks

Videos:

> We Will Rock You
> Greatest Flix I
> Live In Rio
> Live In Japan
> Rare Live
> Live In Budapest
> Live At Wembley
> Box Of Flix
> Rock Classics
> Live At The Brixton Academy

**WE WILL ROCK YOU (Brian May
version)**

(May)

Singles:

> Last Horizon (radio version)/Last

Horizon (live version)/Last
Horizon (album version)/WE
WILL ROCK YOU (live slow
version)/WE WILL ROCK
YOU (live fast version) (CD
single)

WHITE MAN

(May)
Singles:
Somebody To Love/WHITE MAN
Somebody To Love/WHITE MAN/
Tie Your Mother Down (3" CD
single)
Albums:
A Day At The Races
The Complete Works
The Ultimate Queen

WHITE QUEEN (AS IT BEGAN)

(May)
Singles:
Queen's First EP
Albums:
Queen II
The Complete Works
The Ultimate Queen
Videos:
Live At The Rainbow

WHO NEEDS YOU

(Deacon)
Albums:
News Of The World
The Complete Works
The Ultimate Queen

WHO WANTS TO LIVE FOREVER

(May)
Singles:
WHO WANTS TO LIVE FOREVER/
A Kind Of Magic/Killer Queen
WHO WANTS TO LIVE FOREVER
(7" version)/WHO WANTS TO
LIVE FOREVER (album

version)/Killer Queen/
Forever (12" single)
Albums:
A Kind Of Magic
Greatest Hits II
Live At Wembley
The Ultimate Queen
Videos:
WHO WANTS TO LIVE
FOREVER/ A Kind Of Magic
Live In Budapest
Live At Wembley
Greatest Flix II
Box Of Flix
Classic Queen
Is This Love
Missing You

Y

YOU AND I

(Deacon)
Singles:
Tie Your Mother Down/YOU
AND I
Long Away/YOU AND I (US
Single)
Albums:
A Day At The Races
The Complete Works
The Ultimate Queen

YOU DON'T FOOL ME

(Queen)
Singles:
YOU DON'T FOOL ME/YOU
DON'T FOOL ME (dancing divaz
mix)/YOU DON'T FOOL ME
(sexy club mix)/YOU DON'T
FOOL ME (late mix) (CD
single)
Albums:
Made In Heaven
The Ultimate Queen
Videos:

Queen The Films (Made In
Heaven)

YOU HAD TO BE THERE

(Taylor)
Singles:
Foreign Sand/YOU HAD TO BE
THERE
Foreign Sand (single version)/
Foreign Sand (album version)/
YOU HAD TO BE THERE/Final
Destination (12" single)
Albums:
Happiness

YOU TAKE MY BREATH AWAY

(Mercury)
Albums:
A Day At The Races
The Complete Works
The Ultimate Queen
Videos:
Rare Live

YOU'RE MY BEST FRIEND

(Deacon)
Singles:
YOU'RE MY BEST FRIEND/ '39
Bohemian Rhapsody/YOU'RE MY
BEST FRIEND/I'm In Love With
My Car (3" CD single)
A Winter's Tale/Now I'm Here/
YOU'RE MY BEST FRIEND/
Somebody To Love (CD single)
Albums:
A Night At The Opera
Live Killers
Greatest Hits
The Complete Works
The Ultimate Queen
A Night At The Opera (1991
remix) (US CD)
Videos:
Greatest Flix I
Box Of Flix

**(YOU'RE SO SQUARE) BABY I
DON'T CARE**

(Lieber & Stoller)

Albums:

Live At Wembley

The Ultimate Queen

YOUNG LOVE

(Taylor)

Albums:

Strange Frontier

YOUR KIND OF LOVER

(Mercury)

Albums:

Mr Bad Guy

The Freddie Mercury Album

QUEEN
A MUSICAL HISTORY

During a career spanning over three decades, Queen have released fourteen studio albums, three live albums and a soundtrack album. In this section we will trace their musical development from their first release *Queen* through to their final album, *Made In Heaven*.

Queen's debut album was released in July 1973 and before arriving at the final title several others were considered – *Top Fax, Pix And Info* and *Deary Me* – all of which were rejected in favour of *Queen*. This album showed the groups virtuosity with great playing from May and excellent rhythms from Taylor and Deacon. It featured a mix of glam, heavy rock and gentler folk-rock music. *Queen II*, an original title for their second album, featured a slicker production and was generally a more gentle album than it's predecessor. *Sheer Heart Attack* followed and this was their first album to rely on pop songs and, with the inclusion of 'Killer Queen', was the band's turning point musically. Reviews were favourable – 'A feast', 'No duffers, and four songs that will just run and run', claimed the music press. Featuring what was to become their biggest selling single, 'Bohemian Rhapsody', *A Night At The Opera* was guaranteed to be a critical success, and rightly so. This was the first of three albums to be named after Marx Brothers movies, the other two being *A Day At The Races* and *News Of The World*. This was probably their most cohesive album and featured a batch of great pop songs, along with some excellent operatic singing from Mercury. *A Day At The Races* was the first to be produced by the group themselves and continued in the same vein as *Opera*, although many people felt that it was a mistake to try to emulate *Opera's* success. *News Of The World* found them back on form with a heavier rock sound and, with both 'We Will Rock You' and 'We Are The Champions', the album couldn't fail. A complete change of direction for the group emerged when they released *Jazz*, a mix of disco, jazz, rock and rhythm and blues. A double live set *Live Killers* followed, but many felt that this was not really representative of the band live. *The Game* was released to mixed reaction and with the exception of the singles, 'Crazy Little Thing Called Love' and 'Play The Game', it was not up to their usual standard. Queen supplied the soundtrack for the movie *Flash Gordon* in 1980 and, as with most soundtracks, the music stands up better as an accompaniment to the film rather than an album you could just sit back and listen to. Their first *Greatest Hits* package was followed in 1982 by *Hot Space*, a more rhythmic album that featured the hit single

'Under Pressure'. It was received favourably by the media but apparently the band were not entirely happy with the album. Two years later in February 1984 they released *The Works*, an album that spawned several hit singles including 'Radio Ga Ga', 'I Want To Break Free' and 'Hammer To Fall'. There had been a gap of two years between *Hot Space* and *The Works* and it saw a return to the successful pop formula. Queen supplied music for the film *Highlander* in 1986 and these tracks were released on the *A Kind Of Magic* album. Touring to promote the album the band had a chance to record another live album. The result, *Live Magic*, recorded at several venues during the tour, was far superior to their first live release. Although several of their greatest hits were missing, it included excellent renditions of 'One Vision', 'Another One Bites The Dust' and 'Radio Ga Ga'. There was a three-year lay-off before the release of *The Miracle*. Sticking to the successful formula, it produced several hits most notably 'I Want It All'. Entering the charts at number one in 1991, *Innuendo* was a classic Queen album and *Q* magazine even called it 'endearing and enduring'. *Innuendo* was full of class material – the title track, 'Headlong', 'These Are The Days Of Our Lives' and 'The Show Must Go On'. By 1991 Queen had amassed enough hit singles to release their second *Greatest Hits* package and this was followed by their third live set. *Live At Wembley 86* was taped during their successful concerts at Wembley Stadium during the Magic tour and while not being a complete concert was a better representation of the band live than *Live Killers* had been. The group's final studio album, released after the tragic death of Freddie Mercury, was *Made In Heaven*. This collection of material that Freddie Mercury had been working on before his untimely death, was a fitting tribute to one of the greatest rock bands in the world.

THE DISCOGRAPHIES
AN OVERVIEW

Queen's recorded output is, obviously, the most important part of their career and since the release of their first single in 1973 their records have appeared on almost every kind of recorded media - 7" vinyl singles, 12" singles, cassettes, compact discs, coloured vinyl, picture discs and shaped discs.

Their early singles up to and including 'Las Palabras De Amor' ('The Words Of Love') were released only on the popular 7" vinyl format and it wasn't until the release of 'Backchat' in 1982 that the first 12" Queen single appeared. By the late eighties, and with the invention of the compact disc, each Queen single was now appearing on all formats, often with the compact disc offering a different selection of tracks or, as was more common, a selection of extended or remixed versions of the lead title. Some of their early singles were re-issued on compact disc around this time.

Picture bags for Queen singles existed almost from the start of their career and these featured group photos, sometimes live but also portrait shots. More often than not, the foreign releases would feature a different picture sleeve to their English counterpart. The emergence of the two-CD single in the nineties, meant that the same lead title could be sold twice as was the case with the 'A Winter's Tale' and 'Let Me Live' singles, when the first part featured the lead title with other titles, and a few weeks later part two would be released, again with the lead title, along with two or three different tracks as a bonus.

Queen have released many albums during their career and they have all made an appearance on compact disc as well. Throughout the world these releases often featured a different cover or slightly different track selections and in rare cases were pressed on coloured vinyl.

The following discographies detail all the UK releases covering 7", 12", cassette, CD and limited edition singles along with albums and compact discs. This is followed by selected discographies for Japanese singles and US releases as well as a separate discography of their live output. The final section deals with the multitude of bootleg releases that have seen the light of day.

COMPLETE UK DISCOGRAPHY
1973–1997

7" SINGLES

Keep Yourself Alive/Son And Daughter
EMI 2036 July 1973

Seven Seas Of Rhye/See What A Fool I've Been
EMI 2121 February 1974

Killer Queen/Flick Of The Wrist
EMI 2229 October 1974

Now I'm Here/Lily Of The Valley
EMI 2256 January 1975

Bohemian Rhapsody/I'm In Love With My Car
EMI 2375 October 1975

You're My Best Friend/ '39
EMI 2494 June 1976

Somebody To Love/White Man
EMI 2565 November 1976

Tie Your Mother Down/You And I
EMI 2593 March 1977

QUEEN'S FIRST EP:
Good Old Fashioned Lover Boy/Death On Two Legs/Tenement Funster/White Queen (As It Began)
EMI 2623 May 1977

We Are The Champions/We Will Rock You
EMI 2708 October 1977

Spread Your Wings/Sheer Heart Attack
EMI 2575 February 1978

Bicycle Race/Fat Bottomed Girls
EMI 2870 October 1978

Don't Stop Me Now/In Only Seven Days
EMI 2910 January 1979

Love Of My Life (live)**/Now I'm Here** (live)
EMI 2959 June 1979

Crazy Little Thing Called Love/We Will Rock You (live)
EMI 5001 October 1979

Save Me/Let Me Entertain You (live)
EMI 5022 January 1980

Play The Game/A Human Body
EMI 5076 May 1980

Another One Bites The Dust/Dragon Attack
EMI 5102 August 1980

Flash/Football Fight
EMI 5126 November 1980

Under Pressure (w. David Bowie)**/Soul Brother**
EMI 5250 November 1981

Body Language/Life Is Real (Song For Lennon)
EMI 5293 April 1982

Las Palabras de Amor (The Words Of Love)/Cool Cat
EMI 5316 June 1982

Backchat (remix)/Staying Power
EMI 5325 July 1982

Radio Ga Ga (edit)/I Go Crazy
EMI QUEEN 1 January 1984

I Want To Break Free (remix)/Machines (Back To Humans)
EMI QUEEN 2 April 1984

It's A Hard Life/Is This The World We Created...?
EMI QUEEN 3 July 1984

Hammer To Fall (edit)/Tear It Up
EMI QUEEN 4 September 1984

Thank God It's Christmas/Man On The Prowl/Keep Passing The Open Windows
EMI QUEEN 5 November 1984

One Vision (7" mix)/Blurred Vision
EMI QUEEN 6 November 1985

A Kind Of Magic/A Dozen Red Roses For My Darling
EMI QUEEN 7 March 1986

Friends Will Be Friends (7" mix)/Seven Seas Of Rhye
EMI QUEEN 8 June 1986

Who Wants To Live Forever (edit)/Killer Queen
EMI QUEEN 9 September 1986

I Want It All (single version)/Hang On In There
EMI QUEEN 10 May 1989

Breakthru (7" mix)/Stealin'
EMI QUEEN 11 July 1989

Invisible Man (single version)/Hijack My Heart
EMI QUEEN 12 August 1989

Scandal (7" mix)/My Life Has Been Saved
EMI QUEEN 14 – hologram picture sleeve October 1989

The Miracle/Stone Cold Crazy (live)
EMI QUEEN 15 November 1989

Innuendo/Bijou
EMI QUEEN 16 January 1991

I'm Going Slightly Mad/The Hitman
EMI QUEEN 17 March 1991

Headlong/All God's People
EMI QUEEN 18 May 1991

The Show Must Go On/Keep Yourself Alive
EMI QUEEN 19 October 1991

Bohemian Rhapsody/I'm In Love With My Car
PARLOPHONE QUEEN 20 – re-issue December 1991

Heaven For Everyone/It's A Beautiful Day
PARLOPHONE QUEEN 21 October 1995

A Winter's Tale/Thank God It's Christmas
PARLOPHONE QUEEN 22 December 1995

Too Much Love Will Kill You/We Will Rock You
PARLOPHONE QUEEN 23 February 1996

12" SINGLES

Backchat (extended remix)/Staying Power
12EMI 5325 July 1982

Radio Ga Ga (extended)/Radio Ga Ga (dub)/I Go Crazy
EMI 12QUEEN 1 January 1984

I Want To Break Free (extended remix)/Machines (Back To Humans)
EMI 12QUEEN 2 April 1984

It's A Hard Life (extended remix)/**It's A Hard Life/Is This The World We Created...?**
EMI 12QUEEN 3 July 1984

Hammer To Fall (headbangers mix)/**Tear It Up**
EMI 12QUEEN 4 September 1984

Thank God It's Christmas/Man On The Prowl
(extended remix)/**Keep Passing The Open Windows**
(extended)
EMI 12QUEEN 5 November 1984

One Vision (extended)/**Blurred Vision**
EMI 12QUEEN 6 November 1985

A Kind Of Magic (extended)/**A Dozen Red Roses For My Darling**
EMI 12QUEEN 7 March 1986

Friends Will Be Friends (12" mix)/**Friends Will Be Friends** (7" mix)/**Seven Seas Of Rhye**
EMI 12QUEEN 8 June 1986

Who Wants To Live Forever (7" version)/**Who Wants To Live Forever** (album version)/**Killer Queen/Who Wants To Live Forever** (piano version)
EMI 12QUEEN 9 September 1986

I Want It All (single version)/**Hang On In There/I Want It All** (album version)
EMI 12QUEEN 10 May 1989

Breakthru (12" version)/**Breakthru** (single version)/**Stealin'**
EMI 12QUEEN 11 July 1989

Invisible Man (12" version)/**Invisible Man** (single version)/**Hijack My Heart**
EMI 12QUEEN 12 August 1989

Scandal (12" mix)/**Scandal** (7" mix)/**My Life Has Been Saved**
EMI 12QUEEN 14 October 1989

Scandal (12" mix)/**My Life Has Been Saved/Scandal** (7" mix)

EMI 12QUEENS 14 – single-sided disc with group's signatures etched on other side October 1989

The Miracle/Stone Cold Crazy (live)/**My Melancholy Blues** (live)
EMI 12QUEEN 15 November 1989

The Miracle/Stone Cold Crazy (live)/**My Melancholy Blues** (live)
EMI 12QUEEN P15 – with signed print November 1989

Innuendo (explosive version)/**Under Pressure/Bijou**
EMI 12QUEEN 16 January 1991

I'm Going Slightly Mad/The Hitman/Lost Opportunity
EMI 12QUEEN G17 – gatefold sleeve March 1991

Headlong/All God's People/Mad The Swine
EMI 12QUEEN 18 May 1991

The Show Must Go On/Keep Yourself Alive/Queen Talks
EMI 12QUEEN 19 October 1991

The Show Must Go On/Keep Yourself Alive/Queen Talks
EMI 12QUEENSG 19 – single-sided disc with group's signatures etched on other side October 1991

CASSETTE SINGLES

I Want It All (album version)/**Hang On In There**
EMI QUEEN C10 May 1989

Breakthru (7" mix)/**Stealin'**
EMI QUEEN C11 July 1989

Invisible Man (single version)/**Hijack My Heart**
EMI QUEEN C12 August 1989

Scandal (7" mix)/**My Life Has Been Saved**
EMI TCQUEEN 14 October 1989

The Miracle/Stone Cold Crazy (live)
EMI QUEEN C15 November 1989

Innuendo/Bijou
EMI QUEEN C16 January 1991

I'm Going Slightly Mad/The Hitman
EMI QUEEN C17 March 1991

Headlong/All God's People
EMI QUEEN C18 May 1991

The Show Must Go On/Keep Yourself Alive
EMI QUEEN C19 October 1991

Bohemian Rhapsody/I'm In Love With My Car
PARLOPHONE QUEEN C20 December 1991

A Winter's Tale/Thank God It's Christmas/Rock In Rio Blues
PARLOPHONE QUEEN C22 December 1995

Too Much Love Will Kill You/We Will Rock You/We Are The Champions
PARLOPHONE QUEEN C23 February 1996

You Don't Fool Me (album version)**/You Don't Fool Me** (club mix)
PARLOPHONE QUEEN C25 November 1996

CD SINGLES

The Seven Seas Of Rhye/See What A Fool I've Been/Funny How Love Is
EMI QUECD 1 – 3" CD single December 1987

Killer Queen/Flick Of The Wrist/Brighton Rock
EMI QUECD 2 – 3" CD single December 1987

Bohemian Rhapsody/I'm In Love With My Car/You're My Best Friend
EMI QUECD 3 – 3" CD single December 1987

Somebody To Love/White Man/Tie Your Mother Down
EMI QUECD 4 – 3" CD single December 1987

QUEEN'S FIRST EP:
Good Old Fashioned Lover Boy/Death On Two Legs/Tenement Funster/White Queen (As It Began)
EMI QUECD5 – 3" CD single

We Are The Champions/We Will Rock You/Fat Bottomed Girls
EMI QUECD 6 – 3" CD single December 1987

Crazy Little Thing Called Love/Spread Your Wings/Flash
EMI QUECD 7 – 3" CD single December 1987

Another One Bites The Dust/Dragon Attack/Las Palabras de Amor
EMI QUECD 8 – 3" CD single December 1987

Under Pressure/Soul Brother/Body Language
EMI QUECD 9 – 3" CD single December 1987

Radio Ga Ga/I Go Crazy/Hammer To Fall (edit)
EMI QUECD 10 – 3" CD single December 1987

I Want To Break Free (remix)**/Machines** (Back To Humans)**/It's A Hard Life**
EMI QUECD 11 – 3" CD single December 1987

A Kind Of Magic/A Dozen Red Roses For My Darling/One Vision
EMI QUECD 12 – 3" CD single December 1987

I Want It All (album version)**/Hang On In There/I Want It All** (single version)
EMI CDQUEEN 10 May 1989

Breakthru (extended)**/Stealin'/Breakthru** (7" mix)
EMI CDQUEEN 11 July 1989

Invisible Man (extended)**/Hijack My Heart/Invisible Man** (single version)
EMI CDQUEEN 12 August 1989

Scandal (extended)/**My Life Has Been Saved/Scandal** (7" mix)
EMI CDQUEEN 14 October 1989

The Miracle/Stone Cold Crazy (live)/**My Melancholy Blues** (live)
EMI CDQUEEN 15 November 1989

Innuendo (explosive version)/**Under Pressure/Bijou**
EMI CDQUEEN 16 January 1991

I'm Going Slightly Mad/The Hitman/Lost Opportunity
EMI CDQUEEN 17 March 1991

The Show Must Go On/Keep Yourself Alive/Queen Talks/Body Language
EMI CDQUEEN 19 October 1991

The Show Must Go On/Now I'm Here/Fat Bottomed Girls/Las Palabras de Amor
EMI CDQUEENS 19 – CD in box with foldout poster - limited issue of 10,000 October 1991

Bohemian Rhapsody (single version)/**I'm In Love With My Car**
PARLOPHONE CDQUEEN 20 December 1991

FIVE LIVE EP:
Somebody To Love/These Are The Days Of Our Lives/Calling You/Papa Was A Rolling Stone/Killer Medley
PARLOPHONE CDRS 6340 April 1993
(Queen only appear on the first two tracks. The first credits George Michael and Queen and the second George Michael with Lisa Stansfield)

Heaven For Everyone (single version)/**It's A Beautiful Day/Heaven For Everyone** (album version)
PARLOPHONE CDQUEEN 21 – part one of two CD set November 1995

Heaven For Everyone (single version)/**Keep Yourself Alive/Seven Seas Of Rhye/Killer Queen**
PARLOPHONE CDQUEEN 21 – part two of two CD set November 1995

A Winter's Tale/Thank God It's Christmas/Rock In Rio Blues
PARLOPHONE CDQUEEN 22 – part one of two CD set - special Christmas wrap-around digipack December 1995

A Winter's Tale/Now I'm Here/You're My Best Friend/Somebody To Love
PARLOPHONE CDQUEEN 22 – part two of two CD set December 1995

Too Much Love Will Kill You/Spread Your Wings/We Will Rock You/We Are The Champions
PARLOPHONE CDQUEEN 23 March 1996

Let Me Live/Bicycle Race/Fat Bottomed Girls/Don't Stop Me Now
PARLOPHONE CDQUEEN 24 – part one of two CD set June 1996

Let Me Live/My Fairy King/Doin' Alright/Liar
PARLOPHONE CDQUEEN 24 – part two of two CD set June 1996

You Don't Fool Me/You Don't Fool Me (dancing divaz mix)/**You Don't Fool Me** (sexy club mix)/**You Don't Fool Me** (late mix)
PARLOPHONE CDQUEEN 25 November 1996

LIMITED EDITION SINGLES

Bohemian Rhapsody/I'm In Love With My Car
EMI 2375 – blue vinyl – limited edition of 200 July 1978

Bohemian Rhapsody/I'm In Love With My Car
EMI 2375 – blue vinyl – with outer 'EMI International' card sleeve July 1978

Bohemian Rhapsody/I'm In Love With My Car
EMI 2375 – blue vinyl – with invites, outer card sleeve, commemorative scarf and EMI goblets July 1978

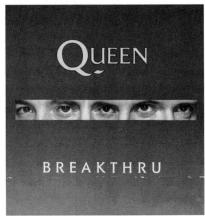

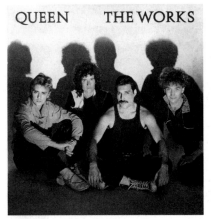

A selection of album sleeves and 12″ single bags from the Queen catalogue (courtesy of Queen Productions)

COLOURED VINYL/ PICTURE DISCS/ SHAPED DISCS

It's A Hard Life/Is This The World We Created...?
EMI 12QUEEN P3 – 12" picture disc July 1984

One Vision (extended)/**Blurred Vision**
EMI 12QUEEN P6 – 12" – pvc cover with red inner sleeve and lyrics November 1985

A Kind Of Magic (extended)/**A Dozen Red Roses For My Darling**
EMI 12QUEEN P7 – 12" picture disc March 1986

Friends Will Be Friends (7" mix)/**Seven Seas Of Rhye**
EMI QUEEN P8 – 7" picture disc June 1986

Breakthru (7" mix)/**Stealin'**
PARLOPHONE QUEEN PD11 – shaped picture disc July 1989

Invisible Man (single version)/**Hijack My Heart**
PARLOPHONE QUEEN X12 – 7" clear vinyl August 1989

Invisible Man (extended)/**Invisible Man** (single)/**Hijack My Heart**
PARLOPHONE 12QUEEN X12 – 12" clear vinyl August 1989

Innuendo (explosive version)/**Under Pressure/Bijou**
PARLOPHONE 12QUEEN PD16 – 12" picture disc January 1991

I'm Going Slightly Mad/The Hitman
PARLOPHONE QUEEN PD17 – shaped picture disc with insert March 1991

Headlong/All God's People/Mad The Swine
PARLOPHONE 12QUEEN PD18 – clear vinyl picture disc May 1991

Too Much Love Will Kill You/We Will Rock You/We Are The Champions
PARLOPHONE QUEEN 23 – pink vinyl March 1996

Let Me Live/Bicycle Race/Fat Bottomed Girls
PARLOPHONE QUEEN P24 – 7" picture disc June 1996

ALBUMS

Queen
EMI EMC 3006 July 1973
Side 1: Keep Yourself Alive/Doing All Right/Great King Rat/My Fairy King/Liar
Side 2: The Night Comes Down/Modern Times Rock 'N' Roll/Son And Daughter/Jesus/Seven Seas Of Rhye

Queen II
EMI EMA 767 March 1974
Side (White) 1: Procession/Father To Son/White Queen (As It Began)/Some Day One Day/The Loser
Side (Black) 2: Ogre Battle/The Fairy Fellers Masterstroke/Nevermore/March Of The Black Queen/Funny How Love Is/Seven Seas Of Rhye

Sheer Heart Attack
EMI EMC 3061 November 1974
Side 1: Brighton Rock/Killer Queen/Tenement Funster/Flick Of The Wrist/Lily Of The Valley/Now I'm Here
Side 2: In The Lap Of The Gods/Stone Cold Crazy/Dear Friends/Misfire/Bring Back That Leroy Brown/She Makes Me (Stormtrooper In Stilettoes)/In The Lap Of The Gods...revisited

A Night At The Opera
EMI EMTC 103 December 1975
Side 1: Death On Two Legs/Lazing On A Sunday Afternoon/I'm In Love With My Car/You're My Best Friend/Sweet Lady/Seaside Rendezvous
Side 2: The Prophets Song/Love Of My Life/ Good Company/Bohemian Rhapsody/God Save The Queen

A Day At The Races

EMI EMTC 104 December 1976
Side 1: Tie Your Mother Down/You Take My Breath Away/Long Away/The Millionaire Waltz/You And I
Side 2: Somebody To Love/White Man/Good Old Fashioned Lover Boy/Drowse/Teo Torriatte (Let Us Cling Together)

News Of The World

EMI EMA 784 October 1977
Side 1: We Will Rock You/We Are The Champions/Sheer Heart Attack/All Dead, All Dead/Spread Your Wings/Fight From The Inside
Side 2: Get Down, Make Love/Sleeping On The Sidewalk/Who Needs You/It's Late/My Melancholy Blues

Jazz

EMI EMA 788 November 1978
Side 1: Mustapha/Fat Bottomed Girls/Jealousy/Bicycle Race/If You Can't Beat Them/Let Me Entertain You
Side 2: Dead On Time/In Only Seven Days/Dreamer's Ball/Fun It/Leaving Home Ain't Easy/Don't Stop Me Now/More Of That Jazz

Live Killers

EMI EMSP 330 June 1979
Side 1: We Will Rock You/Let Me Entertain You/Death On Two Legs/Killer Queen/Bicycle Race/I'm In Love With My Car/Get Down, Make Love/You're My Best Friend
Side 2: Now I'm Here/Dreamer's Ball/Love Of My Life/'39/Keep Yourself Alive
Side 3: Don't Stop Me Now/Spread Your Wings/Brighton Rock/Mustapha
Side 4: Bohemian Rhapsody/Tie Your Mother Down/Sheer Heart Attack/We Will Rock You/We Are The Champions/God Save The Queen

The Game

EMI EMA 795 June 1980
Side 1: Play The Game/Dragon Attack/Another One Bites The Dust/Need Your Loving Tonight/Crazy Little Thing Called Love
Side 2: Rock It/Don't Try Suicide/Sail Away Sweet Sister/Coming Soon/Save Me

Flash Gordon

EMI EMC 3351 December 1980
Side 1: Flash's Theme/In The Space Capsule (The Love Theme)/Ming's Theme (In The Court Of Ming The Merciless)/The Ring (Hypnotic Seduction Of Dale)/Football Fight/In The Death Cell (Love Theme Reprise)/Execution Of Flash/The Kiss (Aura Resurrects Flash)
Side 2: Arboria (Planet Of The Tree Men)/Escape From The Swamp/Flash To The Rescue/Vultan's Theme (Attack Of The Hawk Men)/Battle Theme/The Wedding March/Marriage Of Dale And Ming (And Flash Approaching)/Crash Dive On Mingo Bay/Flash's Theme Reprise (Victory Celebrations)/The Hero

Greatest Hits

EMI EMTV 30 October 1981
Side 1: Bohemian Rhapsody/Another One Bites The Dust/Killer Queen/Fat Bottomed Girls/Bicycle Race/You're My Best Friend/Don't Stop Me Now/Save Me
Side 2: Crazy Little Thing Called Love/Somebody To Love/Now I'm Here/Good Old Fashioned Lover Boy/Play The Game/Flash/Seven Seas Of Rhye/We Will Rock You/We Are The Champions

Hot Space

EMI EMA 797 May 1982
Side 1: Staying Power/Dancer/Back Chat/Body Language/Action This Day
Side 2: Put Out The Fire/Life Is Real (Song For Lennon)/Calling All Girls/Las Palabras de Amor/Cool Cat/Under Pressure

The Works

EMI WORK 1 February 1984
Side 1: Radio Ga Ga/Tear It Up/It's A Hard Life/Machines (Or Back To Humans)
Side 2: I Want To Break Free/Keep Passing The Open Windows/Hammer To Fall/Is This The World We Created...?

A Kind Of Magic

EMI EU 3509 May 1986
Side 1: One Vision/A Kind Of Magic/One Year Of

Love/Pain Is So Close To Pleasure
Side 2: Who Wants To Live Forever/Gimme The Prize
(Kurgan's Theme)/Don't Lose Your Head/Princes Of The
Universe

Live Magic

EMI EMC 3519 December 1986
Side 1: One Vision/Tie Your Mother Down/Seven Seas
Of Rhye/A Kind Of Magic/Under Pressure/Another One
Bites The Dust/I Want To Break Free
Side 2: Is This The World We Created...?/Bohemian
Rhapsody/Hammer To Fall/Radio Ga Ga/We Will Rock
You/Friends Will Be Friends/We Are The
Champions/God Save The Queen

The Miracle

EMI PCSD 107 May 1989
Side 1: Party/Khashoggi's Ship/The Miracle/I Want It
All/The Invisible Man
Side 2: Breakthru/Rain Must Fall/Scandal/My Baby
Does Me/Was It All Worth It

Queen At The Beeb

Band Of Joy BOJLP 001 December 1989
Side 1: My Fairy King/Keep Yourself Alive/Doing All
Right/Liar
Side 2: Ogre Battle/Great King Rat/Modern Times Rock
'N' Roll/Son And Daughter

Innuendo

PARLOPHONE PCSD 115 February 1991
Side 1: Innuendo/I'm Going Slightly Mad/Headlong/I
Can't Live With You/Ride The Wild Wind/All God's
People
Side 2: These Are The Days Of Our Lives/Delilah/Don't
Try Too Hard/The Hitman/Bijou/The Show Must Go On

Greatest Hits II

PARLOPHONE PMTV 2 October 1991
A Kind Of Magic/Under Pressure/Radio Ga Ga/I Want It
All/I Want To Break Free/Innuendo/It's A Hard
Life/Breakthru/Who Wants To Live
Forever/Headlong/The Miracle/I'm Going Slightly
Mad/The Invisible Man/Hammer To Fall/Friends Will Be
Friends/The Show Must Go On/One Vision

Made In Heaven

PARLOPHONE PCSD 167 November 1995
Side 1: It's A Beautiful Day/Made In Heaven/Let Me
Live/Mother Love/My Life Has Been Saved
Side 2: I Was Born To Love You/Heaven For
Everyone/Too Much Love Will Kill You/You Don't Fool
Me/A Winter's Tale

COMPACT DISCS

Queen

EMI CDP 746204 2 December 1986
Keep Yourself Alive/Doing All Right/Great King Rat/My
Fairy King/Liar/The Night Comes Down/Modern Times
Rock 'N' Roll/Son And Daughter/Jesus/Seven Seas Of
Rhye

Queen II

EMI CDP 746205 2 December 1986
Procession/Father To Son/White Queen (As It
Began)/Some Day One Day/The Loser/Ogre Battle/The
Fairy Fellers Masterstroke/Nevermore/March Of The
Black Queen/Funny How Love Is/Seven Seas Of Rhye

Sheer Heart Attack

EMI CDP 746206 2 December 1986
Brighton Rock/Killer Queen/Tenement Funster/Flick Of
The Wrist/Lily Of The Valley/Now I'm Here/In The Lap
Of The Gods/Stone Cold Crazy/Dear
Friends/Misfire/Bring Back That Leroy Brown/She
Makes Me (Stormtrooper In Stilettoes)/In The Lap Of
The Gods...revisited

A Night At The Opera

EMI CDP 746207 2 December 1986
Death On Two Legs/Lazing On A Sunday Afternoon/I'm
In Love With My Car/You're My Best Friend/Sweet
Lady/Seaside Rendezvous/The Prophets Song/Love Of
My Life/Good Company/Bohemian Rhapsody/God Save
The Queen

A Day At The Races

EMI CDP 746208 2 December 1986
Tie Your Mother Down/You Take My Breath Away/Long

Away/The Millionaire Waltz/You And I/Somebody To Love/White Man/Good Old Fashioned Lover Boy/Drowse/Teo Torriatte (Let Us Cling Together)

News Of the World
EMI CDP 746209 2 December 1986
We Will Rock You/We Are The Champions/Sheer Heart Attack/All Dead, All Dead/Spread Your Wings/Fight From The Inside/Get Down, Make Love/Sleeping On The Sidewalk/Who Needs You/It's Late/My Melancholy Blues

Jazz
EMI CDP 746210 2 December 1986
Mustapha/Fat Bottomed Girls/Jealousy/Bicycle Race/If You Can't Beat Them/Let Me Entertain You/Dead On Time/In Only Seven Days/Dreamer's Ball/Fun It/Leaving Home Ain't Easy/Don't Stop Me Now/More Of That Jazz

Live Killers
EMI CDS 746211 8 December 1986
We Will Rock You/Let Me Entertain You/Death On Two Legs/Killer Queen/Bicycle Race/I'm In Love With My Car/Get Down, Make Love/You're My Best Friend/Now I'm Here/Dreamer's Ball/Love Of My Life/ '39/Keep Yourself Alive/Don't Stop Me Now/Spread Your Wings/Brighton Rock/Mustapha/Bohemian Rhapsody/Tie Your Mother Down/Sheer Heart Attack/We Will Rock You/We Are The Champions/God Save The Queen

The Game
EMI CDP 746213 2 December 1986
Play The Game/Dragon Attack/Another One Bites The Dust/Need Your Loving Tonight/Crazy Little Thing Called Love/Rock It/Don't Try Suicide/Sail Away Sweet Sister/Coming Soon/Save Me

Flash Gordon
EMI CDP 746214 2 December 1986
Flash's Theme/In The Space Capsule (The Love Theme)/Ming's Theme (In The Court Of Ming The Merciless)/The Ring (Hypnotic Seduction Of Dale)/Football Fight/In The Death Cell (Love Theme Reprise)/Execution Of Flash/The Kiss (Aura Resurrects

Flash)/Arboria (Planet Of The Tree Men)/Escape From The Swamp/Flash To The Rescue/Vultan's Theme (Attack Of The Hawk Men)/Battle Theme/The Wedding March/Marriage Of Dale And Ming (And Flash Approaching)/Crash Dive On Mingo Bay/Flash's Theme Reprise (Victory Celebrations)/The Hero

Greatest Hits
EMI CDP 74603 2 December 1986
Bohemian Rhapsody/Another One Bites The Dust/Killer Queen/Fat Bottomed Girls/Bicycle Race/You're My Best Friend/Don't Stop Me Now/Save Me/Crazy Little Thing Called Love/Somebody To Love/Now I'm Here/Good Old Fashioned Lover Boy/Play The Game/Flash/Seven Seas Of Rhye/We Will Rock You/We Are The Champions

Hot Space
EMI CDP 746215 2 December 1986
Staying Power/Dancer/Back Chat/Body Language/Action This Day/Put Out The Fire/Life Is Real (Song For Lennon)/Calling All Girls/Las Palabras de Amor/Cool Cat/Under Pressure

The Works
EMI CDP 7460616 2 December 1986
Radio Ga Ga/Tear It Up/It's A Hard Life/Machines (Or Back To Humans)/I Want To Break Free/Keep Passing The Open Windows/Hammer To Fall/Is This The World We Created...?

A Kind Of Magic
EMI CDP 746267 2 December 1986
One Vision/A Kind Of Magic/One Year Of Love/Pain Is So Close To Pleasure/Who Wants To Live Forever/Gimme The Prize (Kurgan's Theme)/Don't Lose Your Head/Princes Of The Universe

Live Magic
EMI CDP 746413 2 December 1986
One Vision/Tie Your Mother Down/Seven Seas Of Rhye/A Kind Of Magic/Under Pressure/Another One Bites The Dust/I Want To Break Free/Is This The World We Created...?/Bohemian Rhapsody/Hammer To Fall/Radio Ga Ga/We Will Rock You/Friends Will Be Friends/We Are The Champions/God Save The Queen

The Miracle

PARLOPHONE CDPCSD 197 December 1986

Party/Khashoggi's Ship/The Miracle/I Want It All/The Invisible Man/Breakthru/Rain Must Fall/Scandal/My Baby Does Me/Was It All Worth It

Greatest Hits II

PARLOPHONE CDP797912 October 1991

A Kind Of Magic/Under Pressure/Radio Ga Ga/I Want It All/I Want To Break Free/Innuendo/It's A Hard Life/Breakthru/Who Wants To Live Forever/Headlong/The Miracle/I'm Going Slightly Mad/The Invisible Man/Hammer To Fall/Friends Will Be Friends/The Show Must Go On/One Vision

Live At Wembley

PARLOPHONE CDPCSP 725 May 1992

One Vision/Tie Your Mother Down/In The Lap Of The Gods/Seven Seas Of Rhye/Tear It Up/A Kind Of Magic/Under Pressure/Another One Bites The Dust/Who Wants To Live Forever/I Want To Break Free/Impromptu/Brighton Rock Solo/Now I'm Here/Love Of My Life/Is This The World We Created...?/(You're So Square) Baby I Don't Care/Hello Mary Lou/Tutti Frutti/Gimme Some Lovin'/Bohemian Rhapsody/Hammer To Fall/Crazy Little Thing Called Love/Big Spender/Radio Ga Ga/We Will Rock You/Friends Will Be Friends/We Are The Champions/God Save The Queen

Innuendo

PARLOPHONE CDPCSD 115 February 1991

Side One: Innuendo/I'm Going Slightly Mad/Headlong/I Can't Live With You/Ride The Wild Wind/All God's People Side Two: These Are The Days Of Our Lives/Delilah/Don't Try Too Hard/The Hitman/Bijou/The Show Must Go On

Greatest Hits 2

PARLOPHONE CDPMTV2 October 1991

A Kind Of Magic/Under Pressure/Radio Ga Ga/I Want It All/I Want To Break Free/Innuendo/It's A Hard Life/Breakthru/Who Wants To Live Forever/Headlong/The Miracle/I'm Going Slightly Mad/The Invisible Man/Hammer To Fall/Friends Will Be Friends/The Show Must Go On/One Vision

Made In Heaven

PARLOPHONE CDPCSD 167 November 1995

It's A Beautiful Day/Made In Heaven/Let Me Live/Mother Love/My Life Has Been Saved/I Was Born To Love You/Heaven For Everyone/Too Much Love Will Kill You/You Don't Fool Me/A Winter's Tale/Yeah/Untitled

Queen Rocks

PARLOPHONE 823 0912 1997

We Will Rock You/Tie Your Mother Down/I Want It All/Seven Seas Of Rhye/I Can't Live With You/Hammer To Fall/Stone Cold Crazy/Now I'm Here/Fat Bottomed Girls/Keep Yourself Alive/Tear It Up/One Vision/Sheer Heart Attack/I'm In Love With My Car/Put Out The Fire/Headlong/It's Late/No One But You

TAPE CASSETTES

Queen

EMI TCPCSD 139 April 1994

Keep Yourself Alive/Doing All Right/Great King Rat/My Fairy King/Liar/The Night Comes Down/Modern Times Rock 'N' Roll/Son And Daughter/Jesus/Seven Seas Of Rhye

Queen II

EMI TCPCSD 140 April 1994

Procession/Father To Son/White Queen (As It Began)/Some Day One Day/The Loser/Ogre Battle/The Fairy Fellers Masterstroke/Nevermore/March Of The Black Queen/Funny How Love Is/Seven Seas Of Rhye

Sheer Heart Attack

EMI TCPCSD 129 September 1993

Brighton Rock/Killer Queen/Tenement Funster/Flick Of The Wrist/Lily Of The Valley/Now I'm Here/In The Lap Of The Gods/Stone Cold Crazy/Dear Friends/Misfire/Bring Back That Leroy Brown/She Makes Me (Stormtrooper In Stilettoes)/In The Lap Of The Gods...revisited

A Night At The Opera

EMI TCPCSD 130 September 1993

Death On Two Legs/Lazing On A Sunday Afternoon/I'm In Love With My Car/You're My Best Friend/Sweet Lady/Seaside Rendezvous/The Prophets Song/Love Of My Life/Good Company/Bohemian Rhapsody/God Save The Queen

A Day At The Races

EMI TCPCSD 131 September 1993

Tie Your Mother Down/You Take My Breath Away/Long Away/The Millionaire Waltz/You And I/Somebody To Love/White Man/Good Old-Fashioned Lover Boy/Drowse/Teo Torriatte (Let Us Cling Together)

News Of The World

EMI TCPCSD 132 September 1993

We Will Rock You/We Are The Champions/Sheer Heart Attack/All Dead, All Dead/Spread Your Wings/Fight From The Inside/Get Down, Make Love/Sleeping On The Sidewalk/Who Needs You/It's Late/My Melancholy Blues

Jazz

EMI TCPCSD 133 February 1994

Mustapha/Fat Bottomed Girls/Jealousy/Bicycle Race/If You Can't Beat Them/Let Me Entertain You/Dead On Time/In Only Seven Days/Dreamer's Ball/Fun It/Leaving Home Ain't Easy/Don't Stop Me Now/More Of That Jazz

Live Killers

EMI TCPCSD 138 April 1994

We Will Rock You/Let Me Entertain You/Death On Two Legs/Killer Queen/Bicycle Race/I'm In Love With My Car/Get Down, Make Love/You're My Best Friend/Now I'm Here/Dreamer's Ball/Love Of My Life/'39/Keep Yourself Alive/Don't Stop Me Now/Spread Your Wings/Brighton Rock/Mustapha/Bohemian Rhapsody/Tie Your Mother Down/Sheer Heart Attack/We Will Rock You/We Are The Champions/God Save The Queen

The Game

EMI TCPCSD 134 February 1994

Play The Game/Dragon Attack/Another One Bites The Dust/Need Your Loving Tonight/Crazy Little Thing Called Love/Rock It/Don't Try Suicide/Sail Away Sweet Sister/Coming Soon/Save Me

Flash Gordon

EMI TCPCSD 137 April 1994

Flash's Theme/In The Space Capsule (The Love Theme)/Ming's Theme (In The Court Of Ming The Merciless)/The Ring (Hypnotic Seduction Of Dale)/Football Fight/In The Death Cell (Love Theme Reprise)/Execution Of Flash/The Kiss (Aura Resurrects Flash)/Arboria (Planet Of The Tree Men)/Escape From The Swamp/Flash To The Rescue/Vultan's Theme (Attack Of The Hawk Men)/Battle Theme/The Wedding March/Marriage Of Dale And Ming (And Flash Approaching)/Crash Dive On Mingo Bay/Flash's Theme Reprise (Victory Celebrations)/The Hero

Greatest Hits

EMI TCPCSD 141 June 1994

Bohemian Rhapsody/Another One Bites The Dust/Killer Queen/Fat Bottomed Girls/Bicycle Race/You're My Best Friend/Don't Stop Me Now/Save Me/Crazy Little Thing Called Love/Somebody To Love/Now I'm Here/Good Old Fashioned Lover Boy/Play The Game/Flash/Seven Seas Of Rhye/We Will Rock You/We Are The Champions

Hot Space

EMI TCPCSD 135 February 1994

Staying Power/Dancer/Back Chat/Body Language/Action This Day/Put Out The Fire/Life Is Real (Song For Lennon)/Calling All Girls/Las Palabras de Amor/Cool Cat/Under Pressure

The Works

EMI TCPCSD 136 February 1994

Radio Ga Ga/Tear It Up/It's A Hard Life/Machines (Or Back To Humans)/I Want To Break Free/Keep Passing The Open Windows/Hammer To Fall/Is This The World We Created...?

A Kind Of Magic

EMI TCEU 3509 June 1986

One Vision/A Kind Of Magic/One Year Of Love/Pain Is So Close To Pleasure/Who Wants To Live

Forever/Gimme The Prize (Kurgan's Theme)/Don't Lose Your Head/Princes Of The Universe

Live Magic
EMI TCEMC 3519 December 1986
One Vision/Tie Your Mother Down/Seven Seas Of Rhye/A Kind Of Magic/Under Pressure/Another One Bites The Dust/I Want To Break Free/Is This The World We Created...?/Bohemian Rhapsody/Hammer To Fall/Radio Ga Ga/We Will Rock You/Friends Will Be Friends/We Are The Champions/God Save The Queen

The Miracle
EMI TCPCSD 107 May 1989
Party/Khashoggi's Ship/The Miracle/I Want It All/The Invisible Man/Breakthru/Rain Must Fall/Scandal/My Baby Does Me/Was It All Worth It

Queen At The Beeb
Band Of Joy BOJLP 001 December 1989
My Fairy King/Keep Yourself Alive/Doing All Right/Liar/Ogre Battle/Great King Rat/Modern Times Rock 'N' Roll/Son And Daughter

Innuendo
EMI TCPCSD 115 February 1991
Innuendo/I'm Going Slightly Mad/Headlong/I Can't Live With You/Ride The Wild Wind/All God's People/These Are The Days Of Our Lives/Delilah/Don't Try Too Hard/The Hitman/Bijou/The Show Must Go On

Greatest Hits II
PARLOPHONE TCPMTV 2 October 1991
A Kind Of Magic/Under Pressure/Radio Ga Ga/I Want It All/I Want To Break Free/Innuendo/It's A Hard Life/Breakthru/Who Wants To Live Forever/Headlong/The Miracle/I'm Going Slightly Mad/The Invisible Man/Hammer To Fall/Friends Will Be Friends/The Show Must Go On/One Vision

Live At Wembley
PARLOPHONE TCPCSP 725 May 1992
One Vision/Tie Your Mother Down/In The Lap Of The Gods/Seven Seas Of Rhye/Tear It Up/A Kind Of Magic/Under Pressure/Another One Bites The

Dust/Who Wants To Live Forever/I Want To Break Free/Impromptu/Brighton Rock Solo/Now I'm Here/ Love Of My Life/Is This The World We Created...?/ (You're So Square) Baby I Don't Care/Hello Mary Lou/Tutti Frutti/Gimme Some Lovin'/Bohemian Rhapsody/Hammer To Fall/Crazy Little Thing Called Love/Big Spender/Radio Ga Ga/We Will Rock You/Friends Will Be Friends/We Are The Champions/God Save The Queen

Made In Heaven
PARLOPHONE TCPCSD 167 November 1995
It's A Beautiful Day/Made In Heaven/Let Me Live/Mother Love/My Life Has Been Saved/I Was Born To Love You/Heaven For Everyone/Too Much Love Will Kill You/You Don't Fool Me/A Winter's Tale

MISCELLANEOUS RELEASES

The Complete Works
EMI QB 1 – 14 LP set December 1985
Disc 1: Keep Yourself Alive/Doing All Right/Great King Rat/My Fairy King/Liar/The Night Comes Down/Modern Times Rock 'N' Roll/Son And Daughter/Jesus/Seven Seas Of Rhye

Disc 2: Procession/Father To Son/White Queen (As It Began)/Some Day One Day/The Loser/Ogre Battle/The Fairy Fellers Masterstroke/Nevermore/March Of The Black Queen/Funny How Love Is/Seven Seas Of Rhye

Disc 3: Brighton Rock/Killer Queen/Tenement Funster/Flick Of The Wrist/Lily Of The Valley/Now I'm Here/In The Lap Of The Gods/Stone Cold Crazy/Dear Friends/Misfire/Bring Back That Leroy Brown/She Makes Me (Stormtrooper In Stilettoes)/In The Lap Of The Gods...revisited

Disc 4: Death On Two Legs/Lazing On A Sunday Afternoon/I'm In Love With My Car/You're My Best Friend/Sweet Lady/Seaside Rendezvous/The Prophets Song/Love Of My Life/Good Company/Bohemian Rhapsody/God Save The Queen

Disc 5: Tie Your Mother Down/You Take My Breath Away/Long Away/The Millionaire Waltz/You And I/Somebody To Love/White Man/Good Old-Fashioned Lover Boy/Drowse/Teo Torriatte (Let Us Cling Together)

Disc 6: We Will Rock You/We Are The Champions/Sheer Heart Attack/All Dead, All Dead/Spread Your Wings/Fight From The Inside/Get Down, Make Love/Sleeping On The Sidewalk/Who Needs You/It's Late/My Melancholy Blues

Disc 7: Mustapha/Fat Bottomed Girls/Jealousy/Bicycle Race/If You Can't Beat Them/Let Me Entertain You/Dead On Time/In Only Seven Days/Dreamer's Ball/Fun It/Leaving Home Ain't Easy/Don't Stop Me Now/More Of That Jazz

Disc 8/9: We Will Rock You/Let Me Entertain You/Death On Two Legs/Killer Queen/Bicycle Race/I'm In Love With My Car/Get Down, Make Love/You're My Best Friend/Now I'm Here/Dreamer's Ball/Love Of My Life/'39/Keep Yourself Alive/Don't Stop Me Now/Spread Your Wings/Brighton Rock/Mustapha/Bohemian Rhapsody/Tie Your Mother Down/Sheer Heart Attack/We Will Rock You/We Are The Champions/God Save The Queen

Disc 10: Play The Game/Dragon Attack/Another One Bites The Dust/Need Your Loving Tonight/Crazy Little Thing Called Love/Rock It/Don't Try Suicide/Sail Away Sweet Sister/Coming Soon/Save Me

Disc 11: Flash's Theme/In The Space Capsule (The Love Theme)/Ming's Theme (In The Court Of Ming The Merciless)/The Ring (Hypnotic Seduction Of Dale)/Football Fight/In The Death Cell (Love Theme Reprise)/Execution Of Flash/The Kiss (Aura Resurrects Flash)/Arboria (Planet Of The Tree Men)/Escape From The Swamp/Flash To The Rescue/Vultan's Theme (Attack Of The Hawk Men)/Battle Theme/The Wedding March/Marriage Of Dale And Ming (And Flash Approaching)/Crash Dive On Mingo Bay/Flash's Theme Reprise (Victory Celebrations)/The Hero

Disc 12: Staying Power/Dancer/Back Chat/Body Language/Action This Day/Put Out The Fire/Life Is Real (Song For Lennon)/Calling All Girls/Las Palabras de Amor/Cool Cat/Under Pressure

Disc 13: Radio Ga Ga/Tear It Up/It's A Hard Life/Machines (Or Back To Humans)/I Want To Break Free/Keep Passing The Open Windows/Hammer To Fall/Is This The World We Created...?

Disc 14: See What A Fool I've Been/Human Body/A Soul Brother/I Go Crazy/Thank God It's Christmas/One Vision/Blurred Vision

Ultimate Queen
PARLOPHONE QUEENBOX – 20 CD set November 1995
CD 1: Queen
Keep Yourself Alive/Doing All Right/Great King Rat/My Fairy King/Liar/The Night Comes Down/Modern Times Rock 'N' Roll/Son And Daughter/Jesus/Seven Seas Of Rhye

CD 2: Queen II
Procession/Father To Son/White Queen (As It Began)/Some Day One Day/The Loser/Ogre Battle/The Fairy Fellers Masterstroke/Nevermore/March Of The Black Queen/Funny How Love Is/Seven Seas Of Rhye

CD 3: Sheer Heart Attack
Brighton Rock/Killer Queen/Tenement Funster/Flick Of The Wrist/Lily Of The Valley/Now I'm Here/In The Lap Of The Gods/Stone Cold Crazy/Dear Friends/Misfire/Bring Back That Leroy Brown/She Makes Me (Stormtrooper In Stilettoes)/In The Lap Of The Gods...revisited

CD 4: A Night At The Opera
Death On Two Legs/Lazing On A Sunday Afternoon/I'm In Love With My Car/You're My Best Friend/Sweet Lady/Seaside Rendezvous/The Prophets Song/Love Of My Life/Good Company/Bohemian Rhapsody/God Save The Queen

CD 5: A Day At The Races
Tie Your Mother Down/You Take My Breath Away/Long Away/The Millionaire Waltz/You And I/Somebody To

Love/White Man/Good Old-Fashioned Lover Boy/Drowse/Teo Torriatte (Let Us Cling Together)

CD 6: News Of the World
We Will Rock You/We Are The Champions/Sheer Heart Attack/All Dead, All Dead/Spread Your Wings/Fight From The Inside/Get Down, Make Love/Sleeping On The Sidewalk/Who Needs You/It's Late/My Melancholy Blues

CD 7: Jazz
Mustapha/Fat Bottomed Girls/Jealousy/Bicycle Race/If You Can't Beat Them/Let Me Entertain You/Dead On Time/In Only Seven Days/Dreamer's Ball/Fun It/Leaving Home Ain't Easy/Don't Stop Me Now/More Of That Jazz

CD 8/9: Live Killers
We Will Rock You/Let Me Entertain You/Death On Two Legs/Killer Queen/Bicycle Race/I'm In Love With My Car/Get Down, Make Love/You're My Best Friend/Now I'm Here/Dreamer's Ball/Love Of My Life/'39/Keep Yourself Alive/Don't Stop Me Now/Spread Your Wings/Brighton Rock/ Mustapha/Bohemian Rhapsody/Tie Your Mother Down/Sheer Heart Attack/ We Will Rock You/We Are The Champions/ God Save The Queen

CD 10: The Game
Play The Game/Dragon Attack/Another One Bites The Dust/Need Your Loving Tonight/Crazy Little Thing Called Love/Rock It/Don't Try Suicide/Sail Away Sweet Sister/Coming Soon/Save Me

CD 11: Flash Gordon
Flash's Theme/In The Space Capsule (The Love Theme)/Ming's Theme (In The Court Of Ming The Merciless)/The Ring (Hypnotic Seduction Of Dale)/Football Fight/In The Death Cell (Love Theme Reprise)/Execution Of Flash/The Kiss (Aura Resurrects Flash)/Arboria (Planet Of The Tree Men)/Escape From The Swamp/ Flash To The Rescue/Vultan's Theme (Attack Of The Hawk Men)/ Battle Theme/The Wedding March/Marriage Of Dale And Ming (And Flash Approaching)/Crash Dive On Mingo Bay/Flash's Theme Reprise (Victory Celebrations)/The Hero

CD 12: Hot Space
Staying Power/Dancer/Back Chat/Body Language/Action This Day/Put Out The Fire/Life Is Real (Song For Lennon)/Calling All Girls/Las Palabras De Amor/Cool Cat/Under Pressure

CD 13: The Works
Radio Ga Ga/Tear It Up/It's A Hard Life/Machines (Or Back To Humans)/I Want To Break Free/Keep Passing The Open Windows/Hammer To Fall/Is This The World We Created...?

CD 14: A Kind Of Magic
One Vision/A Kind Of Magic/One Year Of Love/Pain Is So Close To Pleasure/Who Wants To Live Forever/Gimme The Prize (Kurgan's Theme)/Don't Lose Your Head/Princes Of The Universe

CD 15: Live Magic
One Vision/Tie Your Mother

Down/Seven Seas Of Rhye/A Kind Of Magic/Under Pressure/Another One Bites The Dust/I Want To Break Free/Is This The World We Created...?/Bohemian Rhapsody/Hammer To Fall/Radio Ga Ga/We Will Rock You/Friends Will Be Friends/We Are The Champions/God Save The Queen

CD 16: The Miracle
Party/Khashoggi's Ship/The Miracle/I Want It All/The Invisible Man/Breakthru/Rain Must Fall/Scandal/My Baby Does Me/Was It All Worth It

CD 17: Innuendo
Innuendo/I'm Going Slightly Mad/ Headlong/I Can't Live With You/ Ride The Wild Wind/All God's People/ These Are The Days Of Our Lives/ Delilah/Don't Try Too Hard/The Hitman/Bijou/The Show Must Go On

CD 18/19: Live At Wembley
One Vision/Tie Your Mother Down/In The Lap Of The Gods/Seven Seas Of Rhye/Tear It Up/A Kind Of Magic/Under Pressure/Another One Bites The Dust/Who Wants To Live Forever/I Want To Break Free/Impromptu/Brighton Rock Solo/Now I'm Here/Love Of My Life/Is This The World We Created...?/(You're So Square) Baby I Don't Care/Hello Mary Lou/Tutti Frutti/Gimme Some Lovin'/Bohemian Rhapsody/Hammer To Fall/Crazy Little Thing Called Love/Big Spender/Radio Ga Ga/We Will Rock You/Friends Will Be Friends/We Are The Champions/God Save The Queen

CD 20: Made In Heaven
It's A Beautiful Day/Made In Heaven/Let Me Live/Mother
Love/My Life Has Been Saved/I Was Born To Love
You/Heaven For Everyone/Too Much Love Will Kill
You/You Don't Fool Me/A Winter's Tale

OTHER SPECIAL RELEASES

Box Of Tricks

1992

This special limited edition box set was made available
throughout Europe in 1992 by mail order. It contained
the following items:

Video: Live At The Rainbow 1974
CD: The 12" Collection: Details below
Badge: Purple with Gold Crest
Patch: Purple with Gold Crest
T-Shirt: Black with Queen in gold
Book: Compilation from Greatest Pix Volumes I & II
Poster: Details below

The poster contained pictures of various single
and album sleeves from all over the world and had
16 rows with 11 images on each row. The single
sleeves listed below are 7" unless marked
otherwise:

Row 1 featured: Keep Yourself Alive (Portugal)/Queen/
Seven Seas Of Rhye (Germany)/Seven Seas Of Rhye
(Japan)/Seven Seas Of Rhye (Holland)/Seven Seas Of
Rhye (Yugoslavia)/Queen II/Killer Queen (Italy)/Killer
Queen (France)/Killer Queen (Belgium)/Killer Queen
(Germany)

Row 2 featured: Killer Queen (Japan)/Killer Queen
(Japanese reissue)/Killer Queen (Malta)/Killer Queen
(Holland)/Killer Queen (Spain)/You're My Best Friend-
Killer Queen (UK reissue)/Sheer Heart Attack/Sheer
Heart Attack (Argentina)/Sheer Heart Attack
(Portugese)/Now I'm Here (Belgium)/Now I'm Here
(France)

Row 3 featured: You're My Best Friend(Holland)/Love
Of My Life (Japan)/Now I'm Here (Holland)/Now I'm
Here (Spain)/Bohemian Rhapsody (UK)/Bohemian
Rhapsody (Belgium)/Bohemian Rhapsody
(France)/Bohemian Rhapsody (France)/Bohemian
Rhapsody (Germany)/Bohemian Rhapsody
(Japan)/Bohemian Rhapsody (Holland)

Row 4 featured: Bohemian Rhapsody
(Holland)/Bohemian Rhapsody (Portugal)/Bohemian
Rhapsody (Malta)/Bohemian Rhapsody (UK)/A Night At
The Opera (UK)/A Night At The Opera (France)/A Night
At The Opera (Israel)/You're My Best
Friend(Belgium)/You're My Best Friend(Japan)/You're
My Best Friend(Spain)/You're My Best Friend(Thailand)

Row 5 featured: You're My Best
Friend(Yugoslavia)/Somebody To Love
(Japan)/Somebody To Love (Malta)/Somebody To
Love (Poland)/Somebody To Love (Poland)/Somebody
To Love (Portugal)/Somebody To Love (UK)/A Day At
The Races/Tie Your Mother Down (Holland)/Tie Your
Mother Down (Belgium)/Tie Your Mother Down
(Germany)

Row 6 featured: Tie Your Mother Down (Japan)/Long
Away (Thailand)/Teo Torriatte (Japan)/Queen's First
EP/We Are The Champions (UK)/News Of The World
(UK)/Spread Your Wings (UK)/It's Late (Japan)/It's Late
(USA)/Jazz (UK) /Jazz (France)

Row 7 featured: Jazz (France)/Bicycle Race-Fat
Bottomed Girls (UK)/Mustapha (UK)/Bicycle Race-Fat
Bottomed Girls (Hungary)/Bicycle Race-Fat Bottomed
Girls (Spain)/Bicycle Race-Fat Bottomed Girls
(Belgium)/Don't Stop Me Now (UK)/Don't Stop Me Now
(Argentina)/Don't Stop Me Now (Japan)/Live Killers
(UK)/Live Killers (Japan)

Row 8 featured: Live Killers (Japan)/Jealousy (Russia)/
Mustapha (Spain)/Mustapha (Yugoslavia)/Love Of My
Life (live) (Japan)/Love Of My Life (live) (Holland)/Love
Of My Life (live) (Spain)/Crazy Little Thing Called Love
(UK)/Crazy Little Thing Called Love (Japan)/Queen
(East Germany)/Save Me (UK)

Row 9 featured: Save Me (Japan)/Save Me (Poland)/The Game/Play The Game/Another One Bites The Dust/Another One Bites The Dust (France)/Another One Bites The Dust (Japan)/Another One Bites The Dust (Portugal)/Flash (UK)/Flash (Japan)/Flash (USA)

Row 10 featured: Flash Gordon (UK)/Need Your Loving Tonight (Japan)/Under Pressure (UK)/ Greatest Hits (UK)/The Best Of Queen (Poland)/Greatest Hits (Germany)Greatest Hits (Holland)/ Greatest Hits (Bulgaria)/Greatest Hits (Bulgaria)/Greatest Hits (Bulgaria)/Under Pressure (Japan)

Row 11 featured: Hot Space (UK)/Body Language (Japan)/Body Language (Mexico)/Body Language (USA)/Las Palabras De Amor (UK)/Staying Power (Japan)/Calling All Girls (USA)/Backchat (Japan)/Backchat (UK)/Radio Ga Ga (UK)/The Works (UK)

Row 12 featured: I Want To Break Free (Germany)/I Want To Break Free (UK-Freddie Mercury picture)/I Want To Break Free (UK-Roger Taylor picture)/I Want To Break Free (UK-John Deacon picture)/I Want To Break Free (UK-Brian May picture)/It's A Hard Life (UK)/It's A Hard Life (Japan)/It's A Hard Life (12" picture disc)/It's A Hard Life (12"picture disc)/It's A Hard Life (USA)/Hammer To Fall (UK)

Row 13 featured: Thank God It's Christmas (UK)/One Vision (UK)/Queen Live (Japan)/Queen Live (Brazil)/Queen Live In Concert (New Zealand)/Queen Collection Volume 1 (Holland)/Queen Collection Volume 2 (Holland)/A Kind Of Magic (UK)/A Kind Of Magic (12" picture disc)/A Kind Of Magic (12" picture disc)/A Kind Of Magic (UK)

Row 14 featured: A Kind Of Magic (France)/A Kind Of Magic (USA)/Friends Will Be Friends (UK)/Friends Will Be Friends (7" picture disc)/Friends Will Be Friends (7" picture disc)/Pain Is So Close To Pleasure (UK)/Who Wants To Live Forever (UK)/Live Magic (UK)/Princes Of The Universe (Japan)/One Year Of Love (France)/I Want It All (UK)

Row 15 featured: The Miracle (UK)/Breakthru (UK)/Breakthru (shaped picture disc)/The Invisible Man (UK)/The Invisible Man (clear vinyl)/Scandal (12" single)/The Miracle (hologram sleeve)/The Miracle (UK)/The Miracle (12"

single)/Queen At The Beeb (UK)/Innuendo (12" picture disc)

Row 16 featured: Innuendo (UK)/Innuendo/I'm Going Slightly Mad (UK)/I'm Going Slightly Mad (shaped disc)/Headlong (USA)/Headlong/Headlong (12" picture disc)/The Show Must Go On (UK)/Greatest Hits II (UK)/Bohemian Rhapsody-These Are The Days Of Our Lives (reissue)/Classic Queen (USA)

CD: The 12" Collection

Bohemian Rhapsody / Radio Ga Ga/ Machines (Or Back To Humans) (instrumental version) / I Want To Break Free / It's A Hard Life (extended) / Hammer To Fall (headbangers mix) / Man On The Prowl / A Kind Of Magic / Pain Is So Close To Pleasure / Breakthru / The Invisible Man / The Show Must Go On

Roger live at the Rainbow, 31 March 1974 (© Jill Furmanovsky)

SELECTED US DISCOGRAPHY
1973–1997

7" SINGLES

Keep Yourself Alive/Son & Daughter
ELEKTRA 45863 October 1973

Liar (edit)**/Doing All Right**
ELEKTRA 45884 February 1974

**Seven Seas Of Rhye/See What A Fool
I've Been**
ELEKTRA 45891 June 1974

Killer Queen/Flick Of The Wrist
ELEKTRA 45226 October 1974

Keep Yourself Alive (edit)**/Lily Of The valley**
ELEKTRA 45268 July 1975

**Bohemian Rhapsody/I'm In Love With
My Car**
ELEKTRA 45297 December 1975

You're My Best Friend/ '39
ELEKTRA 45318 June 1976

Somebody To Love/White Man
ELEKTRA 45362 December 1976

Tie Your Mother Down/Drowse
ELEKTRA 45385 March 1977

Long Away/You & I
ELEKTRA 45412 June 1977

We Are The Champions/We Will Rock You
ELEKTRA 45441 October 1977

It's Late/Sheer Heart Attack
ELEKTRA 45478 April 1978

Bicycle Race/Fat Bottomed Girls
ELEKTRA 45541 October 1978

Don't Stop Me Now/More Of That Jazz
ELEKTRA 46008 February 1979

Jealousy/Fun It
ELEKTRA 46039 April 1979

We Will Rock You (live)**/Let Me Entertain
You** (live)
ELEKTRA 46532 August 1979

**Crazy Little Thing Called Love/Spread Your
Wings** (live)
ELEKTRA 46579 December 1979

Play The Game/A Human Body
ELEKTRA 46652 June 1980

Another One Bites The Dust/Don't Try Suicide
ELEKTRA 47031 August 1980

Need Your Loving Tonight/Rock It
ELEKTRA 47086 November 1980

Flash/Football Fight
ELEKTRA 47092 January 1981

Under Pressure/Soul Brother
ELEKTRA 47235 October 1981

Body Language/Life Is Real
ELEKTRA 47452 April 1982

Calling All The Girls/Put Out The Fire
ELEKTRA 69981 July 1982

Staying Power/Back Chat
ELEKTRA 67975 November 1982

Radio Ga Ga/I Go Crazy
CAPITOL B5317 February 1984

I Want To Break Free (remix)**/Machines**
(instrumental)
CAPITOL B5350 April 1984

It's A Hard Life/Is This The World We Created...?
CAPITOL B5372 July 1984

Hammer To Fall/Tear It Up
CAPITOL B5424 October 1984

One Vision (extended remix)**/Blurred Vision**
CAPITOL B5530 November 1985

Princes Of The Universe/A Dozen Red Roses For My Darling
CAPITOL B5568 April 1986

A Kind Of Magic (extended remix)**/Gimme The Prize**
CAPITOL B5590 June 1986

Pain Is So Close To Pleasure (remix)**/Don't Lose Your Head**
CAPITOL B5633 August 1986

Breakthru/I Want It All
CAPITOL 44372 May 1989

Scandal/My Life Has Been Saved
CAPITOL CDP7155142 October 1989

Headlong (edit)**/Under Pressure**
HOLLYWOOD HR64920 January 1991

These Are The Days Of Our Life/Bijou
HOLLYWOOD HR64868 September 1991

Bohemian Rhapsody/The Show Must Go On
HOLLYWOOD HR64794 February 1992

COMPACT DISCS

Sheer Heart Attack
HOLLYWOOD HR61036 March 1991
Brighton Rock/Killer Queen/Tenement Funster/Flick Of The Wrist/Lily Of The Valley/Now I'm Here/In The Lap Of The Gods/Stone Cold Crazy/Dear Friends/Misfire/Bring Back That Leroy Brown/She Makes Me (Stormtrooper In Stilettoes)/In The Lap Of The Gods…revisited
BONUS TRACKS: Stone Cold Crazy (1991 remix)

A Day At The Races
HOLLYWOOD HR61035 March 1991
Tie Your Mother Down/You Take My Breath Away/Long Away/The Millionaire Waltz/You And I/Somebody To Love/White Man/Good Old Fashioned Lover Boy/Drowse/Teo Torriatte (Let Us Cling Together)
BONUS TRACKS: Tie Your Mother Down (remix)/Somebody To Love (remix)

News Of The World
HOLLYWOOD HR61037 March 1991
We Will Rock You/We Are The Champions/Sheer Heart Attack/All Dead, All Dead/Spread Your Wings/Fight From The Inside/Get Down, Make Love/Sleeping On The Sidewalk/Who Needs You/It's Late/My Melancholy Blues
BONUS TRACKS: We Will Rock You (1991 remix)

Hot Space
HOLLYWOOD HR61038 March 1991
Staying Power/Dancer/Back Chat/Body Language/Action This Day/Put Out The Fire/Life Is Real (Song For Lennon)/Calling All Girls/Las Palabras de Amor/Cool Cat/Under Pressure
BONUS TRACKS: Body Language (remix)

Queen

HOLLYWOOD HR61064 June 1991

Keep Yourself Alive/Doing All Right/Great King Rat/My
Fairy King/Liar/The Night Comes Down/Modern Times
Rock 'N' Roll/Son And Daughter/Jesus/Seven Seas Of
Rhye

BONUS TRACKS: Mad The Swine/Keep Yourself Alive
(remake)/Liar (1991 remix)

Jazz

HOLLYWOOD HR61062 1991

Mustapha/Fat Bottomed Girls/Jealousy/Bicycle Race/If
You Can't Beat Them/Let Me Entertain You/Dead On
Time/In Only Seven Days/Dreamer's Ball/Fun
It/Leaving Home Ain't Easy/Don't Stop Me Now/More
Of That Jazz

BONUS TRACKS: Fat Bottomed Girls (1991
remix)/Bicycle Race (1991 remix)

The Game

HOLLYWOOD HR61063 June 1991

Play The Game/Dragon Attack/Another One Bites The
Dust/Need Your Loving Tonight/Crazy Little Thing
Called Love/Rock It/Don't Try Suicide/Sail Away Sweet
Sister/Coming Soon/Save Me

BONUS TRACKS: Dragon Attack (1991 remix)

A Kind Of Magic

HOLLYWOOD HR61152 June 1991

One Vision/A Kind Of Magic/One Year Of Love/Pain
Is So Close To Pleasure/Who Wants To Live
Forever/Gimme The Prize (Kurgan's Theme)/Don't Lose
Your Head/Princes Of The Universe

BONUS TRACKS: Forever/One Vision

A Night At The Opera

HOLLYWOOD HR61065 August 1991

Death On Two Legs/Lazing On A Sunday Afternoon/
I'm In Love With My Car/You're My Best Friend/Sweet
Lady/Seaside Rendezvous/The Prophets Song/Love
Of My Life/Good Company/Bohemian Rhapsody/
God Save The Queen

BONUS TRACKS: I'm In Love With My Car
(1991 remix)/You're My Best Friend (1991
remix)

Flash Gordon

HOLLYWOOD HR61203 August 1991

Flash's Theme/In The Space Capsule (The Love
Theme)/Ming's Theme (In The Court Of Ming The
Merciless)/The Ring (Hypnotic Seduction Of
Dale)/Football Fight/In The Death Cell (Love Theme
Reprise)/Execution Of Flash/The Kiss (Aura Resurrects
Flash)/Arboria (Planet Of The Tree Men)/Escape From
The Swamp/Flash To The Rescue/Vultan's Theme
(Attack Of The Hawk Men)/Battle Theme/The Wedding
March/Marriage Of Dale And Ming (And Flash
Approaching)/Crash Dive On Mingo Bay/Flash's Theme
Reprise (Victory Celebrations)/The Hero

BONUS TRACKS: Flash (1991 remix)

Queen II

HOLLYWOOD HR61232 October 1991

Procession/Father To Son/White Queen (As It
Began)/Some Day One Day/The Loser/Ogre Battle/
The Fairy Fellers Masterstroke/Nevermore/March Of
The Black Queen/Funny How Love Is/Seven Seas Of
Rhye

BONUS TRACKS: Ogre Battle (1991 remix)/The Seven
Seas Of Rhye (1991 remix)/See What A Fool I've
Been

The Miracle

HOLLYWOOD HR61234 October 1991

Party/Khashoggi's Ship/The Miracle/I Want It All/The
Invisible Man/Breakthru/Rain Must Fall/Scandal/My
Baby Does Me/Was It All Worth It

BONUS TRACKS: Hang On In There/Chinese
Torture/Invisible Man (12" mix)/Scandal (12" mix)

Live Killers

HOLLYWOOD HR61066 October 1991

We Will Rock You/Let Me Entertain You/Death On Two
Legs/Killer Queen/Bicycle Race/I'm In Love With My
Car/Get Down, Make Love/You're My Best Friend/Now
I'm Here/Dreamer's Ball/Love Of My Life/'39/Keep
Yourself Alive/Don't Stop Me Now/Spread Your
Wings/Brighton Rock/Mustapha/Bohemian
Rhapsody/Tie Your Mother Down/Sheer Heart
Attack/We Will Rock You/We Are The Champions/God
Save The Queen

The Works
HOLLYWOOD HR61233 December 1991
Radio Ga Ga/Tear It Up/It's A Hard Life/Machines (Or
Back To Humans)/I Want To Break Free/Keep Passing
The Open Windows/Hammer To Fall/Is This The World
We Created...?
BONUS TRACKS: Radio Ga Ga (12" mix)/I Want To
Break Free (12" mix)/I Go Crazy

JAPANESE SINGLES DISCOGRAPHY

The Queen singles released in Japan are highly
collectable as the combination of tracks on
many of them were different to their European
releases, and quite often they featured different
picture sleeves. These editions also included lyric
translations, many of which were not quite
accurate! Most of these singles are long deleted
and fetch anything between £50 and £100, with
the earliest commanding even higher prices for
mint condition copies.

JAPANESE 7" SINGLES

Keep Yourself Alive/Son And Daughter
ELEKTRA P-1290E March 1974

Seven Seas Of Rhye/Loser In The End
ELEKTRA P-1314E June 1974

Killer Queen/Flick Of The Wrist
ELEKTRA P-1357E October 1974

Now I'm Here/Lily Of The Valley
ELEKTRA P-1377E May 1975

Bohemian Rhapsody/I'm In Love With My Car
ELEKTRA P-128E December 1975

Now I'm Here/Keep Yourself Alive
ELEKTRA P-102E April 1976

You're My Best Friend/ '39
ELEKTRA P-16E June 1976

Killer Queen/Seven Seas Of Rhye
ELEKTRA P-103E July 1976

Bohemian Rhapsody/I'm In Love With My Car
ELEKTRA P-1430E October 1976

Somebody To Love/White Man
ELEKTRA P-78E December 1976

Teo Torriatte (Let Us Cling Together)/Good Old Fashioned Lover Boy
ELEKTRA P-157E March 1977

Tie Your Mother Down/Drowse
ELEKTRA P-193E July 1977

We Are The Champions/We Will Rock You
ELEKTRA P-230E November 1977

It's Late (edit)**/Sheer Heart Attack**
ELEKTRA P-271E April 1978

Bicycle Race/Fat Bottomed Girls
ELEKTRA P-350E November 1978

Don't Stop Me Now/More Of That Jazz
ELEKTRA P-381E March 1979

Love Of My Life (live)**/Now I'm Here** (live)
ELEKTRA P-423E May 1979

We Will Rock You (live)**/Let Me Entertain You** (live)
ELEKTRA P-486E October 1979

Crazy Little Thing Called Love/Spread Your Wings (live)
ELEKTRA P-529E January 1980

Save Me/Sheer Heart Attack (live)
ELEKTRA P-550E April 1980

Play The Game/A Human Body
ELEKTRA P-603E July 1980

Another One Bites The Dust/Don't Try Suicide
ELEKTRA P-618E September 1980

Need Your Loving Tonight/Rock It (Prime Jive)
ELEKTRA P-654E November 1980

Flash's Theme/Football Fight
ELEKTRA P-655E January 1981

Under Pressure/Soul Brother
ELEKTRA P-1587E October 1981

Body Language/Life Is For Real (Song For Lennon)
ELEKTRA P-1650 April 1982

Staying Power/Calling All Girls
ELEKTRA P-1678 July 1982

Back Chat/Las Palabras de Amor (The Words Of Love)
ELEKTRA P-1708 October 1982

Radio Ga Ga/I Go Crazy
EMI EMS-17425 February 1984

I Want To Break Free/Machines (Or Back To Humans)
EMI EMS-17452 April 1984

It's A Hard Life/Is This The World We Created...?
EMI EMS-17482 July 1984

One Vision/Blurred Vision
EMI EMS-17594 November 1985

A Kind Of Magic/A Dozen Red Roses For My Darling
EMI EMS-17632 June 1986

Princes Of The Universe/Who Wants To Live Forever
EMI EMS-17663 October 1986

I Want It All/Hang On In There
EMI PRP-1397 May 1989

Headlong/Lost Opportunity
EMI T6801 July 1991

JAPANESE 3″ CD SINGLE

I Want It All/Hang On In There
EMI XP10-20813 May 1989

JAPANESE CD SINGLES

Innuendo (explosive version)/**Under Pressure/Bijou**
EMI TOCP-6571 February 1991

Headlong/Mad The Swine/Lost Opportunity
EMI TOCP-6801 July 1991

Bohemian Rhapsody/These Are The Days Of Our Lives
EMI TOCP-7259 February 1992

MISCELLANEOUS JAPANESE RELEASES

The Queen CD Singles Box
TODP-2251/2262
CD1: Seven Seas Of Rhye/See What A Fool I've Been/Funny How Love Is
CD2: Killer Queen/Flick Of The Wrist/Brighton Rock
CD3: Bohemian Rhapsody/I'm In Love With My Car/You're My Best Friend
CD4: Somebody To Love/White Man/Tie Your Mother Down
CD5: Good Old Fashioned Lover Boy/Death On Two Legs/Tenement Funster/White Queen
CD6: We Are The Champions/We Will Rock You/Fat Bottomed Girls

CD7: Crazy Little Thing Called Love/Spread Your Wings/Flash's Theme
CD8: Another One Bites The Dust/Dragon Attack/Las Palabras de Amor
CD9: Under Pressure/Soul Brother/Body Language
CD10: Radio Ga Ga/I Go Crazy/Hammer To Fall
CD11: I Want To Break Free/Machines (Or Back To Humans)/It's A Hard Life
CD12: A Kind Of Magic/A Dozen Red Roses For My Darling/One Vision
This set was housed in a detachable box and included a Japanese discography, biography and eight-page booklet of lyrics.

LIVE DISCOGRAPHY 1973–1997

7″ SINGLES

Love Of My Life (live)/**Now I'm Here** (live)
EMI 2959 June 1979

Crazy Little Thing Called Love/We Will Rock You (live)
EMI 5001 October 1979

Save Me/Let Me Entertain You (live)
EMI 5022 January 1980

The Miracle/Stone Cold Crazy (live)
EMI QUEEN 15 November 1989

12″ SINGLES

The Miracle/Stone Cold Crazy (live)/**My Melancholy Blues**
EMI 12QUEEN 15 – with signed print November 1989

CASSETTE SINGLE

The Miracle/Stone Cold Crazy (live)
EMI TCQUEEN 15 November 1989

CD SINGLE

The Miracle/Stone Cold Crazy (live)/**My Melancholy Blues** (live)
EMI CDQUEEN 15 November 1989

ALBUMS

Live Killers
EMI EMSP 330 June 1979
Side 1: We Will Rock You/Let Me Entertain You/Death On Two Legs/Killer Queen/Bicycle Race/I'm In Love With My Car/Get Down, Make Love/You're My Best Friend
Side 2: Now I'm Here/Dreamer's Ball/Love Of My Life/'39/Keep Yourself Alive
Side 3: Don't Stop Me Now/Spread Your Wings/Brighton Rock/Mustapha
Side 4: Bohemian Rhapsody/Tie Your Mother Down/Sheer Heart Attack/We Will Rock You/We Are The Champions/God Save The Queen

Live Magic
EMI EMC 3519 December 1986
Side 1: One Vision/Tie Your Mother Down/Seven Seas Of Rhye/A Kind Of Magic/Under Pressure/Another One Bites The Dust/I Want To Break Free/Is This The World We Created...?/Bohemian Rhapsody/Hammer To Fall/Radio Ga Ga/We Will Rock You/Friends Will Be Friends/We Are The Champions/God Save The Queen

Queen At The Beeb
Band Of Joy BOJLP 001 December 1989
Side 1: My Fairy King/Keep Yourself Alive/Doing All Right/Liar/Ogre Battle/Great King Rat/Modern Times Rock 'N' Roll/Son And Daughter

COMPACT DISCS

Live Killers
EMI CDS 746211 8

We Will Rock You/Let Me Entertain You/Death On Two
Legs/Killer Queen/Bicycle Race/I'm In Love With My
Car/Get Down To Make Love/You're My Best
Friend/Now I'm Here/Dreamer's Ball/Love Of My
Life/ '39/Keep Yourself Alive/Don't Stop Me
Now/Spread Your Wings/Brighton Rock/
Mustapha/Bohemian Rhapsody/Tie Your Mother
Down/Sheer Heart Attack/We Will Rock You/We Are
The Champions/God Save The Queen

Live Magic
EMI CDP 746413 2

One Vision/Tie Your Mother Down/Seven Seas Of
Rhye/A Kind Of Magic/Under Pressure/Another One
Bites The Dust/I Want To Break Free/Is This The World
We Created...?/Bohemian Rhapsody/Hammer To
Fall/Radio Ga Ga/We Will Rock You/Friends Will Be
Friends/We Are The Champions/God Save The Queen

Live At Wembley
Parlophone CDPCSP 725 May 1992

One Vision/Tie Your Mother Down/In The Lap Of The
Gods/Seven Seas Of Rhye/Tear It Up/A Kind Of
Magic/Under Pressure/Another One Bites The
Dust/Who Wants To Live Forever/I Want To Break
Free/Impromptu/Brighton Rock Solo/Now I'm
Here/Love Of My Life/Is This The World We
Created...?/(You're So Square) Baby I Don't Care/Hello
Mary Lou/Tutti Frutti/Gimme Some Lovin'/Bohemian
Rhapsody/Hammer To Fall/Crazy Little Thing Called
Love/Big Spender/Radio Ga Ga/We Will Rock
You/Friends Will Be Friends/We Are The
Champions/God Save The Queen

TAPE CASSETTES

Live Killers
EMI TCPCSD 138 April 1994

We Will Rock You/Let Me Entertain You/Death On Two
Legs/Killer Queen/Bicycle Race/I'm In Love With My
Car/Get Down To Make Love/You're My Best
Friend/Now I'm Here/Dreamer's Ball/Love Of My
Life/ '39/Keep Yourself Alive/Don't Stop Me
Now/Spread Your Wings/Brighton Rock/
Mustapha/Bohemian Rhapsody/Tie Your Mother
Down/Sheer Heart Attack/We Will Rock You/We Are
The Champions/God Save The Queen

Live Magic
EMI TCEMC 3519 December 1986

One Vision/Tie Your Mother Down/Seven Seas Of
Rhye/A Kind Of Magic/Under Pressure/Another One
Bites The Dust/I Want To Break Free/Is This The World
We Created...?/Bohemian Rhapsody/Hammer To
Fall/Radio Ga Ga/We Will Rock You/Friends Will Be
Friends/We Are The Champions/God Save The Queen

Queen At The Beeb
Band Of Joy BOJLP 001 December 1989

My Fairy King/Keep Yourself Alive/Doing All
Right/Liar/Ogre Battle/Great King Rat/Modern Times
Rock 'N' Roll/Son And Daughter

Live At Wembley
Parlophone TCPCSP 725 May 1992

One Vision/Tie Your Mother Down/In The Lap Of The
Gods/Seven Seas Of Rhye/Tear It Up/A Kind Of
Magic/Under Pressure/Another One Bites The
Dust/Who Wants To Live Forever/I Want To Break
Free/Impromptu/Brighton Rock Solo/Now I'm
Here/Love Of My Life/Is This The World We
Created...?/(You're So Square) Baby I Don't Care/Hello
Mary Lou/Tutti Frutti/Gimme Some Lovin'/Bohemian
Rhapsody/Hammer To Fall/Crazy Little Thing Called
Love/Big Spender/Radio Ga Ga/We Will Rock
You/Friends Will Be Friends/We Are The
Champions/God Save The Queen

MISCELLANEOUS RELEASES

Where they differ to the standard issues.

The Complete Works
EMI QB 1 – 14 LP set December 1985

Disc 3: Brighton Rock/Killer Queen/Tenement Funster/Flick Of The Wrist/Lily Of The Valley/Now I'm Here/In The Lap Of The Gods/Stone Cold Crazy/Dear Friends/Misfire/Bring Back That Leroy Brown/She Makes Me (Stormtrooper In Stilettoes)/In The Lap Of The Gods…revisited

Disc 4: Death On Two Legs/Lazing On A Sunday Afternoon/I'm In Love With My Car/You're My Best Friend/Sweet Lady/Seaside Rendezvous/The Prophets Song/Love Of My Life/Good Company/Bohemian Rhapsody/God Save The Queen

Ultimate Queen
Parlophone QUEENBOX – 20 CD set November 1995

CD 8: Live Killers
We Will Rock You/Let Me Entertain You/Death On Two Legs/Killer Queen/Bicycle Race/I'm In Love With My Car/Get Down To Make Love/You're My Best Friend/Now I'm Here/Dreamer's Ball/Love Of My Life/ '39/Keep Yourself Alive/Don't Stop Me Now/Spread Your Wings/Brighton Rock/Mustapha/Bohemian Rhapsody/Tie Your Mother Down/Sheer Heart Attack/We Will Rock You/We Are The Champions/God Save The Queen

CD 14: Live Magic
One Vision/Tie Your Mother Down/Seven Seas Of Rhye/A Kind Of Magic/Under Pressure/Another One Bites The Dust/I Want To Break Free/Is This The World We Created…?/Bohemian Rhapsody/Hammer To Fall/Radio Ga Ga/We Will Rock You/Friends Will Be Friends/We Are The Champions/God Save The Queen

CD 17: Live At Wembley
One Vision/Tie Your Mother Down/In The Lap Of The Gods/Seven Seas Of Rhye/Tear It Up/A Kind Of Magic/Under Pressure/Another One Bites The Dust/Who Wants To Live Forever/I Want To Break Free/Impromptu/Brighton Rock Solo/Now I'm Here/Love Of My Life/Is This The World We Created…?/(You're So Square) Baby I Don't Care/Hello Mary Lou/Tutti Frutti/Gimme Some Lovin'/Bohemian Rhapsody/Hammer To Fall/Crazy Little Thing Called Love/Big Spender/Radio Ga Ga/We Will Rock You/Friends Will Be Friends/We Are The Champions/God Save The Queen

MISCELLANEOUS FOREIGN RELEASES

We Will Rock You (live)/**Let Me Entertain You** (live)
P-486E October 1979 – Japanese single

Crazy Little Thing Called Love/Spread Your Wings (live)
P-529E January 1980 – Japanese single

Save Me/Sheer Heart Attack (live)
P-550E April 1980 – Japanese single

We Will Rock You (live)/**We Are The Champions** (live)/**We Will Rock You/We Are The Champions**
Catalogue Number Unknown 1992 – this Dutch single release, 'Live At Wembley '86', featured two live tracks and two studio recordings

We Will Rock You (live)/**Let Me Entertain You** (live)
P-486EE46532 August 1979 – US single

Crazy Little Thing Called Love/Spread Your Wings (live)
E46579 December 1979 – US single

Queen Live
ELEKTRA P13117E
Side 1: We Will Rock You/Let Me Entertain You/Killer Queen/Bicycle Race/You're My Best Friend/Spread

Your Wings/Keep Yourself Alive
Side 2: Don't Stop Me Now/Bohemian Rhapsody/Tie
Your Mother Down/Sheer Heart Attack/We Are The
Champions
This was a Japanese single album featuring an edited
version of the *Live Killers* album

Live Killers
EMI EXTRA 5 1985
Side 1: We Will Rock You/Let Me Entertain You/Killer
Queen/Bicycle Race/You're My Best Friend/Spread
Your Wings/Keep Yourself Alive
Side 2: Don't Stop Me Now/Bohemian Rhapsody/Tie
Your Mother Down/Sheer Heart Attack/We Are The
Champions
This was a South African single album featuring an
edited version of the *Live Killers* album

Queen Live
ELEKTRA 60343/1
Side 1: We Will Rock You/Let Me Entertain You/Killer
Queen/Bicycle Race/You're My Best Friend/Spread
Your Wings/Keep Yourself Alive
Side 2: Don't Stop Me Now/Bohemian Rhapsody/Tie
Your Mother Down/Sheer Heart Attack/We Are The
Champions
This was an Australian single album featuring an edited
version of the *Live Killers* album

Live In Concert
ELEKTRA 60343/1
Side 1: We Will Rock You/Let Me Entertain You/Killer
Queen/Bicycle Race/You're My Best Friend/Spread
Your Wings/Keep Yourself Alive
Side 2: Don't Stop Me Now/Bohemian Rhapsody/Tie
Your Mother Down/Sheer Heart Attack/We Are The
Champions
This was a New Zealand single album featuring an
edited version of the *Live Killers* album

Queen Live: Rock In Rio
4047224 1985
Side 1: We Will Rock You/Let Me Entertain You/Killer
Queen/Bicycle Race/You're My Best Friend/Spread
Your Wings/Keep Yourself Alive

Side 2: Don't Stop Me Now/Bohemian Rhapsody/Tie
Your Mother Down/Sheer Heart Attack/We Are The
Champions
This was a Brazilian single album featuring an edited
version of the *Live Killers* album not the 'Rock In Rio'
concert as the title suggests

SOLO AND PRE-QUEEN DISCOGRAPHIES

ROGER TAYLOR

7″ SINGLES

I Wanna Testify/Turn On The TV
EMI 2679 August 1977

Future Management/Laugh Or Cry
EMI 5157 March 1981

My Country (edit)**/Fun In Space**
EMI 5200 June 1981

Man On Fire/Killing Time
EMI 5478 May 1984

Strange Frontier/I Cry For You (remix)
EMI 5490 July 1984

Nazis 1994/Nazis 1994
PARLOPHONE R 6379 1994

Foreign Sand (single version)**/You Had To Be There**
PARLOPHONE R 6389 1994

Happiness/Ride The Wide Wind (live)
PARLOPHONE R 6399 – (green vinyl) 1994

12″ SINGLES

Man On Fire (extended)/**Killing Time**
EMI 12EMI 5478 May 1984

Strange Frontier (extended)/**I Cry For You** (extended remix)/**Two Sharp Pencils** (Get Bad)
EMI 12EMI 5490 July 1984

Nazis 1994 (single version)/**Nazis 1994** (Radio Mix)/**Nazis 1994** (Makita mix-extended)/**Nazis 1994** (big science mix)
PARLOPHONE 12RC 6379 1994

Foreign Sand (single version)/**Foreign Sand** (album version)/**You Had To Be There/Final Destination**
PARLOPHONE 12R 6389 1994

Happiness/Dear Mr Murdoch/Everybody Hurts Sometime (live)/**Old Friends**
PARLOPHONE 12R 6399 – picture disc 1994

CASSETTE SINGLE

Nazis 1994/Nazis 1994
PARLOPHONE TCR6379 1994

CD SINGLE

Nazis 1994 (single version)/**Nazis 1994** (Radio Mix)/**Nazis 1994** (kick mix)/**Nazis 1994** (Schindlers mix)/**Nazis 1994** (Makita mix-extended)/**Nazis 1994** (big science mix)
PARLOPHONE CDR 6379 1994

ALBUMS

Fun In Space
EMI EMC 3369 April 1981
Side 1: No Violins/Laugh Or Cry/Future Management/Let's Get Crazy/My Country I & II
Side 2: Good Times Are Now/Magic Is Loose/Interlude In Constantinople/Airheads/Fun In Space

Strange Frontier
EMI RTA 1 June 1984
Side 1: Strange Frontier/Beautiful Dreams/Man On Fire/Racing In The Street/Masters Of War
Side 2: Killing Time/Abandon Fire/Young Love/It's An Illusion/I Cry For You

Happiness
PARLOPHONE CDPCSD 157 September 1994
Nazis 1994/Happiness/Revelation/Touch The Sky/Foreign Sand/Freedon Train/You Had To Be There/The Key/Everybody Hurts Sometime/Loneliness/Dear Mr Murdoch/Old Friends

FREDDIE MERCURY

7″ SINGLES

Love Kills/Rotwangs Party (Georgio Moroder)
CBS A4735 September 1984

I Was Born To Love You/Stop All The Fighting
CBS A6019 April 1985

Made In Heaven (remix)/**She Blows Hot And Cold**
CBS A6413 June 1985

Living On My Own/My Love Is Dangerous
CBS A6555 August 1985

Love Me Like There Is No Tomorrow/Let's Turn It On
CBS A6725 November 1985

Time/Time (instrumental)
EMI 5559 April 1986

The Great Pretender/Exercises In Free Love (Mercury vocal)
PARLOPHONE R6151 February 1987

Barcelona/Exercises In Free Love (version 2)
(Montserrat Caballe only)
POLYDOR POSP 887 October 1987

The Golden Boy/The Fallen Priest
POLYDOR POSP 23 October 1988

How Can I Go On/Overture Piccante
POLYDOR POSP 29 December 1988

Barcelona (single version)/**Exercises In Free Love**
(Caballe vocal)/**Barcelona** (edit)
POLYDOR PO 221 1992

How Can I Go On/The Golden Boy
POLYDOR PO 234 1992

In My Defence/Love Kills (wolf euro mix)
PARLOPHONE R 6331 1992

The Great Pretender/Stop All The Fighting
PARLOPHONE R 6336 1993

Living On My Own (radio version)/**Living On My Own**
(album version)
PARLOPHONE R 6355 1994

12″ SINGLES

Love Kills (extended)/**Rotwangs Party** (Georgio
Moroder)
CBS TA4735 September 1984

I Was Born To Love You (extended)/**Stop All The
Fighting**
CBS TA6019 April 1985

Made In Heaven (extended remix)/**Made In Heaven**
(remix)/**She Blows Hot And Cold** (extended)
CBS TA6413 June 1985

Living On My Own (extended)/**My Love Is
Dangerous** (extended)
CBS TA6555 August 1985

Living On My Own (extended)/**My Love Is
Dangerous** (extended)
CBS GTA6555 – gatefold sleeve August 1985

Love Me Like There's No Tomorrow (extended
version)/**Let's Turn It On** (extended version)
CBS TA6725 November 1985

Love Me Like There's No Tomorrow
(extended)/**Let's Turn It On** (extended)/**Living On My
Own** (extended)/**My Love Is Dangerous** (extended)
CBS TA6725 – double-pack shrinkwrapped with TA
6555 November 1985

Time (extended version)/**Time** (7″ version)/**Time**
(instrumental)
EMI 12EMI 5559 April 1986

The Great Pretender (extended)/**The Great
Pretender** (7″ version)/**Exercises In Free Love**
(Mercury vocal)
PARLOPHONE 12R6151 February 1987

Barcelona/Exercises In Free Love (version 2)
(Montserrat Caballe only)/**Barcelona** (extended)
POLYDOR POSPX 887 October 1987

The Golden Boy/The Fallen Priest/The Golden Boy
(instrumental)
POLYDOR POSPX 23 October 1988

**How Can I Go On/Guide Me Home/Overture
Piccante**
POLYDOR POSPX 29 December 1988

Living On My Own (extended version)/**Living On My
Own** (club version)/**Living On My Own** (dub
version)/**Living On My Own** (L.A. version)
PARLOPHONE 12R 6355 1994

CASSETTE SINGLE

Barcelona/Exercises In Free Love (version 2)
(Montserrat Caballe only)**/Barcelona** (extended)
POLYDOR POSPC 887 October 1987

CD SINGLES

Barcelona/Exercises In Free Love (version 2)
(Montserrat Caballe only)**/Barcelona** (extended)
POLYDOR POCD 887 October 1987

The Golden Boy/The Fallen Priest/The Golden Boy
(instrumental)
POLYDOR POCD 23 October 1988

**How Can I Go On/Guide Me Home/Overture
Piccante**
POLYDOR PZCD 29 December 1988

Barcelona (single version)**/Exercises In Free Love**
(Caballe vocal)**/Barcelona** (edit)**/Barcelona/The
Fallen Priest** (edit)
POLYDOR PZCD 221 July 1992

**How Can I Go On/The Golden Boy/The Fallen
Priest**
POLYDOR PZCD 234 November 1992

In My Defence (album version)**/In My Defence**
(original version)**/Love Kills** (wolf euro mix)**/She Blows
Hot And Cold**
PARLOPHONE CDRS 6331 November 1992

The Great Pretender (single version)**/The Great
Pretender** (album version)**/Stop All The
Fighting/Exercises In Free Love** (Mercury vocal)
PARLOPHONE CDRS 6336 – digi-pack January 1993

Living On My Own (radio mix)**/Living On My Own**
(extended mix)**/Living On My Own** (club mix)**/Living
On My Own** (album mix)
PARLOPHONE CDR 6355 July 1993

LIMITED EDITION SINGLE

**I Was Born To Love You/Stop All The
Fighting/Love Kills/Stop All The Fighting**
(extended)
CBS DA6019 – 7" double-pack in gatefold sleeve April
1985

COLOURED VINYL/ PICTURE DISCS/ SHAPED DISCS

Love Kills/Rotwangs Party (Georgio Moroder)
CBS WA4735 – 7" picture disc September 1984

Made In Heaven (remix)**/She Blows Hot And Cold**
CBS WA6413 – shaped picture disc) June 1985

The Great Pretender/Exercises In Free Love
(Mercury vocal)
PARLOPHONE RP6151 – radio-shaped picture disc
February 1987

Barcelona/Exercises In Free Love (version 2)
(Montserrat Caballe only)**/Barcelona** (extended)
POLYDOR POSPP 887 – 12" picture disc October
1987

How Can I Go On/Overture Piccante
POLYDOR POSX 29 – 7" picture disc December 1988

ALBUMS

Mr. Bad Guy
CBS 86312 May 1985
Side 1: Let's Turn It On/Made In Heaven/I Was Born To
Love You/Foolin' Around/Your Kind Of Lover
Side 2: Mr. Bad Guy/Man Made Paradise/There Must
Be More To Life/Living On My Own/My Love Is
Dangerous/Love Me Like There's No Tomorrow

Barcelona
POLYDOR POLH 44 October 1988
Side 1: Barcelona/La Japonaise/The Fallen
Priest/Ensueno
Side 2: The Golden Boy/Guide Me Home/How Can I Go
On/Overture Piccante

The Freddie Mercury Album
PARLOPHONE 7809992 November 1992
Side 1: The Great Pretender/Foolin' Around/Time/Your
Kind Of Lover/Exercises In Free Love/In My Defence
Side 2: Mr. Bad Guy/Let's Turn It On/Living On My
Own/Love Kills/Barcelona

COMPACT DISCS

Mr. Bad Guy
CBS CD 86312 May 1985
Let's Turn It On/Made In Heaven/I Was Born To Love
You/Foolin' Around/Your Kind Of Lover/Mr. Bad
Guy/Man Made Paradise/There Must Be More To
Life/Living On My Own/My Love Is Dangerous/Love Me
Like There's No Tomorrow
BONUS TRACKS: Let's Turn It On (12" mix)/I Was Born
To Love You (12" mix)/Living On My Own (12" mix)

Barcelona
POLYDOR CDPOLH 44 October 1988
Barcelona/La Japonaise/The Fallen Priest/Ensueno/The
Golden Boy/Guide Me Home/How Can I Go On/Overture
Piccante

The Freddie Mercury Album
PARLOPHONE 7809992 November 1992
The Great Pretender/Foolin Around/Time/Your Kind Of
Lover/Exercises In Free Love/In My Defence/Mr. Bad
Guy/Let's Turn It On/Living On My Own/Love
Kills/Barcelona

TAPE CASSETTES

Mr. Bad Guy
CBS 86312 May 1985
Side 1: Let's Turn It On/Made In Heaven/I Was Born To
Love You/Foolin' Around/Your Kind Of Lover
Side 2: Mr. Bad Guy/Man Made Paradise/There Must
Be More To Life/Living On My Own/My Love Is
Dangerous/Love Me Like There's No Tomorrow
BONUS TRACK: I Was Born To Love You (12" mix)

Barcelona
POLYDOR POLH 44 October 1988
Side 1: Barcelona/La Japonaise/The Fallen
Priest/Ensueno
Side 2: The Golden Boy/Guide Me Home/How Can I Go
On/Overture Piccante

SOUNDTRACK ALBUMS

Metropolis
CBS 70252 October 1984
Includes: Love Kills

Teachers
EMI EJ 240271 February 1985
Includes: Fooling Around

Time
EMI AMPM 1 April 1986
Includes: Time/In My Defence/ Time (reprise)

BRIAN MAY

7" SINGLES

Starfleet (single version)/**Son Of Starfleet**
EMI 5436 October 1983

Driven By You/Just One Life
PARLOPHONE R 6304 November 1991

Too Much Love Will Kill You/I'm Scared (single version)
PARLOPHONE R 6320 August 1992

Back To The Light (radio version)**/Back To The Light** (album version)**/Nothin' But Blue** (guitar version)
PARLOPHONE CDRDJ 6329 November 1992

Back To The Light/Starfleet/Let Me Out
PARLOPHONE CDRX 6329 November 1992

Resurrection/Love Token/Too Much Love Will Kill You (live)
PARLOPHONE CDRS 6351 June 1993

Resurrection/Driven By You/Back To The Light (live)**/Tie Your Mother Down** (live)
PARLOPHONE CDR 6351 June 1993

Last Horizon (radio version)**/Last Horizon** (live version)**/Last Horizon** (album version)**/We Will Rock You** (live slow version)**/We Will Rock You** (live fast version)
PARLOPHONE CDRS 6371 November 1993

MINI ALBUM

Starfleet Project
EMI SFLT 1078061 October 1983
Side 1: Starfleet/Let Me Out
Side 2: Bluesbreakers

ALBUM

Back To The Light
PARLOPHONE PCSD 123 September 1992
Side 1: The Dark/Back To The Light/Love Token/Resurrection/Too Much Love Will Kill You/Driven By You
Side 2: Nothing But Blue/I'm Scared/Last Horizon/Let Your Heart Rule Your Head/Just One Life/Rolling Over

TAPE CASSETTE

Starfleet Project
October 1983
Side 1: Starfleet/Let Me Out
Side 2: Bluesbreakers

CD ALBUMS

Back To The Light
PARLOPHONE CDPCSD X123 – gold disc - 10,000 limited edition September 1992
The Dark/Back To The Light/Love Token/Resurrection/Too Much Love Will Kill You/Driven By You / Nothing But Blue/I'm Scared/Last Horizon/Let Your Heart Rule Your Head/Just One Life/Rolling Over

Live At The Brixton Academy
PARLOPHONE CDPCSD 150 February 1994
Back To The Light/Driven By You/Tie Your Mother Down/Love Token/Headlong/Love Of My Life/ '39/Let Your Heart Rule Your Head/Too Much Love Will Kill You/Since You've Been Gone/Now I'm Here/Guitar Extravagance/Resurrection /Last Horizon/We Will Rock You/Hammer To Fall

JOHN DEACON (& IMMORTALS)

Back To The Light/Nothin' But Life
PARLOPHONE R 6329 November 1992

Last Horizon/ '39 (live)**/Let Your Heart Rule Your Head**
PARLOPHONE R 6371 November 1993

12″ SINGLES

Driven By You (single version)/**Driven By You** (Ford advert version)/**Just One Life** (album version)/**Just One Life** (guitar version)
PARLOPHONE 12R 6304 November 1991

Resurrection/Love Token/Too Much Love Will Kill You (live)
PARLOPHONE 12RPF 6351 – picture disc with insert June 1993

CD SINGLES

Driven By You (single version)/**Driven By You** (Ford advert version)/**Just One Life** (album version)/**Just One Life** (guitar version)
PARLOPHONE CDRDJ 6304 November 1991

Too Much Love Will Kill You (album version)**/I'm Scared** (single version)/**Too Much Love Will Kill You** (guitar version)/**Driven By You** (new version)
PARLOPHONE CDR 6320 August 1992

Back To The Light/Nothin' But Blue (guitar version)/**Blues Breaker**
PARLOPHONE CDRX 6329 November 1992

7″ SINGLE

No Turning Back/No Turning Back (chocs away mix)
MCA MCA 1057 May 1986

12″ SINGLE

No Turning Back (joy stick mix)/**No Turning Back** (chocs away mix)/**No Turning Back** (7″ mix)
MCA MCAT 1057 May 1986

SOUNDTRACK ALBUM

Biggles
MCA MCF 3328 June 1986
Includes: No Turning Back

LARRY LUREX DISCOGRAPHY

7″ SINGLE

I Can Hear Music/Goin' Back
EMI 2030 June 1973

SMILE DISCOGRAPHY

7″ SINGLE

Earth/Step On Me
MERCURY 72977 1969
Released in the US only

ALBUM

Gettin' Smile
MERCURY 18PP-1 September 1982
Doin' Alright/Blag/April Lady/Polar Bear/Earth/Step On Me
Japanese release only

THE CROSS DISCOGRAPHY

7″ SINGLES

Cowboys And Indians/Love Lies Bleeding
VIRGIN VS 1007 September 1987

Shove It/Rough Justice
VIRGIN VS 1026 January 1988

Heaven For Everyone/Love On A Tightrope (Like An Animal)
VIRGIN VS 1062 March 1988

Manipulator/Stand Up For Love
VIRGIN VS 1100 July 1988

Power To Love/Passion For Trash
PARLOPHONE R6251 April 1990

12" SINGLES

Cowboys And Indians (full length version)**/Love Lies Bleeding**
VIRGIN VST 1007 September 1987

Shove It/Shove It (metropolix)**/Rough Justice**
VIRGIN VST 1026 January 1988

Heaven For Everyone/Love On A Tightrope (Like An Animal)/Contact
VIRGIN VST 1062 March 1988

Manipulator (extended mix)**/Stand Up For Love/Manipulator** (7" version)
VIRGIN VST 1100 July 1988

Power To Love (extended version)**/Passion For Trash/Power To Love** (7" version)
PARLOPHONE 12R 6251 April 1990

CASSETTE SINGLE

Cowboys And Indians/Love Lies Bleeding
VIRGIN VSTC1007 September 1987

CD SINGLES

Cowboys And Indians/Love Lies Bleeding
VIRGIN CDEP10 September 1987

Shove It/Rough Justice/Cowboys And Indians/Shove It (extended mix)
VIRGIN CDEP20 January 1988

Power To Love (extended version)**/Passion For Trash/Power To Love**
PARLOPHONE CDR6251 April 1990

ALBUMS

Shove It
VIRGIN V2477 February 1988
Side 1: Shove It/Cowboys And Indians/Contact/Heaven For Everyone
Side 2: Stand Up For Love/Love On A Tightrope (Like An Animal)/Love Lies Bleeding (She's A Wicked Wily Waitress)/Rough Justice

Mad, Bad And Dangerous To Know
PARLOPHONE PCS 7342 March 1990
Side 1: Top Of The World Ma/Liar/Closer To You/Breakdown/Penetration Guru/Power To Love
Side 2: Sister Blue/Better Things/Passion For Trash/Old Men/Final Destination

COMPACT DISCS

Mad, Bad And Dangerous To Know
PARLOPHONE CDPCS 7342 March 1990
Top Of The World Ma/Liar/Closer To You/Breakdown/Penetration Guru/Power To Love/Sister Blue/Better Things/Passion For Trash/Old Men/Final Destination/ Foxy Lady

MISCELLANEOUS OR FOREIGN RELEASES

Liar/In Charge Of My Heart
ELECTROLA 14 75167 – German 7" single June 1990

Liar (extended)**/In Charge Of My Heart**
(extended)**/Liar**
ELECTROLA 1C 1475167 – German 12" single June 1990

Liar (extended)**/In Charge Of My Heart**
(extended)**/Liar**
ELECTROLA 560 1475167 – German CD single June 1990

Final Destination/Penetration Guru/Man On Fire
(live)
ELECTROLA 1C 12 560 147529 – European 12" single October 1990

Final Destination/Penetration Guru/Man On Fire
(live)
ELECTROLA 1C 560 147529 – European CD single October 1990

New Dark Ages (single mix)**/Ain't Put Noting Down/Man On Fire** (live)**/New Dark Ages** (album version)
ELECTROLA 1C 560 204372 – German CD single September 1991

Life Changes (7" version)**/Put It All Down To Love/Life Changes** (album version)**/Heartland**
ELECTROLA 560 204572 – Dutch CD single – withdrawn

Blue Rock
ELECTROLA 1C 564–796 6242 – German album October 1991
Side 1: Bad Attitude/New Dark Ages/Dirty Mind/Baby It's Alright/Ain't Putting Nothing Down
Side 2: The Also Rans/Millionaire/Put It All Down To Love/Hand Fools/Life Changes

Blue Rock
ELECTROLA 1C 564-796-6242 – German CD October 1991
Bad Attitude/New Dark Ages/Dirty Mind/Baby It's Alright/Ain't Putting Nothing Down/The Also Rans/Millionaire/Put It All Down To Love/Hand Fools/Life Changes

BOOTLEGS

Queen must be one of the most bootlegged groups in the history of popular music. Many of these bootlegs suffer from inferior sound quality, especially the live concert recordings, but they are, nevertheless, important additions to any Queen collection. Over the years they have been available on vinyl and cassette but in more recent years the trend has been towards CD bootlegs. It is far beyond the scope of this book to list every bootleg ever released along with complete track listings but the following is a guide to what exists. Many of the bootlegs are just copies of other bootlegs and certain shows, i.e. Christmas 1975 and material from the 'Magic' tour appeared on many different releases, in varying quality. Quite often the information given on the sleeves is incorrect and bares little resemblance to what is actually on the disc. We have noted here the details as on the sleeves. Also listed are the audience-recorded cassettes that are available, although there are possibly many more than listed here. These cassettes listed here only give the title and format.

The entries follow the following format:

Title:
Format: (i.e. CD, Vinyl or Cassette)
Catalogue Number:
Comments: (Comments regarding tracks, venue, date and any other relevant information)

Not all entries will contain all this information, neither will complete track listings be given.

18 Greatest Hits Live
Format: Vinyl
Catalogue Number: QMU
Comments: Live concert recorded 26 June 1986

18 Greatest Hits Live
Format: Compact Disc
Catalogue Number: STEN 91 005
Comments: Live tracks from 1986

A Day At The Stadium
Format: Compact Disc
Catalogue Number: KTS 039
Comments: Live concerts recorded in London 1975

A Day In Munich
Format: Cassette

A Night At The Court
Format: Compact Disc
Catalogue Number: TNT 007/8
Comments: Double album featuring live material
recorded in London 1977 and Birmingham 1973

A Night Of Summer Magic
Format: Cassette

Absolutely Enthusiastic
Format: Vinyl
Catalogue Number: TFKRL 9002-2
Comments: Live concert recorded 11 May 1985

Absolutely Perfect
Format: Compact Disc
Catalogue Number: MNS 0292
Comments: Recorded live in Brussels

Absolutely Rare
Format: Vinyl
Catalogue Number: TFKRL 9201
Comments: Recorded at various live concerts

Absolutely Rare
Format: Compact Disc
Catalogue Number: QUCD 9202
Comments: Various shows

Adelaide
Format: Cassette

All Your Love Tonight
Format: Compact Disc
Catalogue Number: RC 2106
Comments: 10 September 1980 concert recorded at
the Milwaukee Stadium

Amphitheatre France
Format: Cassette

Apollo II
Format: Cassette

At The Palace
Format: Cassette

Best Selection
Format: Compact Disc
Catalogue Number: VC 3024
Comments: Live recording from various shows

Big In Japan
Format: Compact Disc
Catalogue Number: NRG 010/11
Comments: May 1975 live concert double CD. Also
included some UK 1985 live material

Bingley Hall
Format: Cassette

Birmingham Town Hall
Format: Cassette

Black & White Queen
Format: Vinyl
Catalogue Number: EEN 98
Comments: Live concert recorded 14 December 1975

Bristol Colston
Format: Cassette

Bristol Hippodrome
Format: Cassette

Budokan
Format: Cassette

By Request: The Ultimate Collection II
Format: Compact Disc
Catalogue Number: RM 002/003
Comments: A mix of live recordings, rare tracks and extended versions

Cardiac Arrest
Format: Vinyl
Catalogue Number: Hip 001
Comments: Various live recordings

Command Performance
Format: Vinyl
Catalogue Number: TAKRL 1997
Comments: Live concert recorded 24 December 1975

Copenhagen
Format: Cassette

Coventry Theatre
Format: Cassette

Coverin'
Format: Compact Disc
Catalogue Number: Ugly Records COW100
Comments: A collection of tracks from various shows from 1977 -1986 along with BBC sessions and studio tracks

Crazy Duck
Format: Vinyl
Catalogue Number: DR 481
Comments: Live concert recorded 26 December 1979

Crazy Tour
Format: Vinyl

Catalogue Number: 26Q
Comments: Double album recorded 26 December 1979

Crowning Glory
Format: Compact Disc
Catalogue Number: KTS 071
Comments: This Italian release contains the 11 July 1986 Wembley show

Cry Argentina
Format: Compact Disc
Catalogue Number: Oh Boy 2-9145
Comments: Most of the tracks on this French release stem from a 1981 concert in Argentina with the addition of some tracks from a 1973 London concert

Dear Friend Goodbye
Format: Vinyl
Catalogue Number: TFMML 001
Comments: Recorded live 7 May 1975

Domo Aragato
Format: Compact Disc
Catalogue Number: Aulica Records A2157
Comments: Another Italian release this time featuring a 1982 concert from Osaka, Japan. This release was a double CD

Done Under Pressure
Format: Vinyl
Catalogue Number: Unknown
Comments: Recorded 21 June 1986

Done Under Pressure
Format: Compact Disc
Catalogue Number: LCD 115-2
Comments: Recorded in Germany June 1986

Duck Soup
Format: Vinyl
Catalogue Number: SLA 007
Comments: Live concert recorded 13 March 1997

Dynasty
Format: Vinyl
Catalogue Number: QN 1-6
Comments: Recorded 27 September 1984

Earls Court
Format: Cassette

Elizabeth II
Format: Vinyl
Catalogue Number: Unknown
Comments: Live concert recorded 14 September 1984

Empire Theatre
Format: Cassette

En Viva Pueblo
Format: Vinyl
Catalogue Number: Unknown
Comments: Recorded 16 October 1981

Eve Of Christmas
Format: Compact Disc
Catalogue Number: TR 256
Comments: Hammersmith Odeon concert from 24 December 1975

Falklands II - The Sequel
Format: Vinyl
Catalogue Number: KQ001
Comments: Recorded March 1981

Flash Alive
Format: Vinyl
Catalogue Number: Q80128
Comments: Double album recorded live 8 December 1980

Flash Freddie
Format: Compact Disc
Catalogue Number: BM 051-052
Comments: Wembley concert recorded 5 July 1986

Freddie Mercury Is Alive
Format: Compact Disc

Catalogue Number: WRCD 001-2
Comments: Various live recordings from unknown dates and venues

Freddie's Boys At The Beeb
Format: Vinyl
Catalogue Number: JOKE 40 HO
Comments: Tracks recorded for various BBC Sessions

Freddie's Last Journey
Format: Vinyl
Catalogue Number: PAN 648-09
Comments: Double album that consisted of the 'Rock In Rio' video tracks

Free In The Park
Format: Vinyl
Catalogue Number: MARC
Comments: Recorded 18 September 1976

Free In The Park
Format: Cassette

From The Beeb To Tokyo
Format: Compact Disc
Catalogue Number: CD17
Comments: BBC sessions and Japanese live recordings

Fukuoka
Format: Cassette

Ga Ga
Format: Vinyl
Catalogue Number: ETS 2563/64
Comments: Double album featuring the 1 September 1984 concert

Geisha Boys
Format: Vinyl
Catalogue Number: SLA 001
Comments: Live concert from 4 April 1976

Geisha Boys
Format: Cassette

Get Down
Format: Vinyl
Catalogue Number: LR 140RC
Comments: Recorded live on 24 October 1982

Glasgow
Format: Cassette

Glasgow Apollo
Format: Cassette

God Save The Queen
Format: Compact Disc
Catalogue Number: OS CD4
Comments: Live recordings from 1980 tours

Golden Demos 1973-76
Format: Compact Disc
Catalogue Number: Steck 001
Comments: BBC live sessions and other early tracks

Gonna Rock
Format: Vinyl
Catalogue Number: QLS 1957
Comments: BBC sessions and 1974 live material.

Goodbye
Format: Compact Disc
Catalogue Number: NE 2211
Comments: Double CD featuring live material from
London in 1973 and 1975 and Tokyo 1985

Greatest Hits USA
Format: Compact Disc
Catalogue Number: GH 1826
Comments: Various live tracks from unknown venues
and dates

Halfpence
Format: Vinyl
Catalogue Number: EEN 98
Comments: Concert recorded 24 December 1975

Halfpence
Format: Cassette

Her Majesties Secret Service
Format: Vinyl
Catalogue Number: TFKRL 9001
Comments: Double album

High Voltage
Format: Vinyl
Catalogue Number: SR 25 703
Comments: Double album of live show from 24
December 1975

Hot Space Tour '82
Format: Vinyl
Catalogue Number: ETS 2511
Comments: Triple live album from 14 September
1982

I Want To Break Free
Format: Compact Disc
Catalogue Number: CD/ON 2223
Comments: Live material from 1984 and 1986 along
with tracks lifted directly from the 'Live In Budapest'
video

I'm In Love With Freddie
Format: Compact Disc
Catalogue Number: MLP 2
Comments: Live recordings from Chicago 19
September 1980

I've Just Got To Have It Now
Format: Vinyl
Catalogue Number: Unknown
Comments: Unknown recording date

Immortal
Format: Compact Disc
Catalogue Number: G53203
Comments: Tracks from various unknown live shows

In The Lap Of The Gods
Format: Compact Disc
Catalogue Number: SCM 01
Comments: Recorded live at the Rainbow Theatre 20
December 1974

In The Lap Of The Queen
Format: Compact Disc
Catalogue Number: CO 25153
Comments: Live recordings from 17 March 1977
in Seattle

Japan 1985 Highlights
Format: Compact Disc
Catalogue Number: TCS CD 001
Comments: Material not from Japan as the title would
suggest but possibly from Wembley in 1986

Killers
Format: Compact Disc
Catalogue Number: FLASH 09-90-0130
Comments: Live tracks from London in 1973-
1975

Kimono My Place Live
Format: Vinyl
Catalogue Number: MARC 75122
Comments: Live recording from 1 May 1975

Kimono My Place Live
Format: Cassette

King's Favourite
Format: Vinyl
Catalogue Number: 141RC
Comments: Live double album recorded 20 September
1984

Kosei Nenkin
Format: Cassette

La Fleur Du Mal
Format: Compact Disc
Catalogue Number: WORK 5538-2
Comments: 11 May 1985 live recordings from
Japan

Lazing On A Sunday Afternoon
Format: Vinyl
Catalogue Number: MARC TQ-76042
Comments: Recorded live on 4 April 1976

Lazing On A Sunday Evening
Format: Cassette

Live
Format: Vinyl
Catalogue Number: OG-860
Comments: 19 April 1975 concert recording

Live At Budokan
Format: Cassette

Live At The Rainbow
Format: Vinyl
Catalogue Number: TAB 001
Comments: Despite the misleading title this concert
from 24 December 1975 was recorded at the
Hammersmith Odeon in London

Live Dates: Vol 17
Format: Compact Disc
Catalogue Number: STONED 012
Comments: December 1975 concert

Live In Budapest
Format: Cassette

Live In Cologne
Format: Compact Disc
Catalogue Number: PRCD 1033
Comments: Live concert from 1 February 1979

Live In Japan
Format: Vinyl
Catalogue Number: S3004
Comments: Live double album from Japanese concerts
in 1982

Live In Montreal
Format: Compact Disc
Catalogue Number: CSCD 10006
Comments: Live concert from 1 December 1978

Live In USA 1977
Format: Compact Disc
Catalogue Number: HL CD014

Comments: Live recordings from 13 March 1977 in Seattle

Live USA
Format: Compact Disc
Catalogue Number: IMT 900.6
Comments: 1977 and 1982 live material from various US concerts

Liverpool Empire
Format: Cassette

London 1975
Format: Compact Disc
Catalogue Number: FBCD 1146
Comments: Hammersmith Odeon concert from 24 December 1975

London 1986
Format: Compact Disc
Catalogue Number: PSCD 1170
Comments: Recorded at Wembley Arena during the 'Magic' Tour

Long Life To The Queen
Format: Vinyl
Catalogue Number: Unknown
Comments: Live triple album from April 1982 concerts

Los Angeles
Format: Cassette

Made In Heaven
Format: Compact Disc
Catalogue Number: P&L 1992
Comments: Alternate demo versions of classic queen songs. (In reality the originals with Mercury's vocals mixed far back)

Made In Japan
Format: Compact Disc
Catalogue Number: RS 9210
Comments: Live recordings from Japan in 1985

Magic At Knebworth
Format: Vinyl
Catalogue Number: RSR 250
Comments: Live double album from the 'Magic' Tour 1986

Magic At Knebworth
Format: Cassette

Magic Moments
Format: Cassette

Maine Road Magic
Format: Cassette

Manchester
Format: Cassette

Mania
Format: Vinyl
Catalogue Number: EGF 1200
Comments: Concert from 13 March 1977

Marquee
Format: Cassette

Mercury Poisoning
Format: Vinyl
Catalogue Number: IMP 1118
Comments: 31 April 1976 concert recording

Mercury Poisoning
Format: Cassette

Merry Christmas
Format: Compact Disc
Catalogue Number: GDR CD 9108
Comments: Hammersmith show from December 1975

Merry Christmas
Format: Cassette

Moet & Chandon
Format: Vinyl
Catalogue Number: TFKRL 9101
Comments: Details unknown

Mott Tour
Format: Cassette

My Favourite Dance Tracks
Format: Compact Disc
Catalogue Number: MMS 0892
Comments: Live material from Buenos Aires in 1981

Nihon
Format: Compact Disc
Catalogue Number: NSCD 0014/15
Comments: Double CD of material from Tokyo 1985 and London 1986

Nikon
Format: Compact Disc
Catalogue Number: LSCD 5250051/2
Comments: Two CD set with same content as Nihon bootleg

No More Heroes
Format: Compact Disc
Catalogue Number: POET 9212
Comments: Live tracks from unknown dates and venues

No More Mananas
Format: Vinyl
Catalogue Number: SA 0009
Comments: Live recordings from unknown dates

No News Is Good News
Format: Vinyl
Catalogue Number: Unknown
Comments: BBC sessions and live recordings

Noblesse Oblige
Format: Compact Disc
Catalogue Number: LLRCD 149
Comments: Live material spanning the period 1973-1986

On Fire
Format: Compact Disc
Catalogue Number: 1018
Comments: 11 July 1986 live recording from Wembley

Opera House
Format: Cassette

Opera Omnia
Format: Compact Disc
Catalogue Number: RPBX 012/13/14/15
Comments: This lavish four CD set contains material from various unknown shows

Over The Best Or Worst
Format: Compact Disc
Catalogue Number: 5556/2/1
Comments: Recorded at various unknown shows

Oxford New Theatre
Format: Cassette

Pacific North Western
Format: Cassette

Paris Pavillion
Format: Cassette

Paris Theatre
Format: Cassette

Pearly Queen
Format: Compact Disc
Catalogue Number: BGS 018
Comments: Live in Rio de Janeiro 1985

Playhouse Theatre
Format: Cassette

Queen
Format: Compact Disc
Catalogue Number: NE1122
Comments: Double CD featuring live material from London in 1973 and 1975 and Tokyo 1985

Queen At St. James' Park
Format: Vinyl
Catalogue Number: Unknown
Comments: Double album released in limited quantities of 9 July 1986 concert

Queen At The Races
Format: Cassette

Queen Elizabeth II
Format: Vinyl
Catalogue Number: Unknown
Comments: Live recording from 14 September 1984

Queen Invite You To A Night At The Bukodan
Format: Vinyl
Catalogue Number: MARC TQ-76059
Comments: Recorded 31 April 1976

Queen Invite You To A Night At The Warehouse
Format: Vinyl
Catalogue Number: STONED 5
Comments: 12 May 1997 live recording

Queen Invite You To A Night At The Warehouse
Format: Cassette

Queen Mania
Format: Cassette

Queen On The Green
Format: Cassette

Queen Reigns The World
Format: Vinyl
Catalogue Number: Miles records
Comments: 21 June 1986 live double album from the 'Magic' Tour

Queen Reigns The World
Format: Compact Disc
Catalogue Number: TCC 028/029
Comments: Compact disc version of vinyl equivalent

Queen's Last Stand
Format: Vinyl
Catalogue Number: ETS 2583/84
Comments: Live double album from 15 May 1985

Queentessance: In Memoriam Of Frederick Bulsara
Format: Compact Disc
Catalogue Number: LL CD 9214
Comments: Various live recordings from the seventies and eighties

Radio Ga Ga
Format: Compact Disc
Catalogue Number: HS 29104
Comments: Live recordings from Japan in 1985

Rainbow Theatre
Format: Cassette

Regina De Ipanema
Format: Compact Disc
Catalogue Number: BC 008
Comments: Live in Rio de Janeiro 11 January 1985

Regina Versus Freddie And The Boys
Format: Compact Disc
Catalogue Number: OTR 75517/18
Comments: Double CD featuring material from Seattle 13 March 1977 and Brussels 20 September 1984

Rhapsody In Gold
Format: Compact Disc
Catalogue Number: LIMES 3001
Comments: Limited edition double CD of 1981 and 1984 concerts in Buenos Aires and Brussels

Rhapsody In Red
Format: Compact Disc
Catalogue Number: BUC 033
Comments: Live material from 1976

Rock In Japan
Format: Compact Disc
Catalogue Number: FLASH 07.91.0156/1/2
Comments: Double CD featuring live material from Osaka, Japan in 1985 and San Diego 1977

Rocking Osaka In 1982
Format: Compact Disc
Catalogue Number: Big 067
Comments: Recorded live at the Tiger Stadium 25
October 1982

Rogues And Scoundrels
Format: Vinyl
Catalogue Number: Aftermath 8
Comments: Various live recordings

Rogues And Scoundrels
Format: Cassette

Rotterdam
Format: Cassette

Royal American Tour
Format: Vinyl
Catalogue Number: WRMB 307
Comments: 22 March 1975 live recording

Royal American Tour
Format: Cassette

Royal Rock Us
Format: Vinyl
Catalogue Number: TAKRL 927
Comments: Live show from 24 December 1975

Saturday Night's Alright For Fighting
Format: Compact Disc
Catalogue Number: BOD CD 214
Comments: Live material from 1977 tour

Save Me
Format: Vinyl
Catalogue Number: Unknown
Comments: Live double of 1 February 1979 show

Sheer Bloody Poetry
Format: Cassette

Sheetkickers
Format: Vinyl
Catalogue Number: TAKRL 1957
Comments: Live album of various recordings from
1974

Sheetkickers
Format: Cassette

Shivers Down My Spine
Format: Compact Disc
Catalogue Number: XX1
Comments: Live recording from Munich 29 June 1986

St. George's Hall
Format: Cassette

Stockholm
Format: Cassette

Stunning
Format: Vinyl
Catalogue Number: BRR 006
Comments: Recorded on 1 May 1975

Stunning Live In Tokyo
Format: Cassette

Tavaszi Szei
Format: Compact Disc
Catalogue Number: LCD 109-2
Comments: Double CD recorded in Europe and as
featured on the 'Budapest' video

Thank You Freddie
Format: Compact Disc
Catalogue Number: PWCD 101/2/3
Comments: Triple CD of Freddie Mercury Tribute
Concert in 1992

Thanks!!!
Format: Compact Disc
Catalogue Number: 9320.23
Comments: Triple CD set featuring BBC material and
other live material

The Carriage Of Mystery
Format: Compact Disc
Catalogue Number: Rex Discs
Comments: Live in Germany 21 June 1986

The Freddie Mercury Tribute
Format: Compact Disc
Catalogue Number: TFKRL 9204-3
Comments: Triple CD with, as the title suggests, the Tribute Concert held in 1992

The Jewels
Format: Compact Disc
Catalogue Number: IST 31/32
Comments: Unknown source

The Mercury Is Rising
Format: Compact Disc
Catalogue Number: ARC 003
Comments: Mainly 1974 live recordings

The Ultimate Collection: Rarities, Oddities And Cover Versions
Format: Compact Disc
Catalogue Number: RMCD 001
Comments: Double CD that the title suggests features rare material but actually is not what it seems

The Ultimate Queen: Back Catalogue Vol 1
Format: Compact Disc
Catalogue Number: Unknown
Comments: Rare material, B-sides and early performances make up this CD

The Ultimate Queen: Back Catalogue Vol 2
Format: Compact Disc
Catalogue Number: Unknown
Comments: As with Volume 1 this CD features more rare material including 12" versions

Tie Your Mother Down
Format: Vinyl
Catalogue Number: KQ 001
Comments: Live recording from 28 February 1981

Tokyo '85
Format: Compact Disc
Catalogue Number: APR 92.006
Comments: 1985 live material from Japan

Tokyo 1985
Format: Compact Disc
Catalogue Number: TKCD 1120
Comments: Live material, although not from November 1985 as you would be led to believe

Tokyo Rampage
Format: Vinyl
Catalogue Number: TKRWM 1801
Comments: Live recordings from various unknown dates

Tokyo Rampage
Format: Cassette

Tornado In The Far East
Format: Vinyl
Catalogue Number: TFKRL 9002 – 2
Comments: Unknown date and venue

Tribute: Rare And Unreleased Tracks
Format: Compact Disc
Catalogue Number: MF 284
Comments: Mainly BBC sessions from 1973–1977

Unauthorised Live: Volume 1
Format: Compact Disc
Catalogue Number: Jok 015-A
Comments: Another CD of the 1975 Christmas show

Unforgettable Music
Format: Compact Disc
Catalogue Number: 10201
Comments: Two CD set of Freddie Mercury Tribute Show

Vancouver
Format: Cassette

Vienna
Format: Cassette

Vienna (2nd Night)
Format: Cassette

Waiting On A Death Trip
Format: Compact Disc
Catalogue Number: TGP 137
Comments: Live recording from
Argentina in 1981

We Still Rock You
Format: Compact Disc
Catalogue Number: Rola 009
Comments: Material from Europe in
1986

We Will Rock You
Format: Compact Disc
Catalogue Number: SKCD 2063
Comments: Live recordings from
Milan in 1984 and London in 1985

We Will Rock You
Format: Compact Disc
Catalogue Number: CD 12018
Comments: Live material from
unknown venues and dates

X-mas 1975
Format: Compact Disc
Catalogue Number: SR 012
Comments: Yet another Christmas
1975 release

Year Of The Opera
Format: Compact Disc
Catalogue Number: AAF 014
Comments: Live tracks from
various unknown shows

You're My Best Friend
Format: Compact Disc
Catalogue Number: CD 12030
Comments: Live material recorded
between 1975 and 1979 in Europe

Zoom Queen
Format: Vinyl
Catalogue Number: LLX 314
Comments: Double album recorded
in Japan in 1976

UNITED KINGDOM CHART FACTS
1973–1997

NUMBER ONE ALBUMS

1975 A Night At The Opera
1976 A Day At The Races
1980 The Game
1981 Greatest Hits
1986 A Kind Of Magic
1989 The Miracle
1991 Innuendo
1991 Greatest Hits II
1995 Made In Heaven

TOP TWENTY ALBUMS

1974 Queen
1974 Sheer Heart Attack
1975 A Night At The Opera
1976 A Day At The Races
1977 News Of The World
1978 Jazz
1979 Live Killers
1980 The Game
1980 Flash Gordon
1981 Greatest Hits
1982 Hot Space
1984 The Works
1986 A Kind Of Magic
1986 Live Magic
1989 The Miracle
1991 Innuendo
1991 Greatest Hits II
1992 Live At Wembley '86
1995 Made In Heaven

ALBUMS THAT FAILED TO REACH THE TOP TWENTY

1974 Queen
1989 Queen At The Beeb

NUMBER ONE SINGLES

1975 Bohemian Rhapsody
1981 Under Pressure (with David Bowie)
1991 Innuendo
1991 Bohemian Rhapsody (Re-issue)
1993 Five Live EP

TOP TWENTY SINGLES

1974 Seven Sea Of Rhye
1974 Killer Queen
1975 Now I'm Here
1975 Bohemian Rhapsody
1976 You're My Best Friend
1976 Somebody To Love
1977 Queen's First EP (EP)
1977 We Are The Champions
1978 Bicycle Race/Fat Bottomed Girls
1979 Don't Stop Me Now
1979 Crazy Little Thing Called Love
1980 Save Me

1980 Play The Game
1980 Another One Bites The Dust
1980 Flash
1981 Under Pressure (with David Bowie)
1982 Las Palabras de Amor
1984 Radio Ga Ga
1984 I Want To Break Free
1984 It's A Hard Life
1984 Hammer To Fall
1985 One Vision
1986 A Kind Of Magic
1986 Friends Will Be Friends
1989 I Want It All
1989 Breakthru
1989 The Invisible Man
1991 Innuendo
1991 Headlong
1991 The Show Must Go On
1991 Bohemian Rhapsody (Re-issue)
1995 Heaven For Everyone
1995 A Winter's Tale
1996 Too Much Love Will Kill You
1996 Let Me Live
1996 You Don't Fool Me

SINGLES THAT FAILED TO REACH THE TOP TWENTY

1977 Tie Your Mother Down
1978 Spread Your Wings

1979 Love Of My Life
1982 Body Language
1982 Backchat
1984 Thank God It's Christmas
1986 Who Wants To Live Forever
1989 Scandal
1989 The Miracle
1991 I'm Going Slightly Mad

CHART TRIVIA

Weeks On The UK Singles Chart: 389

Hits In UK Singles Chart: 47

Number Of Top Tens In Singles Chart: 24

Number Of Number Ones In Singles Chart: 5

Weeks At Number One In UK Singles Chart: 20

Weeks At Number One In UK Singles Chart By One Record Only: 14 ('Bohemian Rhapsody')

Most Weeks At Number One In UK Singles Chart: 9 ('Bohemian Rhapsody')

Gap Between Number Ones In UK Singles Chart: 14 Years

Weeks On The UK Albums Chart: 1111

Weeks On The UK Albums Chart In One Year: 128

Hits In UK Albums Chart: 21

Number Of Top Tens In Albums Chart: 19

Number Of Number Ones In Albums Chart: 9

Weeks At Number One In UK Albums Chart: 21

Weeks In UK Albums Chart By One Album Only: 433 (Greatest Hits)

Albums That Entered UK Album Chart At Number One: 5

SONGS/ALBUMS THAT REPLACED QUEEN AT NUMBER ONE

Singles
'Bohemian Rhapsody' was replaced at number one by 'Mamma Mia' (ABBA)

'Under Pressure' was replaced at number one by 'Begin The Beguine' (Julio Iglesias)

'Innuendo' was replaced at number one by '3 Am Eternal' (KLF featuring Children Of The Revolution)

'Bohemian Rhapsody' (Re-issue) was replaced at number one by 'Goodnight Girl' (Wet Wet Wet)

Albums
A Night At The Opera was replaced at number one by *40 Greatest Hits* (Perry Como)

A Day At The Races was replaced at number one by *Arrival* (ABBA)

The Game was replaced at number one by *Deepest Purple* (Deep Purple)

Greatest Hits was replaced at number one by *Chart Hits '81* (Various Artists)

A Kind Of Magic was replaced at number one by *Invisible Touch* (Genesis)

The Miracle was replaced at number one by *Ten Good Reasons* (Jason Donovan)

Innuendo was replaced at number one by *Circle Of One* (Oleta Adams)

Greatest Hits II was replaced at number one by *Stars* (Simply Red)

Made In Heaven was replaced at number one by *Robson And Jerome* (Robson Green and Jerome Flynn)

UK CHART
POSITIONS

SINGLES

TITLE	POSITION
Keep Yourself Alive	Did Not Chart
Seven Seas Of Rhye	10
Killer Queen	2
Now I'm Here	11
Bohemian Rhapsody	1
You're My Best Friend	7
Somebody To Love	2
Tie Your Mother Down	31
Good Old Fashioned Lover Boy	17
We Are The Champions	2
Spread Your Wings	34
Bicycle Race/Fat Bottomed Girls	11
Don't Stop Me Now	9
Love Of My Life	63
Crazy Little Thing Called Love	2
Save Me	11
Play The Game	14
Another One Bites The Dust	7
Flash	10
Under Pressure	1
Body Language	25
Las Palabras de Amor	17
Backchat	40
Radio Ga Ga	2
I Want To Break Free	3
It's A Hard Life	6
Hammer To Fall	13
Thank God It's Christmas	21
One Vision	7
A Kind Of Magic	3
Friends Will Be Friends	14
Who Wants To Live Forever	24
I Want It All	3
Breakthru	7
The Invisible Man	12
Scandal	25
The Miracle	21
Innuendo	1
I'm Going Slightly Mad	22
Headlong	14
The Show Must Go On	16
Bohemian Rhapsody (re-issue)	1
Heaven For Everyone	2
A Winter's Tale	6
Too Much Love Will Kill You	15
Let Me Live	9
You Don't Fool Me	17

ALBUMS

TITLE	POSITION
Queen	24
Queen II	5
Sheer Heart Attack	2
A Night At The Opera	1
A Day At The Races	1
News Of The World	4
Jazz	2
Live Killers	3
The Game	1
Flash Gordon	10
Greatest Hits	1
Hot Space	4
The Works	2
A Kind Of Magic	1
Live Magic	3
The Miracle	1
Queen At The Beeb	67
Innuendo	1
Greatest Hits II	1
Live At Wembley	2
Greatest Hits I & II (re-issue)	37
Made In Heaven	1

SOLO AND PRE-QUEEN CHART POSITIONS

UK unless where noted

FREDDIE MERCURY

Singles

Love Kills	10
	76 (in USA)
	32 (in Holland)
I Was Born To Love You	11
	55 (in USA)
	34 (in Holland)
Made In Heaven	57
Living On My Own	50
Love Me Like There's No Tomorrow	76
Time	32
The Great Pretender	4
	9 (in Holland)
Barcelona	8
The Golden Boy	80
How Can I Go On	95
Barcelona (Olympic re-issue)	2
	42 (in Australia)
	2 (in Holland)
In My Defence	8
How Can I Go On (re-issue)	Did Not Chart
The Great Pretender (re-issue)	29
	18 (in Holland)
Living On My Own (re-issue)	1
	2 (in Holland)

Albums

Mr Bad Guy	6
	20 (Japan)
	20 (Holland)
Barcelona	15
	9 (in Holland)
The Freddie Mercury Album	4
	8 (in Holland)

BRIAN MAY

Singles

Starfleet	65
Driven By You	6
	10 (in Holland)
Too Much Love Will Kill You	5
	18 (in Japan)
	1 (in Holland)
Back To The Light	19
	31 (in Holland)
Resurrection	23
Last Horizon	51

Albums

Starfleet Project	35
	125 (in USA)
Back To The Light	6
	159 (in USA)
	42 (in Japan)
Live At The Brixton Academy	20

ROGER TAYLOR

Singles

I Wanna Testify	Did Not Chart
Future Management	49
My Country I & II	Did Not Chart
Man On Fire	66
Strange Frontier	98
Nazis	22
Foreign Sand	26
Happiness	32

Albums

Fun In Space	18
	121 (in USA)
Strange Frontier	30
Happiness	22

JOHN DEACON

Singles

No Turning Back	Did Not Chart

LARRY LUREX

Singles

I Can Hear Music	Did Not Chart

THE CROSS

Singles

Cowboys And Indians	74
Shove It	82
Heaven For Everyone	83
Manipulator	Did Not Chart
Power To Love	85

Albums

Shove It	58
Mad, Bad And Dangerous To Know	Did Not Chart

US CHART POSITIONS

SINGLES

TITLE	POSITION
Keep Yourself Alive	Did Not Chart
Liar	Did Not Chart
Seven Seas Of Rhye	Did Not Chart
Killer Queen	12
Bohemian Rhapsody	9
You're My Best Friend	16
Somebody To Love	13
Tie Your Mother Down	49
Long Away	Did Not Chart
We Are The Champions	4
It's Late	74
Bicycle Race/Fat Bottomed Girls	24

Don't Stop Me Now	86
Jealousy	Did Not Chart
We Will Rock You (live)	Did Not Chart
Crazy Little Thing Called Love	1
Play The Game	42
Another One Bites The Dust	1
Need Your Loving Tonight	44
Flash	42
Under Pressure	29
Body Language	11
Calling All Girls	60
Staying Power	Did Not Chart
Radio Ga Ga	16
I Want To Break Free	45
It's A Hard Life	72
Hammer To Fall	Did Not Chart
One Vision	61
A Kind Of Magic	42
Princes Of The Universe	Did Not Chart
Pain Is So Close To Pleasure	Did Not Chart
I Want It All	50
Breakthru	Did Not Chart
Scandal	Did Not Chart
Innuendo	Did Not Chart
Headlong	Did Not Chart
The Show Must Go On	2
These Are The Days Of Our Lives	Did Not Chart
Bohemian Rhapsody (re-issue)	2
We Are The Champions (live)	52
Heaven For Everyone	Did Not Chart

ALBUMS

Queen	83
Queen II	49
Sheer Heart Attack	12
A Night At The Opera	4
A Day At The Races	5
News Of The World	3
Jazz	6
Live Killers	16
The Game	1
Flash Gordon	23
Greatest Hits	11

Hot Space	22	Flash	73
The Works	23	Under Pressure	88
A Kind Of Magic	26	Body Language	Did Not Chart
The Miracle	24	Backchat	Did Not Chart
Queen At The Beeb	Did Not Chart	Staying Power	Did Not Chart
Innuendo	30	Radio Ga Ga	89
Classic Queen	4	I Want To Break Free	Did Not Chart
Live At Wembley	53	It's A Hard Life	Did Not Chart
Made In Heaven	58	One Vision	Did Not Chart
		A Kind Of Magic	Did Not Chart
		Princes Of The Universe	Did Not Chart
		I Want It All	Did Not Chart
		Innuendo	Did Not Chart
		Heaven For Everyone	Did Not Chart

JAPANESE CHART POSITIONS

SINGLES

TITLE	POSITION
Keep Yourself Alive	Did Not Chart
Seven Seas Of Rhye	Did Not Chart
Killer Queen	27
Now I'm here	87
Bohemian Rhapsody	48
You're My Best Friend	90
Somebody To Love	51
Tie Your Mother Down	Did Not Chart
Teo Torriatte	49
We Are The Champions	72
It's Late	Did Not Chart
Bicycle Race/Fat Bottomed Girls	Did Not Chart
Don't Stop Me Now	Did Not Chart
Love Of My Life (live)	Did Not Chart
We Will Rock You (live)	Did Not Chart
Crazy Little Thing Called Love	64
Save Me	96
Play The Game	Did Not Chart
Another One Bites The Dust	Did Not Chart
Need Your Loving Tonight	Did Not Chart

ALBUMS

Queen	52
Queen II	Unknown
Sheer Heart Attack	23
A Night At The Opera	9
A Day At The Races	1
News Of The World	3
Jazz	5
Live Killers	9
The Game	5
Flash Gordon	12
Greatest Hits	9
Hot Space	6
The Works	7
A Kind Of Magic	25
Live Magic	49
The Miracle	20
Queen At The Beeb	Did Not Chart
Innuendo	13
Greatest Hits II	80
Live At Wembley	80
Made In Heaven	10

DUTCH CHART POSITIONS

SINGLES

TITLE	POSITION
Keep Yourself Alive	Did Not Chart
Seven Seas Of Rhye	Did Not Chart
Killer Queen	3
Now I'm here	32
Bohemian Rhapsody	1
You're My Best Friend	9
Somebody To Love	1
Tie Your Mother Down	14
Good Old Fashioned Lover Boy	Did Not Chart
We Are The Champions	2
Spread Your Wings	20
Bicycle Race/Fat Bottomed Girls	7
Don't Stop Me Now	14
Love Of My Life (live)	Did Not Chart
Crazy Little Thing Called Love	1
Save Me	5
Play The Game	15
Another One Bites The Dust	14
Flash	18
Under Pressure	1
Body Language	6
Las Palabras de Amor	26
Backchat	Did Not Chart
Radio Ga Ga	1
I Want To Break Free	1
One Vision	21
A Kind Of Magic	4
Friends Will Be friends	17
Pain Is So Close To Pleasure	26
Who Wants To Live Forever	Did Not Chart
I Want It All	2

Breakthru	4
The Invisible Man	4
Scandal	16
The Miracle	20
Innuendo	4
I'm Going Slightly Mad	13
Headlong	Did Not Chart
The Show Must Go On	7
These Are The Days Of Our Lives	2
Who Wants To Live Forever (re-issue)	7
We Are The Champions (live)	12
We Are The Champions (World Cup re-issue)	32
Heaven For Everyone	3
We Are The Champions (2nd re-issue)	Did Not Chart

ALBUMS

Queen	Did Not Chart
Queen II	Did Not Chart
Sheer Heart Attack	6
A Night At The Opera	1
A Day At The Races	1
News Of The World	1
Jazz	4
Live Killers	10
The Game	2
Flash Gordon	13
Greatest Hits	1
Hot Space	2
The Works	1
A Kind Of Magic	2
Live Magic	17
The Miracle	1
Queen At The Beeb	Did Not Chart
Innuendo	1
Greatest Hits II	1
Live At Wembley	9
Made In Heaven	1

UNRELEASED SOLO SONGS

This list of unreleased solo recordings does not aim to be complete nor does it claim that the tracks mentioned are complete or even more than just fragments of songs.

FREDDIE MERCURY

Victory
State Of Shock
There Must Be More To Life Than This
These three tracks originate from recordings made around 1982 with Michael Jackson. Of the three tracks 'Victory' was subsequently recorded by the Jacksons, 'State Of Shock' by Michael Jackson and Mick Jagger and 'There Must Be More To Life Than This' by Queen (not released) and by Freddie.

Smoke Gets In Your Eyes
In 1986 he was reportedly working on an album of covers and the only track to see release was 'The Great Pretender'.

BRIAN MAY

My Boy
This demo comes from the planned solo album that Brian was working on in 1988.

Slot Machine
This track originates from sessions with Steve Hackett. There may be more unissued songs in the vaults.

Hard Business
This was the theme song from the TV series *Frank Stubbs Promotes*.

Cyborg
This track is only available on a computer game. Written for 'Rise 2-Resurrection' it has not been made available as a proper release.

Rolling Stone
Let Your Heart Rule Your Head
Both these tracks are from Lonnie Donegan sessions that Brian played on.

Lady Of Leisure
This track was recorded with Gareth Marks.

Fork In The Road
Recorded with Jonathan Kelly.

Whistle Down The Wind
This track was recorded with the unlikely combination of Andrew Lloyd Webber and Jim Steinman.

Whatever Happened To Saturday Night
This was intended for a remake of the *Rocky Horror Show* soundtrack.

Brian also recorded some TV incidental music for the 1992 Olympic Games

ROGER TAYLOR

Keep On Running
This Spencer Davis Group classic was recorded for but not used on Roger's *Strange Frontier* album.

Nazis 1994
This version may be the banned version that did not make the album.

Roger also recorded some TV incidental music for the 1992 Olympic Games

JOHN DEACON

This Is Your Time
This is from work John recorded with Errol Brown.

QUEEN ON VIDEO

Greatest Flix

Catalogue Number: TVD 90 0504 2 19 October 1981
(Also released on Betamax TXD 90 0504 4 in
November 1981/Picture Music International MVP 99
1011 2 in 1984/Beta MXP 99 1011 4 in 1984/CED
Videodisc Format 33064 in 1983)
Tracks: Killer Queen/Bohemian Rhapsody/You're My
Best Friend/Somebody To Love/Tie Your Mother
Down/We Are The Champions/We Will Rock
You/Spread Your Wings/Bicycle Race/Fat Bottomed
Girls/Don't Stop Me Now/Love Of My Life (Live)/Crazy
Little Thing Called Love/Save Me/Play The
Game/Another One Bites The Dust/Flash's Theme
This video release brought together all Queen's promo
videos covering the period 1975 to 1980. When it was
released it reached the top of the video rental chart.
Interestingly the video of 'Bohemian Rhapsody' on the
video is slightly different to the one featured on future
videos.

Live In Japan

1983
Tracks: Flash's Theme/Now I'm Here/Put Out The
Fire/Dragon Attack/Now I'm Here/Love Of My Life/Save
Me/Guitar Solo/Under Pressure/Crazy Little Thing
Called Love/Bohemian Rhapsody/Tie Your Mother
Down/Teo Torriatte/We Will Rock You/We Are The
Champions
Filmed at the Seibu Lions Stadium in 1982. Released in
Japan only.

We Will Rock You

Catalogue Number: Peppermint Music Video 6122 10
September 1984
(Also released on Betamax in September 1984/The
Video Collection VC 4012 in September 1986/Music
Club MC 2032 in October 1989)
Tracks: We Will Rock You/Let Me Entertain You/Play
The Game/Somebody To Love/Killer Queen/I'm In Love
With My Car/Get Down, Make Love/Save Me/Now I'm
Here/Dragon Attack/Love Of My Life/Under
Pressure/Keep Yourself Alive/Crazy Little Thing Called

Love/Bohemian Rhapsody/Tie Your Mother
Down/Another One Bites The Dust/Sheer Heart
Attack/We Will Rock You/We Are The Champions/God
Save The Queen
Filmed during 'The Game' tour in 1981 this video
featured an almost complete concert.

The Works Video EP

Catalogue Number: Picture Music International (MVT 99
0010 2) 19 November 1984
(Also released on Betamax MXT 99 1101 4)
Tracks: Radio Ga Ga/I Want To Break Free/It's A Hard
Life/Hammer To Fall
This four-track video featured the four biggest tracks
lifted from *The Works* and all four subsequently appeared
on the *Greatest Flix II* and *Box Of Flix* video's released
later on.

Live In Rio

Catalogue Number: Picture Music International (MVP 99
1079 2) 13 May 1985
(Also released on Betamax MXP 99 1079 4 in May
1985/Video 8 MSP 99 1079 5/Laservision MLP 99
1079 1)
Tracks: Tie Your Mother Down/Seven Seas Of
Rhye/Keep Yourself Alive/Liar/It's A Hard Life/Now I'm
Here/Is This The World We Created...?/Love Of My
Life/Brighton Rock/Hammer To Fall/Bohemian
Rhapsody/Radio Ga Ga/I Want To Break Free/We Will
Rock You/We Are The Champions/God Save The Queen
This video was filmed at the Sao Paulo Stadium, Rio de
Janeiro, Brazil on 12 January 1985 during Queen's South
American Tour. A crowd of over 250,000 turned out to
see the group, the largest turn out for a single concert.
The concert opened the ten day 'Rock In Rio' Festival.

Who Wants To Live Forever/A Kind Of Magic

Catalogue Number: PMI MVW9900592 October 1986
Tracks: Who Wants To Live Forever/A Kind Of Magic
Queen's first video single featured two tracks lifted from
the album *A Kind Of Magic*.

Live In Budapest

Catalogue Number: Picture Music International (MVN 99 1146 2) 16 February 1987

(Also released on Video 8 MSN 99 1146 5/12" CD Video 080 510 1)

Tracks: Tavaszi Szel Vizet Araszt/One Vision/Tie Your Mother Down/In The Lap Of The Gods…revisited/Seven Seas Of Rhye/Tear It Up/A Kind Of Magic/Tavaszi Szel Vizet Araszt/Under Pressure/Who Wants To Live Forever/I Want To Break Free/Now I'm Here/Love Of My Life/Tavaszi Szel Vizet Araszt/Is This The World We Created…?/Tutti Frutti/Bohemian Rhapsody/Hammer To Fall/Crazy Little Thing Called Love/Radio Ga Ga/We Will Rock You/Friends Will Be Friends/We Are The Champions/God Save The Queen

Queen's third live video was recorded at the Nepstadion in Budapest during the band's successful 'Magic' tour in 1986. As well as giving a complete show the video also included some great off-stage footage.

Bohemian Rhapsody/Crazy Little Thing Called Love

Catalogue Number: Gold Rushes (PM 0022) 30 March 1987

Tracks: Bohemian Rhapsody/Crazy Little Thing Called Love

This was the group's second two-track video single.

The Magic Years: Boxed Set

Catalogue Number: Picture Music International (MVB 99 1157 2) 30 November 1987

This three video set aimed to trace the story of Queen through their 17-year career and included rare interview footage, promo videos, TV appearances, out-takes from video shoots, early live appearances and footage of the group in the studio. These videos were also made available separately (see below).

The Magic Years: Volume One – The Foundations

Catalogue Number: Picture Music International (MVP 99 1154 2) 30 November 1987

The Magic Years: Volume Two – Live Killers In The Making

Catalogue Number: Picture Music International (MVP 99 1155 2) 30 November 1987

The Magic Years: Volume Three – Crowned In Glory

Catalogue Number: Picture Music International (MVP 99 1156 2) 30 November 1987

Rare Live – A Concert Through Time And Space

Catalogue Number: Picture Music International (MVN 99 1189 3) 21 August 1989

Tracks: I Want It All/Crazy Little Thing Called Love/Liar/Another One Bites The Dust/Big Spender/Jailhouse Rock/Stupid Cupid/My Melancholy Blues/Hammer To Fall/Killer Queen/We Will Rock You/Somebody To Love/Tie Your Mother Down/Keep Yourself Alive/Love Of My Life/Stone Cold Crazy/Radio Ga Ga/You Take My Breath Away/Sheer Heart Attack/We Are The Champions

This unique video traces Queen's live appearances from 1973 to 1986, and features rehearsal and live performances. Footage is taken from all over the world and includes many first-time live performances.

The Miracle Video EP

Catalogue Number: Picture Music International (MVL 99 0084 3) 27 November 1989

Tracks: I Want It All/Breakthru/The Invisible Man/Scandal

As with *The Works Video EP* this featured four tracks taken from the group's current album. No video for the title track had been filmed when the video was released.

Queen Live At Wembley

Catalogue Number: Picture Music International (MVN 99 1259 3) 3 December 1990

Tracks: Brighton Rock/One Vision/Tie Your Mother Down/In The Lap Of The Gods…revisited/Seven Seas Of Rhye/A Kind Of Magic/Under Pressure/Another One Bites The Dust/Who Wants To Live Forever/I Want To Break Free/Is This The World We Created…?/Tutti Frutti/Bohemian Rhapsody/Hammer To Fall/Crazy Little Thing Called Love/Radio Ga Ga/We Will Rock You/Friends Will Be Friends/We Are The Champions/God Save The Queen

A good record of the group's sell-out concerts at Wembley Stadium in 1986, although severely edited with many tracks left out.

Greatest Flix II

Catalogue Number: Picture Music International (VC 4112) 28th October 1991

Tracks: A Kind Of Magic/Under Pressure/Radio Ga Ga/I Want It All/I Want To Break Free/Innuendo/It's A Hard Life/Breakthru/Headlong/The Miracle/I'm Going Slightly Mad/The Invisible Man/Hammer To Fall/Friends Will Be Friends/The Show Must Go On/One Vision/Who Wants To Live Forever

The second compilation of promo videos covering 1981 to 1991.

Box Of Flix

Catalogue Number: Picture Music International (MVB 99 1324 3) October 1991

Greatest Flix: Tracks: Killer Queen/Bohemian Rhapsody/You're My Best Friend/Somebody To Love/Tie Your Mother Down/We Are The Champions/We Will Rock You/Spread Your Wings/Bicycle Race/Fat Bottomed Girls/Don't Stop Me Now/Love Of My Life/Crazy Little Thing Called Love/Save Me/Play The Game/Another One Bites The Dust/Flash

Greatest Flix II: Tracks: A Kind Of Magic/Under Pressure/Radio Ga Ga/I Want It All/I Want To Break Free/Innuendo/It's A Hard Life/Breakthru/Who Wants To Live Forever/Headlong/The Miracle/I'm Going Slightly Mad/The Invisible Man/Hammer To Fall/Friends Will Be Friends/The Show Must Go On/One Vision

BONUS TRACKS: Keep Yourself Alive/Liar/Killer Queen/Now I'm Here

This deluxe two-video set combined the previously available Greatest Flix I & II adding four bonus tracks along the way. A 12-page booklet accompanied the set giving information on the videos featured along with reproductions of the original single picture sleeves.

Queen The Films (Made In Heaven)

Catalogue Number: Wienerworld (WNR 2066) November 1996

Tracks: I Was Born To Love You/Heaven For Everyone/Too Much Love Will Kill You/My Life Has Been Saved/You Don't Fool Me/A Winter's Tale/Let Me Live/Mother Love/Made In Heaven

This video, presented by Queen Films and The British Film Institute, is a unique music video companion to the award-winning platinum album *Made In Heaven*. It featured eight films produced by some of the most exciting film-makers in Britain.

Classic Queen

Catalogue Number: Hollywood Music Video HR 40143-3 1992

Tracks: A Kind Of Magic/Bohemian Rhapsody/Under Pressure/Hammer To Fall/Stone Cold Crazy/One Year Of Love/Radio Ga Ga/I'm Going Slightly Mad/I Want It All/Tie Your Mother Down/The Miracle/These Are The Days Of Our Lives/One Vision/Keep Yourself Alive/Headlong/Who Wants To Live Forever/The Show Must Go On

This American video release contained many of Queen's promo videos.

The Freddie Mercury Tribute Concert

Catalogue Number: PMI MVB 49 1062 3 Hollywood Music Video HR (1780 1992)

Tracks: Enter Sandman/Sad But True/Nothing Else Matters/Queen Medley/Now I'm Here/Paradise City/Knockin' On Heaven's Door/Speech/Tie Your Mother Down/I Want It All/Hammer To Fall/Stone Cold Crazy/Kashmir Intro/Crazy Little Thing Called Love/Too Much Love Will Kill You/Radio Ga Ga/Who Wants To Live Forever/I Want To Break Free/Under Pressure/All The Young Dudes/Heroes/ '39/These Are The Days Of Our Lives/Somebody To Love/Bohemian Rhapsody/The Show Must Go On/We Will Rock You/We Are The Champions

Filmed at Wembley Stadium on 20 April 1992 this concert featured some of the greatest music talent in the world paying tribute to Freddie Mercury. The concert was held to raise awareness of AIDS and raise money to help AIDS sufferers. Broadcast live on radio and television to over 75 countries around the world.

Queen – Champions Of The World

Catalogue Number: Picture Music International (MVD 4915053) 1995

This documentary video, running a full two hours, traced the history of the group through their videos, live and TV appearances and rare footage. It also gave a private look at the world of Queen.

THE
PROMOTIONAL
VIDEOS

Title	Director	Location/date
Bohemian Rhapsody	Bruce Gowers	Elstree Studios – November 1975
You're My Best Friend	Bruce Gowers	Elstree Studios – April 1976
Somebody To Love	Bruce Gowers	Sarm East Studios – October 1977
Tie Your Mother Down	Bruce Gowers	Nassau, USA – February 1977
We Are The Champions	Derek Burbridge	New London Theatre Centre – October 1977
We Will Rock You (slow)	Rock Flicks	Surrey – January 1978
We Will Rock You (fast)	Rock Flicks	The Summit, Houston – December 1977
Spread Your Wings	Rock Flicks	Surrey – January 1978
Bicycle Race	Dennis De Vallance	London – May 1978
Fat Bottomed Girls	Dennis De Vallance	Convention Centre, Dallas – October 1978
Don't Stop Me Now	J. Kliebenst	Forest Nationalle, Brussels – January 1979
Love Of My Life	Dennis De Vallance	Budokan, Tokyo – April 1979
Crazy Little Thing Called Love	Dennis De Vallance	Trillion Studios, London – September 1979
Save Me	Keith McMillan	Alexandra Palace, London – December 1979
Play The Game	Brian Grant	Trillion Studios – May 1980
Another One Bites The Dust	Daniella	Dallas, Texas – August 1980
Flash	Don Norman	Anvil Studios, London – November 1980
Keep Yourself Alive	Mike Mansfield	St. John's Wood Studios – 1973
Liar	Bruce Gower	Brewer Street Studios – 1973
Killer Queen	Robin Nash	BBC, Shepherds Bush – October 1974
Now I'm Here	Bruce Gower	The Rainbow Theatre – November 1973
A Kind Of Magic	Russell Mulcahy	Playhouse Theatre, London – March 1986
Under Pressure	David Mallet	———
Radio Ga Ga	David Mallet	Carlton TV Studios, London – January 1984
I Want It All	David Mallet	Elstree Studios – April 1989
I Want To Break Free	David Mallet	Limehouse Studios, London – March 1984
Innuendo	Jerry Hibbert	——— - December 1990
It's A Hard Life	Tim Pope	Munich – June 1984
Breakthru	Rudi Dolezal	Nene Valley Railway – June 1989
Who Wants To Live Forever	David Mallet	Tobacco Wharf, London – September 1986
Headlong	Rudi Dolezal	Metropolis Studios – April 1991
The Miracle	Rudi Dolezal	Elstree Studios – November 1989
I'm Going Slightly Mad	Rudi Dolezal	Wembley Studios – February 1991
The Invisible Man	Rudi Dolezal	Pinewood Studios – July 1989
Hammer To Fall	David Mallet	Forest Nationalle, Brussels – August 1984
Friends Will be Friends	Rudi Dolezal	JVC Studios, Wembley – May 1986
The Show Must Go On	Rudi Dolezal	———
One Vision	Rudi Dolezal	Munich – September 1985

THE PROMOTIONAL VIDEOS – TRIVIA

• Both 'We Will Rock You (slow)' and 'Spread Your Wings' were filmed in the back garden of Roger Taylor's mansion in Surrey.

• Hundreds of candles were used during the filming of 'You're My Best Friend'. It was a mammoth task to keep them all lit during shooting.

• The video for 'Bohemian Rhapsody' cost just £4,000 to make and was filmed and edited over two days.

• 'Bohemian Rhapsody' was shown for nine consecutive weeks on BBC's *Top Of The Pops*.

• An out take of 'Spread Your Wings' has the director commenting 'Could you tell him to move, the guitarist, the tall one, what's his name…?'

• 'Don't Stop Me Now' and 'Love Of My Life' were taped during the 'Live Killers' tour.

• For the filming of 'Bicycle Race' fifty girls were recruited, Wimbledon Stadium was hired and the fifty naked girls cycled round the track!

• For the 'Play The Game' video Freddie was smeared with vaseline and had buckets of water thrown over him. All this for a 30-second section of the video!

• 'Killer Queen' was the groups first experience of a video shoot and the final version was never used.

• 'A Kind Of Magic' utilised computer animation to bring the characters from the front of the album alive.

• The BBC refused to use the 'Under Pressure' video as it contained scenes of explosions in Ireland.

• Fan club members were used for the 'Radio Ga Ga' video shoot. For the hand-clapping sequence they were dressed in white boiler suits and sprayed in silver paint.

This video also included scenes from the film *Metropolis*.

• 'I Want To Break Free' was based on the TV programme *Coronation Street*. As with 'Radio Ga Ga' fans were used, this time dressed in black boiler suits and miners' helmets.

• Computers were usen on the 'Innuendo' video to turn live action into animation.

• 'The Miracle' features four lookalikes, minatures of the band themselves, and this prompted Freddie to say, 'Could they do the whole tour for us?'

• The band turned up as characters in a computer game for 'The Invisible Man' video.

• 'The Show Must Go On' edited together various clips of Queen from the eighties.

THE SOLO VIDEOS

Starlicks
Catalogue Number: Starlicks Master Series 1986
Tracks: Various Queen classics
This video features Brian May demonstrating the guitar licks from eleven of Queen's classic tracks.

Video EP
Catalogue Number: Picture Music International (MVS 99 0055 2) July 1986
(Also released on Betamax MXS 99 0055 4)
Tracks: Made In Heaven/Living On My Own/Time

The Great Pretender
Catalogue Number: Picture Music International (MVP 99 0066 2) March 1987
Tracks: The Great Pretender/Exercises In Free Love

The Barcelona EP
Catalogue Number: Channel 5 (CFV 00932) February 1989
Tracks: Barcelona/The Golden Boy/How Can I Go On

Barcelona

Catalogue Number: Polygram 080 548-2 April 1989
Tracks: Barcelona
This CD video single feature three audio tracks as well
as the 'Barcelona' video

The Golden Boy

Catalogue Number: Polygram 080 580-2 May
1989
Tracks: The Golden Boy
This CD video single feature three audio tracks as well
as the 'Barcelona' video

Brian May Live At The Brixton Academy

Catalogue Number: Picture Music International (PMI
7243 4911873 7) February 1994
Tracks: Back To The Light/Driven By You/Tie Your
Mother Down/Love Token/Headlong/Love Of My
Life/'39/Let Your Heart Rule Your Head/Too Much Love
Will Kill You/Since You've Been Gone/Now I'm
Here/Resurrection/Last Horizon/We Will Rock
You/Hammer To Fall

OTHER VIDEOS
FEATURING QUEEN
AND SOLO MEMBERS

The Awards 1992

Catalogue Number: Wienerworld WNR 2026 1992
Tracks: Innuendo

Flash Gordon

Catalogue Number: Thorn EMI TVA 90 0300 2
(Also released on Betamax TXA 90 0300 4/Video 2000
TPS 90 03003/4Front LED 50052)
The soundtrack to this film featured music performed
by Queen

Greenpeace Non-Toxic Video Hits

Catalogue Number: Vestron Music Video 11032
Tracks: Is This The World We Created...?/Strange
Frontier

Hard 'n' Heavy Volume 3

Catalogue Number: Picture Music International MVP 99
1192 3
Tracks: Various numbers

Hard 'n' Heavy Volume 5

Catalogue Number: Picture Music International MVP 99
1203 3
Tracks: Smoke On The Water

Having Your Cake

Catalogue Number: Pinnacle 1990
Tracks: Liar
This video was given away free with *Music Week*
magazine.

Hell's Bells – The Dangers Of Rock 'n'
Roll

Catalogue Number: International Films
Tracks: Another One Bites The Dust

Is This Love

Catalogue Number: Picture Music International MVP 99
1175 2
Tracks: Who Wants To Live Forever

Missing You

Catalogue Number: Picture Music International MVP 99
1251 3
Tracks: Who Wants To Live Forever

Now That's What I Call Music 4

Catalogue Number: Picture Music International/Virgin
MVNOW 4
Tracks: It's A Hard Life

Now That's What I Call Music 6

Catalogue Number: Picture Music International/Virgin
MVNOW 6
Tracks: One Vision

Now That's What I Call Music 7

Catalogue Number: Picture Music International/Virgin
MVNOW 7
Tracks: A Kind Of Magic

Now That's What I Call Music 9

Catalogue Number: Picture Music International/Virgin
MVNOW 9

Tracks: The Great Pretender

Now That's What I Call Music 10

Catalogue Number: Picture Music International/Virgin
MVNOW 10

Tracks: Barcelona

Now That's What I Call Music 15

Catalogue Number: Picture Music International/Virgin
MVNOW 15

Tracks: I Want It All

Now You Can See The Music

Catalogue Number: CD Video Single 080 546 1

Tracks: Barcelona

The Prince's Trust Rock Gala 1988

Catalogue Number: MSD V 9122 1988

This video features Brian May supporting several other
artists

Rock Aid Armenia – Smoke On The Water: The Video Collection

Catalogue Number: Virgin Music Video VVD 636

Tracks: Smoke On The Water

Rock Classics

Catalogue Number: Polygram Music Video 083 102-3

Tracks: We Will Rock You

Rock Idols

Catalogue Number: Video Gems R 1051

Tracks: Killer Queen

Sexy Shorts

Catalogue Number: Picture Music International MVP 99
1076 2

Tracks: Body Language/Killer Queen

Smash Hits – Now That's What I Call Music

Catalogue Number: Virgin Music Video VVD 267

Tracks: Under Pressure

UNOFFICIAL VIDEOS – QUEEN

Takin' Your Breath Away

Tracks: Killer Queen/Keep Yourself Alive/Back
Chat/Innuendo/Liar/Good Old Fashioned Lover
Boy/Bohemian Rhapsody/Las Palabras de Amor/Stone
Cold Crazy/Body Language/One Vision/Princes Of The
Universe/Keep Yourself Alive/One Year Of Love/Calling
All Girls/Killer Queen/These Are The Days Of Our Lives

This video, running at approximately 82 minutes,
featured a compilation of rare clips and live
performances

Cheers! A Toast From Queen

Tracks: Now I'm Here/Ogre Battle/Medley: Bohemian
Rhapsody-Killer Queen-March Of The Black Queen-
Bohemian Rhapsody/Bring Back That Leroy
Brown/Brighton Rock/Son And Daughter/Keep Yourself
Alive/Liar/In The Lap Of The Gods/Medley: Big
Spender-Jailhouse Rock-Stupid Cupid-Be Bop A Lula-
Jailhouse Rock

Running at 56 minutes, this was the show from the
Hammersmith Odeon 24 December 1975 which was
subsequently broadcast on *The Old Grey Whistle Test*

Free In The Park

Tracks: Intro: Bohemian Rhapsody/Ogre Battle/Sweet
Lady/White Queen/Flick Of The Wrist/Medley: You're My
Best Friend-Bohemian Rhapsody-Killer Queen-March Of
The Black Queen-Bohemian Rhapsody/Bring Back That
Leroy Brown/Brighton Rock/Son And Daughter/ '39/
You Take My Breath Away/The Prophet's Song/Stone
Cold Crazy/Keep Yourself Alive/Liar/In The Lap Of The
Gods... revisited

This is a video of the group's 18 September 1976 show
held in London's Hyde Park

Keep Dancin'

Tracks: Intro: Procession/Tie Your Mother Down/Ogre
Battle/White Queen/Somebody To Love/Medley: Killer
Queen-Good Old Fashioned Lover Boy-The Millionaire
Waltz-You're My Best Friend-Bring Back That Leroy
Brown/Death On Two Legs/Doing All Right/Brighton

Rock/ '39/You Take My Breath Away/White Man/The Prophet's Song/Bohemian Rhapsody/Keep Yourself Alive/Stone Cold Crazy/In The Lap Of The Gods...revisited/Now I'm Here/Liar/Medley: Jailhouse Rock-Saturday Night's All Right For Fighting-Stupid Cupid-Be Bop A Lula-Jailhouse Rock/God Save The Queen
London's Earls Court 7 June 1977

Down In The City

Tracks: Now I'm Here/Another One Bites The Dust/You're My Best Friend/Flash/We Will Rock You/Let Me Entertain You/Don't Stop Me Now/Killer Queen/I'm In Love With My Car/Crazy Little Thing Called Love/Somebody To Love/Sheer Heart Attack/Save Me/We Will Rock You/We Are The Champions/God Save The Queen
The 26 December 1979 show from the Hammersmith Odeon, better known as the 'Concert For The People Of Kampuchea'

Rockin' In Buenos Aires

Tracks: Overture/We Will Rock You/Let Me Entertain You/Play The Game/Somebody To Love/I'm In Love With My Car/Get Down Make Love/Need Your Loving Tonight/Save Me/Now I'm Here/Dragon Attack/Now I'm Here/Fat Bottomed Girls/Love Of My Life/Do You Feel It's All Right/Keep Yourself Alive/Instrumental/Flash's Theme/The Hero/Crazy Little Thing Called Love/Bohemian Rhapsody/Tie Your Mother Down/We Will Rock You/We Are The Champions/God Save The Queen
Velez Sarfield Stadium 28 February 1981

Let's Play Games

Tracks: Intro: Flash/The Hero/We Will Rock You/Play The Game/Staying Power/Somebody To Love/Now I'm Here/Dragon Attack/Love Of My Life/Save Me/Guitar Solo/Under Pressure/Fat Bottomed Girls/Bohemian Rhapsody/Tie Your Mother Down/We Will Rock You/We Are The Champions/God Save The Queen
Milton Keynes 5 June 1982

Blow It Out

Tracks: Intro: Flash/The Hero/Now I'm Here/Put Out The Fire/Dragon Attack/Love Of My Life/Save

Me/Guitar Solo/Under Pressure/Crazy Little Thing Called Love/Bohemian Rhapsody/Tie Your Mother Down/Teo Torriatte/We Will Rock You/We Are The Champions
Tokyo 3 November 1982

Vienna Rock

Tracks: Intro: Machines/Tear It Up/Tie Your Mother Down/Under Pressure/Somebody To Love/Killer Queen/Seven Seas Of Rhye/Keep Yourself Alive/Liar/Rock In Rio (Instrumental)/It's A Hard Life/Dragon Attack/Now I'm Here/Is This The World We Created...?/Love Of My Life/Stone Cold Crazy/Machines (Or Back To Humans)/Instrumental/Brighton Rock/Another One Bites The Dust/Hammer To Fall/Crazy Little Thing Called Love/Saturday Night's All Right For Fighting/Bohemian Rhapsody/Radio Ga Ga/I Want To Break Free/Jailhouse Rock/We Will Rock You/We Are The Champions/God Save The Queen
Stadthalle, Vienna 29 September 1984

Breakin' Free

Tracks: Intro: Tear It Up/Tie Your Mother Down/Under Pressure/Somebody To Love/Killer Queen/Seven Seas Of Rhye/Keep Yourself Alive/Liar/Rock In Rio (Instrumental)/It's A Hard Life/Dragon Attack/Now I'm Here/Is This The World We Created...?/Love Of My Life/Instrumental/Brighton Rock/Another One Bites The Dust/Hammer To Fall/Crazy Little Thing Called Love/Bohemian Rhapsody/Radio Ga Ga/I Want To Break Free/Jailhouse Rock/We Will Rock You/We Are The Champions/God Save The Queen
Sydney Entertainment Centre 28 April 1985

Final Live In Japan

Tracks: Tear It Up/Tie Your Mother Down/Under Pressure/Somebody To Love/Killer Queen/Seven Seas Of Rhye/Keep Yourself Alive/Liar/It's A Hard Life/Now I'm Here/Is This The World We Created...?/Love Of My Life/Another One Bites The Dust/Hammer To Fall/Crazy Little Thing Called Love/Bohemian Rhapsody/Radio Ga Ga/I Want To Break Free/Jailhouse Rock/We Will Rock You/We Are The Champions/God Save The Queen
Tokyo 11 May 1985

Final Magic

Tracks: One Vision/Tie Your Mother Down/In The Lap Of The Gods/Seven Seas Of Rhye/Tear It Up/A Kind Of Magic/Under Pressure/ Another One Bites The Dust/Who Wants To Live Forever/I Want To Break Free/Guitar Solo/Now I'm Here/Love Of My Life/Is This The World We Created...?/You're So Square/Hello Mary Lou/Tutti Frutti/Bohemian Rhapsody/Hammer To Fall/Crazy Little Thing Called Love/Radio Ga Ga/We Will Rock You/Friends Will Be Friends/We Are The Champions/God Save The Queen
Knebworth Park 9 August 1986

Unforgettable Performances

Tracks: Crazy Little Thing Called Love (Hippodrome, Bristol 1979)/Crazy Little Thing Called Love (Saturday Night Show, USA 1982)/Under Pressure (Saturday Night Show, USA 1982)/It's A Hard Life (Golden Rose Pop Festival, Montreuz 1984)/I Want To Break Free (Golden Rose Pop Festival, Montreuz 1984)/Tear It Up (Golden Rose Pop Festival, Montreuz 1984)/Radio Ga Ga (Golden Rose Pop Festival, Montreuz 1984)/Rehearsal and Interview (Live Aid, 1985)/Bohemian Rhapsody (Live Aid, 1985)/Radio Ga Ga (Live Aid, 1985)/Hammer To Fall (Live Aid, 1985)/Crazy Little Thing Called Love (Live Aid, 1985)/We Will Rock You-We Are The Champions (Live Aid, 1985)/Is This The World We Created...? (Live Aid, 1985)/Interview With Brian May (Live Aid, 1985)/One Vision (Golden Rose Pop Festival, Montreuz 1986)/A Kind Of Magic (Golden Rose Pop Festival, Montreuz 1986)/Friends Will Be Friends (Golden Rose Pop Festival, Montreuz 1986)/Hammer To Fall (Golden Rose Pop Festival, Montreuz 1986)/We Are The Champions

UNOFFICIAL VIDEOS – SOLO

BRIAN MAY

Unforgettable Performances

Tracks: Intro: The Dark/Tie Your Mother Down/Driven By You/Back To The Light/Love Token/Let Me Out/Love Of My Life/Let Your Heart Rule Your Head/Too Much Love Will Kill You/Since You've Been Gone/Rollin' Over/Guitar Extravaganza/ Resurrection/Last Horizon/Hammer To Fall/Now I'm Here/BONUS: Interview With Brian May/Too Much Love Will Kill You (German TV Broadcast)/Live Rock Festival (6 tracks)
Velez Sarfield, Buenos Aires 6 November 1992

Touring Through South America

Tracks: Back To The Light/Love Token/Let Your Heart Rule Your Head/Driven By You/Tie Your Mother Down/Love Of My Life/Let Me Out/Too Much Love Will Kill You/Guitar Extravaganza/Resurrection/Hammer To Fall/Last Horizon

Civic Center, Hartford USA

Tracks: Back To The Light/Driven By You/Tie Your Mother Down/Love Token/'39/Too Much Love Will Kill You/Now I'm Here/Guitar Solo/Ressurection/ Bohemian Rhapsody/Resurrection/Introductions/ We Will Rock You
9 March 1993

Hammersmith Apollo Theatre

Tracks: The Dark/Back To The Light/Driven By You/Tie Your Mother Down/Love Token/Headlong/Love Of My Life/'39/Let Your Heart Rule Your Head/Too Much Love Will Kill You/Keyboard Solo/Since You've Been Gone/Now I'm Here/Guitar Solo/Resurrection/Bohemian Rhapsody/Resurrection/Band Introductions/Last Horizon/We Will Rock You/The Dream Is Over/Hammer To Fall
16 June 1993

Philipshalle, Dusseldorf
Tracks: The Dark/Back To The Light/Tie Your Mother Down/Love Token/Headlong/Love Of My Life/'39/Let Your Heart Rule Your Head/Too Much Love Will Kill You/Keyboard Solo/Since You've Been Gone/Now I'm Here/Guitar Solo/Resurrection/Bohemian Rhapsody/Resurrection/Band Introductions/Last Horizon/We Will Rock You/Teo Torriatte/Hammer To Fall
30 November 1993

Regreso A La Luz
Tracks: The Dark/Back To The Light/Tie Your Mother Down/Love Token/Headlong/Love Of My Life/'39/Let Your Heart Rule Your Head/Too Much Love Will Kill You/Keyboard Solo/Since You've Been Gone/Now I'm Here/Guitar Solo/Resurrection/Bohemian Rhapsody/Resurrection/Band Introductions/Last Horizon/We Will Rock You/Hammer To Fall
Zeleste Barcelona 14 December 1993

ROGER TAYLOR

Takin' You To Happiness
Tracks: I Wanna Testify/Future Management/Man On Fire/Strange Frontier/Happiness/Nazis 1994/Foreign Sand/Happiness (Paris Live 1995)/Foreign Sand (Germany)/Love Don't Live Here Anymore (Jimmy Nail)/Smoke On The Water/Radio (Shakin' Stevens)
Various clips, interviews and live performances

Takin' You To The Top Of The World
Tracks: Blue Rock (Press Kit)/Cowboys And Indians/Shove It/Heaven For Everyone/Power To Love/New Dark Ages/Cowboys And Indians (live)/Manipulator (live)/Heaven For Everyone (live)/New Dark Ages (live)/Liar (live)/Top Of The World Ma (live)/Shove It (live)/Cowboys And Indians (live)/Love On A Tightrope (live)/Stand Up For Love (live)/Feel The Force (live)/I'm In Love With My Car (live)
Various clips, interviews and live performances

The Vienna Gig
Tracks: In Charge Of My Heart/Top Of The World Ma/Closer To You/Cowboys And Indians/Breakdown/Penetration Guru/Power To Love/Liar/Heaven For Everyone/Better Things/Man On Fire/Old Man (Lay Down)/Sister Blue/Strange Frontier/Foxy Lady/Final Destination/Shove It/I'm In Love With My Car
Outdoor Festival 16 June 1990

Mad, Fab And Marvellous
Tracks: In Charge Of My Heart/Top Of The World Ma/Closer To You/Cowboys And Indians/Breakdown/Penetration Guru/Power To Love/Liar/Heaven For Everyone/Better Things/Man On Fire/Old Man (Lay Down)/Sister Blue/Strange Frontier/Foxy Lady/Final Destination
Geneva 1990

The Final Gig
Tracks: In Charge Of My Heart/Love Lies Bleeding/Ain't Put Notin' Down/A Kind Of Magic/Power To Love/Better Things/Hand Of Fools/Life Changes/Cowboys And Indians/New Dark Ages/Sister Blue/Radio Ga Ga/We Will Rock You/Top Of The World Ma/Kansas City/These Are The Days Of Our Lives/Final Destination
Gosport Festival 29 June 1993

Touchin' The Sky
Tracks: Viva Television (German special on Roger)/Nazis 1994/Foreign Sand
Video Compilation

Meeting Old Friends
Tracks: A Kind Of Magic/Touch The Sky/Everybody Hurts Sometimes/Ride The Wild Wind/Tenement Funster/Loneliness/It's A Hard Rain/You Had To Be There/I Want To Break Free/Soul/Dear Mr Murdoch/Foreign Sand/Happiness/The Key/The Show Must Go On/Revelation/These Are The Days Of Our Lives/We Will Rock You/Radio Ga Ga/Old Friends/Nazis 1994
Shepherds Bush Empire 15 September 1994

QUEEN ON COMPACT DISC VIDEO

Rock In Rio
Catalogue Number: MLP 99 10791 (PMI 12" Disc)
Tracks: Tie Your Mother Down/Seven Seas Of Rhye/Keep Yourself Alive/Liar/It's A Hard Life/Now I'm Here/Is This The World We Created...?/Love Of My Life/Brighton Rock/Hammer To Fall/Bohemian Rhapsody/Radio Ga Ga/I Want To Break Free/We Will Rock You/We Are The Champions/God Save The Queen

Greatest Flix
Catalogue Number: VLP 1018 M (PMI 12" Disc)
Tracks: Killer Queen/Bohemian Rhapsody/You're My Best Friend/Somebody To Love/Tie Your Mother Down/We Are The Champions/We Will Rock You/Spread Your Wings/Bicycle Race/Fat Bottomed Girls/Don't Stop Me Now/Love Of My Life (Live)/Crazy Little Thing Called Love/Save Me/Play The Game/Another One Bites The Dust/Flash's Theme

We Will Rock You
Catalogue Number: VLP 1116 M (PMI 12" Disc)
Tracks: We Will Rock You/Let Me Entertain You/Play The Game/Somebody To Love/Killer Queen/I'm In Love With My Car/Get Down, Make Love/Save Me/Now I'm Here/Dragon Attack/Love Of My Life/Under Pressure/Keep Yourself Alive/Crazy Little Thing Called Love/Bohemian Rhapsody/Tie Your Mother Down/Another One Bites The Dust/Sheer Heart Attack/We Will Rock You/We Are The Champions/God Save The Queen

Live In Budapest
Catalogue Number: 0805101 (PMI 12" Disc)
Tracks: Tavaszi Szel Vizet Araszt/One Vision/Tie Your Mother Down/In The Lap Of The Gods...revisited/Seven Seas Of Rhye/Tear It Up/A Kind Of Magic/Tavaszi Szel Vizet Araszt/Under Pressure/Who Wants To Live Forever/I Want To Break Free/Now I'm Here/Love Of My Life/Tavaszi Szel Vizet Araszt/Is This The World We Created...?/Tutti Frutti/Bohemian Rhapsody/Hammer To Fall/Crazy Little Thing Called Love/Radio Ga Ga/We Will Rock You/Friends Will Be Friends/We Are The Champions/God Save The Queen

The Highlander Selection
Catalogue Number: EMCDV2 (PMI 5" Disc)
Tracks: Princes Of The Universe (audio)/One Year Of Love (audio)/Who Wants To Live Forever (audio)/Don't Lose Your Head (audio)/A Kind Of Magic (video)

UNRELEASED QUEEN AND SOLO VIDEOS/ PERFORMANCES

Many of these have been broadcast on TV but have not seen an official release on video

Concerts

The Rainbow
November 1974

Budokan, Tokyo, Japan
April 1975, March 1979 & March 1985

Hammersmith Odeon, London
December 1975 & December 1979

Hyde Park, London
September 1976

Earls Court, London
June 1977

Houston, Texas
December 1977

Paris
March 1979

Argentina
April 1981

Milton Keynes
July 1982

Osaka, Japan
November 1982

Manheim, Germany
July 1986

PROMOTIONAL VIDEOS
UNAVAILABLE ON
HOME VIDEO RELEASE

Body Language
Back Chat
Calling All Girls
Starfleet (Brian May)
Man On Fire (Roger Taylor)
Strange Frontier (Roger Taylor)
Princes Of The Universe
No Turning Back (The Immortals)
Cowboys And Indians (The Cross)
Shove It (The Cross)
Heaven For Everyone (The Cross)
Power To Love (The Cross)
New Dark Ages (The Cross)
Happiness (Roger Taylor)
Back To The Light (Brian May)
Resurrection (Brian May)
Last Horizon (Brian May)
Seven Seas Of Rhye
Good Old Fashioned Lover Boy
Living On My Own (Freddie Mercury)
Nazis 1994 (Roger Taylor)
Foreign Sand (Roger Taylor)
Heaven For Everyone
A Winter's Tale
Too Much Love Will Kill You
Liar (The Cross)
Driven By You (Brian May)
Too Much Love Will Kill You (Brian May)

QUEEN – A RECORDING
HISTORY 1971–1997

Includes video tapings

Studio Sessions
Trident Studios/De Lane Lea Studios
November 1971

Keep Yourself Alive	A-Side/*Queen*
Doing All Right	*Queen*
Great King Rat	*Queen*
My Fairy King	*Queen*
Liar	*Queen*
The Night Comes Down	*Queen*
Modern Times Rock 'N' Roll	*Queen*
Son And Daughter	B-Side/*Queen*
Jesus	*Queen*
Seven Seas Of Rhye	*Queen*
Silver Salmon	Unissued

Additional Musicians/Vocalists: John Anthony – Backing vocals on 'Modern Times Rock 'n' Roll'

Producers: John Anthony/Roy Baker/Louie Austin ('The Night Comes Down')/Queen
Engineers: Roy Baker/Mike Stone/Ted Sharpe/David Hentschel

Live Session for BBC Radio
Langham 1 Studio, London
5 February 1973

My Fairy King	Radio Broadcast/ *Queen At The Beeb*
Keep Yourself Alive	Radio Broadcast/ *Queen At The Beeb*
Doing All Right	Radio Broadcast/ *Queen At The Beeb*
Liar	Radio Broadcast/ *Queen At The Beeb*

Producer: Bernie Andrews
Engineer: John Etchells

Live Session for BBC Radio
Langham 1 Studio, London
25 July 1973

See What A Fool I've Been	Radio Broadcast/ Unissued
Liar	Radio Broadcast/ Unissued
Son And Daughter	Radio Broadcast/ Unissued
Keep Yourself Alive	Radio Broadcast/ Unissued

Producer: Jeff Griffin/Chris Lycett
Engineer: John Etchells

Studio Sessions
Trident Studios
August 1973

Procession	Queen II
Father To Son	Queen II
White Queen (As It Began)	Queen II
Someday One Day	Queen II
The Loser In The End	Queen II
Ogre Battle	Queen II
The Fairy Fellers Masterstroke	Queen II
Nevermore	Queen II
The March Of The Black Queen	Queen II
Funny How Love Is	Queen II
Seven Seas Of Rhye	A-side/Queen II

Producers: Robin Geoffrey Cable/Roy Thomas Baker/Queen
Engineer: Mike Stone

Live Session for BBC Radio One (In Concert)
Hippodrome, Golders Green, London
13 September 1973

Procession	Radio Broadcast
Father To Son	Radio Broadcast
Son And Daughter	Radio Broadcast
Ogre Battle	Radio Broadcast
Hangman	Radio Broadcast
Stone Cold Crazy	Radio Broadcast
Keep Yourself Alive	Radio Broadcast
Liar	Radio Broadcast
See What A Fool I've Been	Radio Broadcast
Medley: Jailhouse Rock/Stupid Cupid/Bama Lama Bama Loo/ Jailhouse Rock	Radio Broadcast

Live Session for BBC Radio One (In Concert)
Paris Theatre, London
20 October 1973

TRACKS UNKNOWN

Live Session for BBC Radio
Langham 1 Studio, London
3 December 1973

Ogre Battle	Radio Broadcast/ Queen At The Beeb
Great King Rat	Radio Broadcast/ Queen At The Beeb
Modern Times Rock 'n' Roll	Radio Broadcast/ Queen At The Beeb
Son And Daughter	Radio Broadcast/ Queen At The Beeb

Producer: Bernie Andrews/Mike Franks
Engineer: Nick Griffiths

Live Session for BBC Radio
Langham 1 Studio, London
3 April 1974

Modern Times Rock 'n' Roll	Radio Broadcast/ Unissued
March Of The Black Queen	Radio Broadcast/ Unissued
Nevermore	Radio Broadcast/ Unissued
White Queen	Radio Broadcast/ Unissued

Live Session for BBC Radio
Maida Vale Studio 4, London
16 October 1974

Now I'm Here	Radio Broadcast/ Unissued
Stone Cold Crazy	Radio Broadcast/ Unissued
Flick Of The Wrist	Radio Broadcast/ Unissued
Tenement Funster	Radio Broadcast/ Unissued

Live Session for BBC Radio
Maida Vale Studio, London
28 October 1974

Spread Your Wings	Radio Broadcast/ Unissued
It's Late	Radio Broadcast/ Unissued
My Melancholy Blues	Radio Broadcast/ Unissued
We Will Rock You	Radio Broadcast/ Unissued

Studio Sessions
Trident Studios/Wessex Studios/Rockfield
Studios/Air Studios
July–September 1974

Brighton Rock	*Sheer Heart Attack*
Killer Queen	A-Side/*Sheer Heart Attack*
Tenement Funster	*Sheer Heart Attack*
Flick Of The Wrist	B-Side/*Sheer Heart Attack*
Lily Of The Valley	B-Side/*Sheer Heart Attack*
Now I'm Here	A-Side/*Sheer Heart Attack*
In The Lap Of The Gods	*Sheer Heart Attack*
Stone Cold Crazy	*Sheer Heart Attack*
Dear Friends	*Sheer Heart Attack*
Misfire	*Sheer Heart Attack*

Bring Back That Leroy Brown	*Sheer Heart Attack*
She Makes Me (Stormtrooper In Stilettoes)	*Sheer Heart Attack*
In The Lap Of The Gods...revisited	*Sheer Heart Attack*

Producers: Roy Baker/Queen
Engineer: Mike Stone

Live Recordings
Rainbow Theatre, London
20 November 1974

Procession	Unissued
Now I'm Here	Unissued
Ogre Battle	Unissued
Father To Son	Unissued
White Queen	Unissued
Flick Of The Wrist	Unissued
Medley: In The Lap Of The Gods – Killer Queen – The March Of The Black Queen – Bring Back That Leroy Brown	Unissued
Son And Daughter	Unissued
Keep Yourself Alive	Unissued
Seven Seas Of Rhye	Unissued
Stone Cold Crazy	Unissued
Liar	Unissued
In The Lap Of The Gods...revisited	Unissued
Medley: Big Spender – Modern Times Rock 'n' Roll	Unissued
Jailhouse Rock	Unissued
God Save The Queen	Unissued

Filming for Japanese Documentary
Budokan Hall, Tokyo
19 April 1975

Procession	Unissued
Now I'm Here	Unissued
Ogre Battle	Unissued
Father To Son	Unissued
White Queen	Unissued
Flick Of The Wrist	Unissued
Hangman	Unissued
Great King Rat	Unissued

Medley: In The Lap Of The Gods – Killer Queen – The March Of The Black Queen – Bring Back That Leroy Brown	Unissued
Son & Daughter	Unissued
Doing All Right	Unissued
Stone Cold Crazy	Unissued
Keep Yourself Alive	Unissued
Seven Seas Of Rhye	Unissued
Liar	Unissued
In The Lap Of The Gods…revisited	Unissued
Jailhouse Rock	Unissued
See What A Fool I've Been	Unissued
God Save The Queen	Unissued

Studio Sessions
Sarm/Roundhouse/Olympic/Rockfield/Scorpio/
Lansdowne
August–November 1975

Death On Two Legs	*A Night At The Opera*
Lazing On A Sunday Afternoon	*A Night At The Opera*
I'm In Love With My Car	B-Side/*A Night At The Opera*
You're My Best Friend	A-Side/*A Night At The Opera*
'39	B-Side/*A Night At The Opera*
Sweet Lady	*A Night At The Opera*
Seaside Rendezvous	*A Night At The Opera*
The Prophet's Song	*A Night At The Opera*
Love Of My Life	*A Night At The Opera*
Good Company	*A Night At The Opera*
Bohemian Rhapsody	A-Side/*A Night At The Opera*
God Save The Queen	*A Night At The Opera*

Producers: Roy Baker/Queen
Engineers: Mike Stone/Gary Lyona

Live Session for BBC Radio One
Hammersmith Odeon, London
24 December 1975

Now I'm Here	Radio Broadcast/ Unissued
Ogre Battle	Radio Broadcast/ Unissued
White Queen	Radio Broadcast/ Unissued
Medley: Bohemian Rhapsody – Killer Queen – The March Of The Black Queen – Bohemian Rhapsody – Bring Back That Leroy Brown	Radio Broadcast/ Unissued
Son And Daughter	Radio Broadcast/ Unissued
Keep Yourself Alive	Radio Broadcast/ Unissued
Liar	Radio Broadcast/ Unissued
In The Lap Of The Gods…revisited	Radio Broadcast/ Unissued
Medley: Big Spender-Jailhouse Rock – Stupid Cupid-Be Bop A Lula-Shake Rattle And Roll-Jailhouse Rock	Radio Broadcast/ Unissued
Seven Seas Of Rhye	Radio Broadcast/ Unissued
See What A Fool I've Been	Radio Broadcast/ Unissued
God Save The Queen	Radio Broadcast/ Unissued

Studio Sessions
The Manor/Wessex/Sarm East
July–November 1976

Tie Your Mother Down	A-Side/*A Day At The Races*
You Take My Breath Away	*A Day At The Races*

Long Away	*A Day At The Races*
The Millionaire Waltz	*A Day At The Races*
You And I	*B-Side/A Day At The Races*
Somebody To Love	*A-Side/A Day At The Races*
White Man	*B-Side/A Day At The Races*
Good Old Fashioned Lover Boy	*A Day At The Races*
Drowse	*A Day At The Races*
Teo Torriatte (Let Us Cling Together)	*A Day At The Races*

Additional Musicians/Vocalists: Mike Stone – Backing vocals on 'Good Old Fashioned Lover Boy'

Producers: Queen
Engineer: Mike Stone

Studio Sessions
Basing Street Studios/Wessex Studios
July–September 1977

We Will Rock You	*B-Side/News Of The World*
We Are The Champions	*A-Side/News Of The World*
Sheer Heart Attack	*B-Side/News Of The World*
All Dead, All Dead	*News Of The World*
Spread Your Wings	*A-Side/News Of The World*
Fight From The Inside	*News Of The World*
Get Down, Make Love	*News Of The World*
Sleeping On The Sidewalk	*News Of The World*
Who Needs You	*News Of The World*
It's Late	*News Of The World*
My Melancholy Blues	*News Of The World*

Producers: Queen
Engineer: Mike Stone

Studio Sessions
Mountain/Superbear
July–October 1978

Mustapha	*Jazz*
Fat Bottomed Girls	*A-Side/Jazz*
Jealousy	*Jazz*
Bicycle Race	*B-Side/Jazz*
If You Can't Beat Them	*Jazz*
Let Me Entertain You	*Jazz*
Dead On Time	*Jazz*
In Only Seven Days	*B-Side/Jazz*
Dreamer's Ball	*Jazz*
Fun It	*Jazz*
Leaving Home Ain't Easy	*Jazz*
Don't Stop Me Now	*A-Side/Jazz*
More Of That Jazz	*Jazz*

Producers: Queen/Roy Baker
Engineer: Geoff Workman

Live Recordings
Stadthalle, Bremen, Germany
20 January 1979

We Will Rock You	Unissued
Let Me Entertain You	Unissued
Somebody To Love	Unissued
If You Can't Beat Them	Unissued
Medley: Death On Two Legs-Killer Queen – Bicycle Race – I'm In Love With My Car – Get Down, Make Love – You're My Best Friend	Unissued
Now I'm Here	Unissued
Don't Stop Me Now	*Live Killers*
Spread Your Wings	*B-Side/Live Killers*
Dreamer's Ball	Unissued
Love Of My Life	Unissued
'39	Unissued
It's Late	Unissued
Brighton Rock	*Live Killers*
Keep Yourself Alive	Unissued

Bohemian Rhapsody	Unissued
Tie Your Mother Down	Unissued
Sheer Heart Attack	Unisued
We Will Rock You	Unissued
We Are The Champions	Unissued
God Save The Queen	Unissued

Producers: Queen
Engineers: John Etchells/David Richards

Live Recordings
Festhalle, Frankfurt, Germany
2 February 1979

We Will Rock You	Unissued
Let Me Entertain You	Unissued
Somebody To Love	Unissued
Medley: Death On Two Legs – Killer	
Queen – Bicycle Race – I'm In Love	
With My Car – Get Down, Make	
Love – You're My Best Friend	Unissued
Now I'm Here	B-Side/*Live Killers*
Don't Stop Me Now	Unissued
Spread Your Wings	Unissued
Dreamer's Ball	Unissued
Love Of My Life	Unissued
'39	*Live Killers*
It's Late	Unissued
Brighton Rock	Unissued
Keep Yourself Alive	Unissued
Bohemian Rhapsody	Unissued
Tie Your Mother Down	Unissued
Sheer Heart Attack	Unisued
We Will Rock You	Unissued
We Are The Champions	Unissued
God Save The Queen	Unissued

Producers: Queen
Engineers: John Etchells/David Richards

Filming for Documentary
Pavilion De Paris, Paris
27 February 1979

We Will Rock You	Unissued

Let Me Entertain You	Unissued
Somebody To Love	Unissued
Fat Bottomed Girls	Unissued
Medley: Death On Two Legs – Killer	
Queen – Bicycle Race – I'm In Love	
With My Car – Get Down, Make	
Love – You're My Best Friend	Unissued
Now I'm Here	Unissued
Don't Stop Me Now	Unissued
Spread Your Wings	Unissued
Dreamer's Ball	Unissued
Love Of My Life	Unissued
'39	Unissued
It's Late	Unissued
Brighton Rock	Unissued
Keep Yourself Alive	Unissued
Fun It	Unissued
Bohemian Rhapsody	Unissued
Tie Your Mother Down	Unissued
Sheer Heart Attack	Unisued
We Will Rock You	Unissued
We Are The Champions	Unissued
God Save The Queen	Unissued

Filming for Documentary
Pavilion De Paris, Paris
28 February 1979

We Will Rock You	Unissued
Let Me Entertain You	Unissued
Somebody To Love	Unissued
If You Can't Beat Them	Unissued
Medley: Death On Two Legs – Killer	
Queen – Bicycle Race – I'm In Love	
With My Car – Get Down, Make	
Love – You're My Best Friend	Unissued
Now I'm Here	Unissued
Don't Stop Me Now	Unissued
Spread Your Wings	Unissued
Dreamer's Ball	Unissued
Love Of My Life	Unissued
'39	Unissued
It's Late	Unissued
Brighton Rock	Unissued
Keep Yourself Alive	Unissued

Bohemian Rhapsody	Unissued
Tie Your Mother Down	Unissued
Sheer Heart Attack	Unisued
We Will Rock You	Unissued
We Are The Champions	Unissued
God Save The Queen	Unissued

Filming for Documentary
Pavilion De Paris, Paris
1 March 1979

We Will Rock You	Unissued
Let Me Entertain You	Unissued
Somebody To Love	Unissued
Fat Bottomed Girls	Unissued
Medley: Death On Two Legs – Killer	
Queen – Bicycle Race – I'm In Love	
With My Car – Get Down, Make	
Love – You're My Best Friend	Unissued
Now I'm Here	Unissued
Don't Stop Me Now	Unissued
If You Can't Beat Them	Unissued
Spread Your Wings	Unissued
Dreamer's Ball	Unissued
Love Of My Life	Unissued
'39	Unissued
It's Late	Unissued
Brighton Rock	Unissued
Keep Yourself Alive	Unissued
Fun It	Unissued
Mustapha	Unissued
Bohemian Rhapsody	*Live Killers*
Tie Your Mother Down	Unissued
Sheer Heart Attack	Unisued
We Will Rock You	Unissued
We Are The Champions	Unissued
God Save The Queen	Unissued

Live Recordings
Various Locations
January-March 1979

We Will Rock You	*Live Killers*
Let Me Entertain You	B-Side/*Live Killers*
Death On Two Legs	*Live Killers*

Killer Queen	*Live Killers*
Bicycle Race	*Live Killers*
I'm In Love With My Car	*Live Killers*
Get Down, Make Love	*Live Killers*
You're My Best Friend	*Live Killers*
Dreamer's Ball	*Live Killers*
Love Of My Life	A-Side/*Live Killers*
Keep Yourself Alive	*Live Killers*
Tie Your Mother Down	*Live Killers*
Sheer Heart Attack	*Live Killers*
We Will Rock You	*Live Killers*
We Are The Champions	*Live Killers*
God Save The Queen	*Live Killers*

Producers: Queen
Engineers: John Etchells/David Richards

Studio Sessions
Musicland
June-July 1979/February-May 1980

Play The Game	A-Side/*The Game*
Dragon Attack	B-Side/*The Game*
Another One Bites The Dust	A-Side/*The Game*
Need Your Loving Tonight	*The Game*
Crazy Little Thing Called Love	A-Side/*The Game*
Rock It	*The Game*
Don't Try Suicide	*The Game*
Sail Away Sweet Sister	*The Game*
Coming Soon	*The Game*
Save Me	A-Side/*The Game*
A Human Body	B-Side/*The Game*
Play The Game #2	Unissued

Additional Musicians/Vocalists: Andy Gibb – Vocals on
'Play The Game #2'

Producers: Queen/Mack
Engineer: Mack

Studio Sessions
Unknown Studio
October-November 1980

Flash's Theme	A-Side/*Flash Gordon* (OST)
In The Space Capsule	*Flash Gordon* (OST)
Ming's Theme	*Flash Gordon* (OST)
The Ring	*Flash Gordon* (OST)
Football Fight	B-Side/*Flash Gordon* (OST)
In The Death Cell	*Flash Gordon* (OST)
Execution Of Flash	*Flash Gordon* (OST)
The Kiss	*Flash Gordon* (OST)
Arboria	*Flash Gordon* (OST)
Escape From The Swamp	*Flash Gordon* (OST)
Flash To The Rescue	*Flash Gordon* (OST)
Vultan's Theme	*Flash Gordon* (OST)
Battle Theme	*Flash Gordon* (OST)
The Wedding March	*Flash Gordon* (OST)
Marriage Of Dale And Ming	*Flash Gordon* (OST)
Crash Dive On Mingo City	*Flash Gordon* (OST)
Flash's Theme (Reprise)	*Flash Gordon* (OST)
The Hero	*Flash Gordon* (OST)

Producers: Queen/Mack
Engineer: Anvil

Studio Sessions
Mountain/Musicland
September 1981-March 1982

Staying Power	B-Side/*Hot Space*
Dancer	*Hot Space*
Back Chat	A-Side/*Hot Space*
Body Language	A-Side/*Hot Space*
Action This Day	*Hot Space*
Put Out The Fire	*Hot Space*
Life Is Real	B-Side/*Hot Space*
Calling All Girls	*Hot Space*
Las Palabras De Amor	A-Side/*Hot Space*
Cool Cat	B-Side/*Hot Space*
Under Pressure	*Hot Space*
Cool Cat #2	Unissued

Additional Musicians/Vocalists: David Bowie – Vocals on 'Under Pressure' and 'Cool Cat #2'; Arif Martin – Horns on 'Staying Power'

Producers: Queen/Mack (Queen/David Bowie – 'Under Pressure')
Engineers: Mack/David Richards

Live Recordings for Video
Seibu Lions Stadium, Tokyo
3 November 1982

Flash	*Live In Japan*
The Hero	Unissued
Rock It	Unissued
We Will Rock You	Unissued
Action This Day	Unissued
Somebody To Love	Unissued
Now I'm Here	*Live In Japan*
Improvisation	Unissued
Put Out The Fire	*Live In Japan*
Dragon Attack	*Live In Japan*
Now I'm Here (Reprise)	*Live In Japan*
Love Of My Life	*Live In Japan*
Save Me	*Live In Japan*
Get Down, Make Love	Unissued
Guitar Solo	*Live In Japan*
Body Language	Unissued
Back Chat	Unissued
Under Pressure	*Live In Japan*
Fat Bottomed Girls	Unissued
Crazy Little Thing Called Love	*Live In Japan*
Bohemian Rhapsody	*Live In Japan*
Tie Your Mother Down	*Live In Japan*
Teo Torriatte	*Live In Japan*
We Will Rock You	*Live In Japan*
We Are The Champions	*Live In Japan*
God Save The Queen	Unissued

Studio Sessions
Record Plant/Musicland
August 1983–January 1984

Radio Ga Ga	A-Side/*The Works*
Tear It Up	B-Side/*The Works*
It's A Hard Life	A-Side/*The Works*
Man On The Prowl	B-Side/*The Works*
Machines (Or Back To Humans)	B-Side/*The Works*
I Want To Break Free	A-Side/*The Works*
Keep Passing The Open Windows	B-Side/*The Works*
Hammer To Fall	A-Side/*The Works*
Is This The World We Created...?	B-Side/*The Works*
I Go Crazy	B-Side/*The Works*
There Must Be More To Life Than This	Unissued

Additional Musicians/Vocalists: Fred Mandel – Piano on 'Man On The Prowl'/Synths on 'I Want To Break Free' & 'Radio Ga Ga'; Mack – Fairlight Programming on 'Machines'

Producers: Queen/Mack
Engineers: Mack/Mike Beiriger

Live Recordings for Video
Rio de Janeiro
12 & 19 January 1985

Machines	Unissued
Tear It Up	Unissued
Tie Your Mother Down	*Rock In Rio*
Under Pressure	Unissued
Medley: Somebody To Love – Killer Queen Seven Seas Of Rhye – Keep Yourself Alive – Liar	*Rock In Rio*
Rock In Rio Blues	Unissued
It's A Hard Life	*Rock In Rio*
Dragon Attack	Unissued
Now I'm Here	*Rock In Rio*
Is This The World We Created...?	*Rock In Rio*
Love Of My Life	*Rock In Rio*
Improvisation	Unissued
Brighton Rock	*Rock In Rio*
Guitar Solo	Unissued

Another One Bites The Dust	Unissued
Hammer To Fall	*Rock In Rio*
Crazy Little Thing Called Love	Unissued
Bohemian Rhapsody	*Rock In Rio*
Radio Ga Ga	*Rock In Rio*
I Want To Break Free	*Rock In Rio*
We Will Rock You	*Rock In Rio*
We Are The Champions	*Rock In Rio*
God Save The Queen	*Rock In Rio*

Live Session for BBC Radio
Wembley Stadium
13 July 1985

Bohemian Rhapsody	Radio Broadcast/ Unissued
Radio Ga Ga	Radio Broadcast/ Unissued
Hammer To fall	Radio Broadcast/ Unissued
Crazy Little Thing Called Love	Radio Broadcast/ Unissued
We Will Rock You	Radio Broadcast/ Unissued
We Are The Champions	Radio Broadcast/ Unissued

Studio Session
Unknown
Unknown

Thank God It's Christmas	A-Side

Studio Sessions
Musicland/Mountain/Townhouse
November 1985–April 1986

One Vision	A-Side/*A Kind Of Magic*
A Kind Of Magic	A-Side/*A Kind Of Magic*
One Year Of Love	*A Kind Of Magic*
Pain Is So Close To Pleasure	*A Kind Of Magic*
Friends Will Be Friends	A-Side/*A Kind Of Magic*

Who Wants To Live Forever	A-Side/*A Kind Of Magic*
Gimme The Prize	*A Kind Of Magic*
Don't Lose Your Head	*A Kind Of Magic*
Princes Of The Universe	*A Kind Of Magic*
Blurred Vision	B-Side/*A Kind Of Magic*
A Dozen Red Roses For My Darling	B-Side/*A Kind Of Magic*

Additional Musicians/Vocalists: Joan Armatrading – Backing vocals on 'Don't Lose Your Head'; Lynton Naiff – Strings on 'One Year Of Love'; Steve Gregory – Saxophone on 'One Year Of Love'; Royal Philharmonic Orchestra – Orchestra on 'Who Wants To Live Forever'

Producers: Queen/Mack/David Richards
Engineers: Mack/David Richards

Live Session for German Radio
Mairmarktgelande, Mannheim, Germany
21 June 1986

One Vision	Radio Broadcast/ Unissued
Tie Your Mother Down	Radio Broadcast/ Unissued
Medley: In The Lap Of The Gods… revisited – Seven Seas Of Rhye	Radio Broadcast/ Unissued
A Kind Of Magic	Radio Broadcast/ Unissued
Under Pressure	Radio Broadcast/ Unissued
Another One Bites The Dust	Radio Broadcast/ Unissued
Who Wants To Live Forever	Radio Broadcast/ Unissued
I Want To Break Free	Radio Broadcast/ Unissued
Now I'm Here	Radio Broadcast/ Unissued
Love Of My Life	Radio Broadcast/ Unissued

Is This The World We Created…?	Radio Broadcast/ Unissued
Medley: (You're So Square) Baby I Don't Care – Hello Mary Lou-Tutti Frutti	Radio Broadcast/ Unissued
Gimme Some Lovin'	Radio Broadcast/ Unissued
Bohemian Rhapsody	Radio Broadcast/ Unissued
Hammer To Fall	*Live Magic*/Radio Broadcast
Crazy Little Thing Called Love	Radio Broadcast/ Unissued
Big Spender	Radio Broadcast/ Unissued
Radio Ga Ga	Radio Broadcast/ Unissued
We Will Rock You	Radio Broadcast/ Unissued
Friends Will Be Friends	Radio Broadcast/ Unissued
We Are The Champions	Radio Broadcast/ Unissued
God Save The Queen	Radio Broadcast/ Unissued

Producers: Queen/Trip Khalaf
Engineer: John Brough

Live Session for BBC Radio
Wembley Stadium
11 July 1986

One Vision	*Live At Wembley '86*
Tie Your Mother Down	*Live At Wembley '86*
Medley: In The Lap Of The Gods… revisited – Seven Seas Of Rhye-Tear It Up	*Live At Wembley '86*
A Kind Of Magic	*Live At Wembley '86*
Under Pressure	*Live At Wembley '86*
Another One Bites The Dust	*Live At Wembley '86*
Who Wants To Live Forever	*Live At Wembley '86*
I Want To Break Free	*Live At Wembley '86*
Brighton Rock	*Live At Wembley '86*

Now I'm Here	*Live At Wembley '86*	Who Wants To Live Forever	Radio Broadcast/ *Queen At Wembley Video*
Love Of My Life	*Live At Wembley '86*		
Is This The World We Created...?	*Live Magic/Live At Wembley '86*	I Want To Break Free	Radio Broadcast/ Unissued
Medley: (You're So Square) Baby I Don't Care-Hello Mary Lou – Tutti Frutti	*Live At Wembley '86*	Now I'm Here	Radio Broadcast/ Unissued
Bohemian Rhapsody	*Live At Wembley '86*	Love Of My Life	Radio Broadcast/ *Queen At Wembley Video*
Hammer To Fall	*Live At Wembley '86*		
Crazy Little Thing Called Love	*Live At Wembley '86*		
Big Spender	*Live At Wembley '86*	Is This The World We Created...?	Radio Broadcast/ *Queen At Wembley Video*
Radio Ga Ga	*Live At Wembley '86*		
We Will Rock You	*Live At Wembley '86*		
Friends Will Be Friends	*Live At Wembley '86*	Medley: (You're So Square) Baby I Don't Care – Hello Mary Lou – Tutti Frutti	Radio Broadcast/ Unissued
We Are The Champions	*Live At Wembley '86*		
God Save The Queen	*Live At Wembley '86*		
		Tutti Frutti	Radio broadcast/ *Queen At Wembley Video*
Producers: Queen/Trip Khalaf Engineer: John Brough			
		Gimme Some Lovin'	Radio Broadcast/ Unissued

Live Session for BBC Radio
Wembley Stadium
12 July 1986

		Bohemian Rhapsody	Radio Broadcast/ *Queen At Wembley Video*
One Vision	Radio Broadcast/ *Queen At Wembley Video*		
		Hammer To Fall	Radio Broadcast/ *Queen At Wembley Video*
Tie Your Mother Down	Radio Broadcast/ *Queen At Wembley Video*		
		Crazy Little Thing Called Love	Radio Broadcast/ *Queen At Wembley Video*
Medley: In The Lap Of The Gods... revisited – Seven Seas Of Rhye	Radio Broadcast/ *Queen At Wembley Video*	Big Spender	Radio Broadcast/ Unissued
A Kind Of Magic	Radio Broadcast/ *Queen At Wembley Video*	Radio Ga Ga	Radio Broadcast/ *Queen At Wembley Video*
Under Pressure	Radio Broadcast/ *Queen At Wembley Video*	We Will Rock You	Radio Broadcast/ *Queen At Wembley Video*
Another One Bites The Dust	Radio Broadcast/ *Queen At Wembley Video*	Friends Will Be Friends	Radio Broadcast/ *Queen At Wembley Video*
		We Are The Champions	Radio Broadcast/ *Queen At Wembley Video*

God Save The Queen — Radio Broadcast/ *Queen At Wembley Video*

Producers: Queen/Trip Khalaf
Engineer: John Brough

Live Recordings & Video Taping
Nepstadion, Budapest
27 July 1987

One Vision	*Live In Budapest Video*
Tie Your Mother Down	*Live In Budapest Video*
Medley: In The Lap Of The Gods... revisited – Seven Seas Of Rhye – Tear It Up	*Live In Budapest Video*
A Kind Of Magic	*Live Magic/Live In Budapest Video*
Tavaszi Szel Vizet Araszt	*Live In Budapest Video*
Under Pressure	*Live Magic/Live In Budapest Video*
Another One Bites The Dust	Unissued
Who Wants To Live Forever	*Live In Budapest Video*
I Want To Break Free	*Live In Budapest Video*
Now I'm Here	*Live In Budapest Video*
Love Of My Life	*Live In Budapest Video*
Tavaszi Szel Vizet Araszt	*Live In Budapest Video*
Is This The World We Created...?	*Live In Budapest Video*
Medley: (You're So Square) Baby I Don't Care – Hello Mary Lou- Tutti Frutti	Unissued / *Live In Budapest Video*
Bohemian Rhapsody	*Live In Budapest Video*
Hammer To Fall	*Live In Budapest Video*
Crazy Little Thing Called Love	*Live In Budapest Video*
Radio Ga Ga	*Live In Budapest Video*
We Will Rock You	*Live In Budapest Video*
Friends Will Be Friends	*Live In Budapest Video*
We Are The Champions	*Live In Budapest Video*
God Save The Queen	*Live In Budapest Video*

Producers: Queen/Trip Khalaf
Engineer: John Brough

Live Recordings
Knebworth Park, Stevenage, Hertfordshire
9 August 1986

One Vision	*Live Magic*
Tie Your Mother Down	*Live Magic*
Medley: In The Lap Of The Gods... revisited – Seven Seas Of Rhye	*Live Magic*
Tear It Up	Unissued
A Kind Of Magic	Unissued
Under Pressure	Unissued
Another One Bites The Dust	*Live Magic*
Who Wants To Live Forever	Unissued
I Want To Break Free	*Live Magic*
Now I'm Here	Unissued
Love Of My Life	Unissued
Is This The World We Created...?	Unissued
Medley: (You're So Square) Baby I Don't Care – Hello Mary Lou – Tutti Frutti	Unissued
Gimme Some Lovin'	Unissued
Bohemian Rhapsody	*Live Magic*
Hammer To Fall	Unissued
Crazy Little Thing Called Love	Unissued
Radio Ga Ga	*Live Magic*
We Will Rock You	*Live Magic*
Friends Will Be Friends	*Live Magic*
We Are The Champions	*Live Magic*

God Save The Queen	Unissued

Producers: Queen/Trip Khalaf
Engineer: John Brough

Studio Sessions
Olympic/Townhouse/Mountain
January 1988-January 1989

Party	*The Miracle*
Khashoggi's Ship	*The Miracle*
The Miracle	A-Side/*The Miracle*
I Want It All	A-Side/*The Miracle*
The Invisbile Man	A-Side/*The Miracle*
Breakthru	A-Side/*The Miracle*
Rain Must Fall	*The Miracle*
Scandal	A-Side/*The Miracle*
My Baby Does	*The Miracle*
Was It All Worth It	*The Miracle*
Hang On In There	B-Side
Stealin'	B-Side
Hijack My Heart	B-Side
My Life Has Been Saved	B-Side
Stone Cold Crazy	B-Side
Too Much Love Will Kill You	Unissued

Producers: Queen/David Richards
Engineers: David Richards/Andrew Bradfield/John Brough/Angelique Cooper/Claude Rider/Andy Mason/Justin Shirley-Smith

Studio Sessions
Metropolis/Mountain
March 1989-November 1990

Innuendo	A-Side/*Innuendo*
I'm Going Slightly Mad	A-Side/*Innuendo*
Headlong	A-Side/*Innuendo*
I Can't Live With You	*Innuendo*
Don't Try So hard	*Innuendo*
Ride The Wild Wind	*Innuendo*

All God's People	*Innuendo*
These Are The Days Of Our Lives	B-Side/*Innuendo*
Delilah	*Innuendo*
The Hitman	B-Side/*Innuendo*
Bijou	B-Side/*Innuendo*
The Show Must Go On	A-Side/*Innuendo*
Mad The Swine	B-Side/*Innuendo*

Additional Musicians/Vocalists: Mike Moran – Piano on 'All God's People'; Steve Howe – Spanish Guitar on 'Innuendo'

Producers: Queen/David Richards
Engineers: David Richards/Noel Harris/Justin Shirley-Smith

Studio Sessions
Unknown
Unknown

It's A Beautiful Day	*Made In Heaven*
Made In Heaven	*Made In Heaven*
Let Me Live	*Made In Heaven*
Mother Love	*Made In Heaven*
My Life Has Been Saved	*Made In Heaven*
I Was Born To Love You	*Made In Heaven*
Heaven For Everyone	*Made In Heaven*
Too Much Love Will Kill You	*Made In Heaven*
You Don't Fool Me	*Made In Heaven*
A Winter's Tale	*Made In Heaven*
It's A Beautiful Day (Reprise)	*Made In Heaven*

Additional Musicians/Vocalists: Catherine Porter – Backing vocals on 'Let Me Live'; Gary Martin – Backing vocals on 'Let Me Live'; Miriam Stockley – Backing vocals on 'Let Me Live'; Rebecca Leigh-White – Backing vocals on 'Let Me Live'

Producers: Queen
Engineers: Mack/David Richards/Justin Shirley-Smith/Joshua J. Macrae

QUEEN AS GUEST ARTISTS

Throughout Queen's twenty-year life Roger Taylor, Brian May, Freddie Mercury and, to a lesser degree, John Deacon have all involved themselves in other artists' projects. This involvement ranges from simple guest appearances through to complete production on a project. In many cases they are not credited, and if they are, there is no information on which tracks they appeared. This makes the task of listing all their guest appearances almost impossible. However, in this section we attempt to trace their career as 'guests' and follow this with a discography listing the various releases and formats.

The first member to undertake outside work was Roger Taylor. In 1972 he appeared on the Al Stewart album *Past, Present and Future,* adding percussion to a couple of the tracks. Unfortunately it is unknown which tracks he worked on. Three years later Freddie Mercury turned his hand to production. Mercury, ably assisted by the other members of Queen, produced material for the London- based soul group Trax. Nothing from the session was released and the tapes were wiped.

During the sessions for *A Night At The Opera* Mercury produced a single for Eddi Howell. 'Man From Manhattan' was released in 1976 and subsequently re-released in 1995. Also recording at Sarm around this time was the pop group led by Noosha Fox. Fox had two hit singles under their belt, 'Only You Can' and 'S-S-S-Single Bed' when they approached Roger Taylor to add backing vocals on a track from their album *Tails Of Illusion*. He can be heard on 'Survival' during the refrain.

Mott The Hoople front-man Ian Hunter was an old friend of the group and during Mott The Hoople's 1973–74 tours they featured Queen as a support group giving them much needed exposure. During a tour of the US in 1976 Taylor, May and Mercury joined Hunter at the Electric Lady studios in New York and played on the track 'You Nearly Did Me In' which appeared on Hunter's album *All American Alien Boy* and was also released as a single.

The 1977 Peter Straker album *This One's On Me* featured Mercury, albeit not in his role as a musician – he invested money in this album of post-glam rock.

Skiffle king Lonnie Donegan enlisted the help of Brian May in 1977, for an album of re-recordings that also featured guest appearances by Ringo Starr and Elton John. Produced by Adam Faith, May appeared on 'Diggin' My Potatoes' and a track that remains unreleased, 'Rolling Stone'. Twelve years later Donegan and May worked together again on 'Let Your Heart Rule Your Head', a song written by May for Lonnie. May later recorded his own version of the song but the Lonnie Donegan version has not been released.

Roger Taylor's solo production career began in 1979 with female vocalist Hilary Hilary for whom he produced 'How Come You're So Dumb'. He played drums and keyboards as well as co-writing the track and its B-side 'Rich Kid Blues'. Two years later he found himself in the studio with comedian Mel Smith playing on two tracks, and the same year he worked with Gary Numan playing drums on 'Crash' and 'You Are You Are'. Taylor has also played, produced or written material for Kansas' album *Vinyl Confessions*, Roger Daltrey's *Under A Raging Moon,* and various releases by Jimmy Nail, Sideway Look and Camy Todro. Along with John Deacon, he also worked on Elton John's *Ice On Fire* and *Leather Jackets* albums.

Meanwhile Brian May was lending a hand to several projects. In 1983 he added guitar to soul singer Jeffrey Osborne's album *Stay With Me Tonight* and the following year undertook the same task for ex-Manfred Mann's Earth Band vocalist Chris Thompson on *A Shift In The Wind*. Meatloaf and Bad News were helped out by Brian May in 1987 when he played guitar on 'A Time For Heroes', the theme song for the International Summer Special Olympic Games, and on the spoof heavy metal group's *Bad News* LP.

The late eighties saw Roger Taylor working with the Birmingham-based band Magnum and heavy rock band Virginia Wolf, and in 1992 he lent a hand on Shakin' Stevens' hit 'Radio'.

Hank Marvin, Paul Rodgers, Cozy Powell, Judie Tzuke, ex-Eastenders star Anita Dobson and even Hale and Pace kept Brian May busy during the second half of the eighties.

An early picture of Queen. Left to right: John, Roger, Freddie and Brian
(E.Echenberg/Redferns)

GUEST DISCOGRAPHY

This discography lists all the singles and albums on which the individual members of Queen either played or did production work. It does not list all the different formats of singles, although many of them were released as 12", cassette, CD and special limited issues. Many entries also include the relevant member and their involvement.

ROGER TAYLOR

Al Stewart
Past, Present And Future CBS 32036 1973
Roger Taylor – Percussion

Fox
Tails Of Illusion GTO GTLP 006 1975
Roger Taylor – Backing Vocals

Eugene Wallace
Dangerous EMIEMC 3067 1975
Roger Taylor – Percussion

Hilary Hilary
How Come You're So Dumb/Rich Kid Blues Modern STP 2 1980
Roger Taylor – Produced

Mel Smith
Mel Smith's Greatest Hits/Richard & Joey Mercury MEL 1 1981
Roger Taylor – Backing Vocals and Instruments

Gary Numan
Dance Beggars Banquet BEGA 28 1981
Roger Taylor – Drums

Kansas
Audio Visions Kirshner KIR 84500 1980
Roger Taylor – Backing Vocals and Drums

Vinyl Confessions Kirshner KIR 85714 1982

Jimmy Nail
Love Don't Live Here Anymore/Night For Day Virgin VS 764 1985
Roger Taylor – Co-produced

Take It Or Leave Virgin V 2407 1986

Feargal Sharkey
Loving You/Is This An Explanation? Virgin VS 770 1985

Feargal Sharkey Virgin V 2360 1985
Roger Taylor – Producer

Camy Todorow
Bursting At The Seams/Bursting At The Seams (instrumental) Virgin VS 816
Roger Taylor – Producer and played drums

Elton John
Ice On Fire Phonogram HISPD 26 1985

Leather Jackets Phonogram EJLP 1 1986
Roger Taylor – Drums

Roger Daltrey
Under A Raging Moon/Move Better In The Night 10 TEN 81 1986

Under A Raging Moon 10 DIX 17 1985
Roger Taylor – Percussion

Magnum
Lonely Night/Dans Le Mort Polydor POSP 798 1986

Midnight (You Must Be Sleeping)/Backstreet Kid Polydor POSP 833 1986

When The World Comes Down/Vigilante Polydor POSP 850 1987

Vigilante Polydor POLP 5198 1986
Roger Taylor – Producer and Backing Vocals

Virginia Wolf
Waiting For You Love/Take A Chance Atlantic A 9459 1986

Virginia Wolf Atlantic 781 274-1 1986
Roger Taylor – Producer

Sigue Sigue Sputnik
Dancerama/Barbarandroid Parlophone SSS 5 1989
Roger Taylor – Remixed Track

Shakin' Stevens
Radio/Oh Baby Don't Epic 658436 1992

The Epic Years Epic 472422-1 1992
Roger Taylor – Drums

BRIAN MAY

Lonnie Donegan
Puttin' On The Style Chrysalis CHR 1158 1978
Brian May – Guitar and Backing Vocals

Jeffrey Osborne
Stay With Me Tonight/Ready For Your Love A&M AM 157 1983

Stay With Me Tonight A&M AMLX 64940 1983
Brian May – Guitar

Heavy Pettin'
In And Out Of Love/Love On The Run Polydor HEP 1 1983

Rock Me/Shadows Of The Night Polydor HEP 2 1983

Love Times Two/Shout It Out Polydor HEP 3 1984

Lettin' Loose Polydor HEPLP 1 1983
Brian May – Production

Billy Squier
Signs Of Life Capitol EJ 2401 1984
Brian May – Guitar

Chris Thompson
Radio Voices Ultraphone 6.25922 1986
Brian May – Guitar

Minako Honda
Cancel Eastworld WTP 90433 1986

Golden Days/Crazy Nights Columbia DB 9153 1987
Brian May – Production

Ramoncin
Camo Un Susrro/A Diez Pases EMI 006 1986

La Vider Er El Filo EMI 1986
Brian May – Guitar

Meatloaf
A Time For Heroes/Tangerine Dreams Orpheum 060 187 1987
Brian May – Guitar

Jose Lucas
Electric Rumba/Tour De Monde New Deal Carrere 14.305-CA 171 1987
Brian May – Guitar

Bad News
Bohemian Rhapsody/Live With Brian EMI EM 24 1987

Cashing In On Christmas/Bad News EMI EM 36 1987

Bad News EMI EMC 3535 1987

Bootleg EMIEMC 3542 1988
Brian May – Production

Anita Dobson
Talking Of Love/Sweet Talking Parlophone R 6159 1987

I Dream Of Christmas/Silly Christmas Parlophone R 6172 1987

Talking Of Love Odeon ODN 1007 1987

In One Of My Weaker Moments/In One Of My Weaker Moments MCA MCA 1260 1988

To Know Him Is To Love Him/Funny Old Life Ain't It Odeon ODO 111 1988
Brian May – Production and Guitar

Fuzzbox
Self/Wait And See WEA YZ 408 1989
Brian May – Guitar

Holly Johnson
Love Train/Murder In Paradise MCA MCA 1306 1989
Brian May – Guitar

Living In A Box
Blow The House Down/Dance The Mayonnaise Chrysalis LIB 5 1989
Brian May – Guitar

Ian & Belinda
Who Wants To Live Forever?/Who Wants To Live Forever? (instrumental) Odeon ODO 112 1989
Brian May – Guitar

Black Sabbath
Headless Cross IRS EIRSA 1002 1989
Brian May – Guitar

Artists United For Nature
Yes We Can/Yes We Can (instrumental) Virgin 662 764 1989
Brian May – Very brief Guitar part

Rock Aid Armenia
Smoke On The Water/Paranoid ARMEN 001 1989
Brian May – Guitar

R. A. Repatriation
Sailing/Sailing (instrumental) IRS EIRA 139 1989
Brian May – Guitar

Hale and Pace
The Stonk/The Smile Song London LON 296 1991
Brian May – Production

D-Rok
Get Out Of My Way/Renegade/Get Out Of My Way Warhammer DROK 08722 1991

Oblivion Warhammer DROK 08746 1991
Brian May – Guitar

Extreme
Song For Love/Love Of My Life A&M AM 698 1992
Brian May – Guitar

Cozy Powell
The Drums Are Back EMI Odeon CDODN 1008 1992
Brian May – Guitar

Judie Tzuke
Wonderland Essential ESSCD 184 1992
Brian May – Guitar

Steve Hackett
The Unauthorized Biography Charisma CDVM 9014 1992
Brian May – Guitar

Hank Marvin
We Are The Champions/Into The Light Polydor PO 229 1992

Into The Light Polydor 517 148-1 1992
Brian May – Guitar

Phenomena
Phenomena III: Innervision Parachute CDPAR 002 1992

Tony Martin
Is There A Heaven/India Polydor 863 056-7 1992

Back Where I Belong Polydor 513 518-2 1992
Brian May – Guitar

Paul Rodgers
Muddy Water Blues Victory 828 414-1 1992
Brian May – Guitar

Various Artists
Greenpeace Alternative NRG Hollywood

Os Paralamas Do Successo
Severino 1994

Dos Margaritas 1994
Brian May – Guitar and Backing Vocals

Jennifer Rush
Out Of My Hands Electrola 724303 112623 1994
Brian May – Vocals

MC Spy D + Friends
The Amazing Spider-Man Mastermix/The Amazing Spider-Man Sad Bit Parlophone CDR 6404 1995
Brian May – Composer and Producer

FREDDIE MERCURY

Eddie Howell
Man From Manhattan/Waiting In The Wings Warner Brothers K 16701 1976
Freddie Mercury – Production

Ian Hunter
You Nearly Did Me In/Letter From Brittania To The Union Jack CBS S 4479 1976

All American Alien Boy CBS 81310 1976
Freddie Mercury – Backing Vocals

Peter Straker
Ragtime Piano Joe/Saddest Clown EMI 2700 1977

Jackie/I've Been To Hell And Back EMI 2758 1978

This One's On Me EMI EMC 2758
Freddie Mercury – Production

Billy Squier
Emotions In Motion/Catch 22 Capitol CL 261 1982

Love Is The Hero/Learn How To Love Capitol PJ 12483 1986

Emotions In Motion Capitol EST 12217 1982

Enough Is Enough Capitol EST 2024
Freddie Mercury – Backing Vocals

Original Soundtracks
Zabou 1C 0664 2407281 1986

JOHN DEACON

Man Friday & Jive Junior
Picking Up Sounds/Picking Up Sounds Malaco MAL 011 1983
John Deacon – Bass

The Immortals
No Turning Back/No Turning Back MCA 1057 1986

Original Soundtracks
Biggles MCA MCF 3328 1986

OTHER MUSICIANS ON QUEEN RECORDS

Andy Gibb – Backing vocals on the unissued version of 'Play The Game'.

Arif Martin – Horns on the track 'Staying Power' from the *Hot Space* album.

Catherine Porter – Backing vocals on 'Let Me Live', from *Made In Heaven*.

David Bowie – Vocals on the hit single 'Under Pressure' and also backing vocals on the unissued cut of 'Cool Cats'.

Fred Mandel – Piano on 'Man On The Prowl', 'I Want To Break Free' and 'Radio Ga Ga'.

Gary Martin – Backing vocals on 'Let Me Live'

Joan Armatrading – Supplied backing vocals on 'Don't Lose Your Head'.

John Anthony – Backing vocals on 'Modern Times Rock 'n' Roll'.

Lynton Naiff – Strings on 'One Year Of Love'.

Mack – Fairlight Programming on 'Machines (Or Back To Humans)'.

Mike Moran – Played keyboards on 'All God's People'.

Mike Stone – Backing vocals on 'Good Old Fashioned Lover Boy'.

Miriam Stockley – Backing vocals on 'Let Me Live'.

Rebecca Leigh-White – Backing vocals on 'Let Me Live'.

Steve Gregory – Played the saxophone on 'One Year Of Love'.

Steve Howe – Provided the Spanish guitar on 'Innuendo'.

GUEST MUSICIANS ON SOLO RECORDS

Alan Gratzer – Played drums on Brian's *Starfleet Project* album.

Andy Pask – Bass player on 'In My Defence'.

Barry Castle – Horns on the Freddie Mercury/Montserrat Caballe duet 'Barcelona'.

Brett Morgan – Played drums on the album *Time*.

Brian May – Guitar on Taylor's 'Love Lies Bleeding'.

Candy Yates – Backing vocals on 'Baby It's Alright' and 'The Also Rans'.

Carol Woods – Backing vocals on Freddie Mercury's 'The Golden Boy'.

Catherine Porter – Backing vocals on 'Old Friends' and 'Everybody Hurts Sometime'.

Chris Thompson – Vocals and backing vocals on 'Rollin' Over'. Also provided backing vocals on early Brian May gigs.

Clare Yates – Backing vocals on 'Baby It's Alright' and 'The Also Rans'.

Cozy Powell – Drums on 'Resurrection', 'Nothing But Blue', 'Back To The Light', 'I'm Scared, Love Token' and the new version of 'Driven By You'.

Curt Cress – Drums on Freddie Mercury's *Mr Bad Guy* album.

David Richards – Played nearly half the keyboards on the *Fun In Space* release.

Debbie Bishop – Backing vocals on 'The Golden Boy'.

Deborah Ann Johnston – Played the cello on the Mercury/Caballe duet 'Barcelona'.

Dick Marx – String arrangement on 'Foreign Sand' and 'Final Destination'.

Don Airy – Played keyboards on 'Resurrection' and 'Nothing But Blue'.

Edward Van Halen – Played guitar on the *Starfleet Project* album.

Frank Ricotti – Percussionist on the Mercury/Caballe duet 'Barcelona'.

Fred Mandel – Keyboards on Brian's *Starfleet Project* album and also synths and guitar on Mercury's *Mr Bad Guy*.

Freddie Mercury – Backing vocals on 'Heaven For Everyone' and 'Killing Time'.

Gary Tibbs – Bass on 'Back To The Light', 'Let Your Heart Rule Your Head' and 'Rolling Over'.

Geoff Dugmore – Drums on 'Let Your Heart Rule Your Head' and 'Rolling Over'.

Geoffrey Richardson – Violin and viola on 'Baby It's Alright' and 'Life Changes'.

Gill O'Donovan – Provided backing vocals for the *Shove It* album and also 'Back To The Light' and 'Let Your Heart Rule Your Head'. Backing vocals for 'The Cross' during their 1988 tour.

Giorgio Moroder – Keyboards on the Freddie Mercury track 'Love Kills'.

Graham Jarvis – Drums on 'In My Defence'.

Helen Liebman – Played the cello on 'Baby It's Alright' and 'Life Changes'.

Homi Kanga – Violins on 'Barcelona'.

Jason Fallon – Guitar on most of the *Happiness* album. Did not appear on 'Foreign Sand' and 'Final Destination'.

Jim Cregan – Played guitar on 'Foreign Sand' and 'Final Destination'.

Jo Burt – Bass on 'Man Made Paradise'.

John Christie – Backing vocalist on 'Time'.

John Deacon – Bass on 'How Can I Go On', 'Nothing But Blue' and some tracks on the *Shove It* album.

Joshua J. Macrae – Programming on *Happiness* album, except 'Foreign Sand' and 'Final Destination'.

Lance Ellington – Backing vocals on 'The Golden Boy'.

Laurie Lewis – Violin on 'Barcelona'.

Madeleine Bell – Backing vocals on 'The Golden Boy'.

Maggie Ryder – Backing vocals on 'Back To The Light' and 'Rolling Over'. Also sang backing vocals on early Brian May gigs.

Mark Williamson – Backing vocals on 'The Golden Boy'.

Mike Crossley – Keyboards on 'Happiness', 'Touch The Sky', 'Freedom Train', 'The Key', 'Old Friends'.

Mike Moran – Keyboards on 'Time 'and 'In My Defence'. Also played piano on the 'Barcelona' duet and 'Rolling Over', 'Last Horizon' and 'Love Token.'

Miriam Stockley – Backing vocals on 'The Golden Boy', 'Back To The Light' and 'Rolling Over'.

Neil Murray – Played bass on 'I'm Scared', 'Love Token' and the new version of 'Driven By You'.

Paul Vincent – Lead guitarist on *Mr Bad Guy* and played guitar on 'In My Defence'.

Peter Banks – Synthesizer on 'In My Defence'.

Peter Straker – Backing vocals on 'Time' and 'The Golden Boy'.

Phil Chen – Bass player on *Starfleet Project* album, also 'Foreign Sand' and 'Final Destination'.

Phil Spalding – Bass on 'Revelation', 'The Key' and 'Old Friends'.

Ray Russell – Played guitar on 'Time'.

Rick Parfitt – Played guitar on 'It's An Illusion'.

Roger Taylor – Backing vocals on both the *Starfleet Project* and *Great Pretender* albums.

Stephen Wissnet – Bass on *Mr Bad Guy* album.

Suzie O'List – Backing vocals on *Shove It* album. Also appeared on 'Back To The Light' and 'Let Your Heart Rule Your Head'.

Yoshiki – Drum programming on 'Foreign Sand' and 'Final Destination'.

QUEEN COVER VERSIONS

'39
The Eleventh Plague
Pretty Maids

A Kind Of Magic
Mr President
Elaine Page
Music Of Queen (orchestral)
Queen's Rhapsody (orchestral)

All Dead, All Dead
Queen Songs (orchestral)

Another One Bites The Dust
Bany & Demo
Batfish Boys
B-Legged
Captain Jack
Hot 'n' Cold
Illya Kurayki
Die Original Deutschmacher
John Petrucci
Weird Al Yankovic
Queen Classic (orchestral)
Queen's Rhapsody (orchestral)

Barcelona
Music Of Queen (orchestral)

Bicycle Race
Blumchen
Open Windows (orchestral)
Queen Classic (orchestral)

Bohemian Rhapsody
Bad News
Braids
Corporation of One
De Dannen
Dream Theatre
Fuzzbox
Rolf Harris
Magic Affair
M. K. All Stars
Elaine Page
Frank Sidebottom
Tater Totz
Weird Al Yankovic
Music Of Queen (orchestral)
Queen Classic (orchestral)
Queen Collection (orchestral)
Quenn's Rhapsody (orchestral)
Treorchy (orchestral)

Crazy Little Thing Called Love
Pablo Dagnino
Lolitas
Freddy Orion
Queen Classic (orchestral)
Queen Collection (orchestral)
Treorchy (orchestral)

Death On Two Legs
Open Windows

Don't Stop Me Now
Fobia
Queen Classic (orchestral)
Queen Collection (orchestral)
Treorchy (orchestral)

Dragon Attack
Bob Burns
La Lupita

Fat Bottomed Girls
Marga Dredd

Flash
The Creatures of Hollywood Hills
Frank Sidebottom
U96
Music Of Queen (orchestral)
Queen Classic (orchestral)
Queen Collection (orchestral)
Queen's Rhapsody (orchestral)
Treorchy (orchestral)

Friends Will Be Friends
Music Instructor

Get Down, Make Love
Haunted Henschel
Glen Hughes
Nine Inch Nails

Good Old Fashioned Lover Boy
Queen Songs (orchestral)
Treorchy (orchestral)

I Want It All
Ex-It
Heros Del Silencio
Chris Impellitteri
Music Of Queen (orchestral)
Queen's Rhapsody (orchestral)

I Want To Break Free
Masterboy
Maldita Vecinidad
Music Of Queen (orchestral)
Queen's Rhapsody (orchestral)

I Was Born To Love You
Salena Jones
Worlds Apart

If You Can't Beat Them
Throw That Beat

In The Lap Of The Gods...revisited
Circus Ripper

Innuendo
Music Of Queen (orchestral)
Open Windows (orchestral)
Queen's Rhapsody (orchestral)

Is This The World We Created...?
Elaine Page

It's Late
Freddy Bastone
Scott Ian

Keep Passing The Open Windows
Open Windows (orchestral)

Keep Yourself Alive
Mark Boals

Killer Queen
Music Of Queen (orchestral)
Open Windows (orchestral)
Queen Classic (orchestral)

Queen Collection (orchestral)
Queen's Rhapsody (orchestral)

Las Palabras de Amor
Elaine Page

Lily Of The Valley
Pluto And Venus

Living On My Own
Squeezer

Love Of My Life
Extreme
Elaine Page
Mark Slaughter
Antonio Vega
Open Windows (orchestral)
Queen Classic (orchestral)
Queen Collection (orchestral)
Queen Songs (orchestral)

Man On The Prowl
Streetwise

My Melancholy Blues
Elaine Page
Scooters

Nevermore
Queen Songs (orchestral)

Now I'm Here
Def Leppard
Open Windows (orchestral)

One Vision
Bruce Bouillet
Laibach

One Year Of Love
Elaine Page
Zucchero

Play The Game
Aterciopolados
Queen Classic (orchestral)
Queen Collection (orchestral)
Queen's Rhapsody (orchestral)

Radio Ga Ga
DJ Bobo
Elaine Page
Frank Sidebottom
Music Of Queen (orchestral)
Queen's Rhapsody (orchestral)
Treorchy (orchestral)

Sail Away Sweet Sister
Guns 'N' Roses

Save Me
Bruce Kulick
Frank Sidebottom
Soraya
Music Of Queen (orchestral)
Queen's Rhapsody (orchestral)
Treorchy (orchestral)

Scandal
Voice

She Makes Me
Taste Of Cindy

Sheer Heart Attack
Ben Hur And The Goonies
James LaBrie

Somebody To Love
Fits Of Gloom
Man Freddy
Open Windows (orchestral)
Queen Classic (orchestral)

Some Day One Day
Soda Stereo

Spread Your Wings
Blind Guardian

Stone Cold Crazy
Big Balls
Metallica

Teo Torriatte
Queen Collection (orchestral)
Queen Songs (orchestral)

The Great Pretender
Music Of Queen (orchestral)

The Invisible Man
Chassalla
Scatman John

The Show Must Go On
Shirley Bassey
Elton John

Tie Your Mother Down
Lemmy Kilminster
Lynch Mob
Toxin
Open Windows (orchestral)

Too Much Love Will Kill You
Blue Mountain Panpipe Ensemble

We Are The Champions
Acts United
Alvis Basket
Black Fooss
Eiskalte Gaste
Robby Krieger
Hank Marvin
Die Original Deutschmacher
Frank Sidebottom
Andrew White and FC Bayern Munich
Music Of Queen (orchestral)
Open Windows (orchestral)
Queen Classic (orchestral)
Queen Collection (orchestral)

Queen Songs (orchestral)
Queen's Rhapsody (orchestral)
Treorchy (orchestral)

We Will Rock You
Bassline Boys
The Benzedrine Monks Of Santo Domonica
Broiler Gang
Deeva
Disco Magic Records
El General
Guns N' Roses
Interactive
Bob Kulick
Peter Nagy
Panic Zone
Q For F
Linda Ronstadt
Frank Sidebottom
Sly Fox
The Smurfs
Viper
Warrant
Andrew White and FC Bayern Munich
Queen Classic (orchestral)
Queen's Rhapsody (orchestral)
Treorchy (orchestral)

White Man
Der Dritte Raum

Who Wants To Live Forever
Ballerina
Shirley Bassey
Sarah Brightman
Dune
E-rotic
Giorgia
Michael Kamen
Elaine Page
Jennifer Rush
Open Windows (orchestral)

You And I
Queen Songs (orchestral)

You Take My Breath Away
Elaine Page
Herman van Veen

You're My Best Friend
Fito Paez
Queen Classic (orchestral)
Queen Collection (orchestral)
Queen Songs (orchestral)
Treorchy (orchestral)

THE ORCHESTRAL ALBUMS

Music Of Queen
The Royal Philharmonic Orchestra

Open Windows
The Royal Philharmonic Orchestra conducted by David Palmer

Queen Classic
The Royal Philharmonic Orchestra conducted by Louis Clark

Queen Collection
The Royal Philharmonic Orchestra with The Royal Choral Society conducted by Louis Clark

Queen Songs
Makoto Yano/Akiko Yano

Queen's Rhapsody
The Royal Philharmonic Orchestra and Great Empire conducted by Hermann Weindorf

Treorchy
Treorchy

RARE QUEEN RELEASES

Queen are one of the top collectable groups with high prices paid for radio shows, acetates, picture discs and coloured vinyl issues. Many of these were only issued in foreign territories such as France, Japan and Australia/New Zealand. Below, listed under different values, are some of the rarer items.

Acetates are used by the record companies and artists as test pressings of their new recordings. With a very short playing life they are highly collectable and in very rare cases feature a different version to the one that was eventually released. With the invention of DAT, acetates are not being used as much now.

MINT VALUE OVER £1000

Bohemian Rhapsody
EMI 'Queen's Award For Export' limited edition UK blue vinyl hand numbered
1978

Bohemian Rhapsody
EMI 'Queen's Award For Export' limited edition UK blue vinyl hand numbered with 'EMI International' carrying envelope
1978

Bohemian Rhapsody
EMI 'Queen's Award For Export' limited edition UK blue vinyl hand numbered with 'EMI International' carrying envelope including invites, matches, pen, ticket, menu, outer card sleeve, scarf and EMI goblets
1978

MINT VALUE OVER £100

A Day In The Park
Capital Radio Show
1976

Love Kills
One-sided acetate

Live In London
Westwood One US Radio Show
3 Albums

Bohemian Rhapsody
Acetate

Rock Hour
US Radio Show
1973

Live At Milton Keynes
Radio Show`
1982

News Of The World
Promo box set

Magic At Wembley
Capital Radio Show
1986

Seven Seas Of Rhye
Acetate

Keep Yourself Alive
Acetate

Time
Acetate

The Great Pretender
Acetate

I Can Hear Music
EMI demo

Hammer To Fall
Acetate

Sheer Heart Attack
Japanese red vinyl promo LP
1974

Keep Yourself Alive
Dutch picture sleeve single
1973

News Of The World
UK & USA promo box set
1977

Radio Ga Ga
Japanese picture sleeve promo featuring two
versions
1984

I Want It All
Japanese picture sleeve promo
1989

Greatest Hits
Bulgarian picture disc
1984

Jazz
French issue promo picture disc with red
bicycles
1978

Greatest History
Japanese promo CD
1996

Ultimate Collection
Japanese promo CD
1996

Highlander Selection
UK promo CD/Video
1986

A Kind Of Magic
Blue vinyl LP
1986

A Kind Of Magic
French red vinyl issue
1986

Seven Seas Of Rhye
French picture sleeve
1974

Live Magic
New Zealand red vinyl issue
1986

Five Live
US Media Box featuring shirt/CD/Box/
Press Kit
1993

We Will Rock You/We Are The Champions
12" French picture sleeve promo
1992

Innuendo
US promo carrier bag featuring CD/Cassette/
Shirt
1991

Rocks
US 4 promo CDs in box
1991

Disco Hits
Japanese promo LP
1982

**Man On The Prowl/Keep Passing The Open
Windows**
UK 7" single – withdrawn

Their Best
US 2 CD promo briefcase
1992

Classic Queen
US promo carrier bag featuring CD/Cassette/Shirt
1992

Wembley 1986
US promo carrier bag featuring CD/Cassette/
Shirt
1992

One Year Of Love
French 2 track 12" picture sleeve promo
1986

Queen II
Venezuelan LP
1974

Bohemian Rhapsody
UK purple vinyl numbered limited edition
1995

Keep Yourself Alive
Japanese picture sleeve
1973

Now I'm Here
Portuguese picture sleeve
1974

Seven Seas Of Rhye
Japanese picture sleeve
1974

A Kind Of Magic
Australian orange vinyl LP
1986

Hammer To Fall
UK 7" and 12" live sleeve – withdrawn
1986

Tie Your Mother Down
French picture sleeve
1977

Greatest Hits II
UK promo box
1991

Innuendo
UK promo box
1991

The Miracle
UK promo box
1989

Golden Collection Vol 1 & Vol 2
Dutch 2xLP sets
1983

MINT VALUE
BETWEEN £50-£100

In Concert 1973
BBC transcription disc

In Concert 1975
BBC transcription

Killer Queen
Acetate

Somebody To Love
Acetate

Las Palabras de Amour
Acetate

Rock Around The World
US radio show
1977

Off The Record Parts 1 & 2
US radio shows

Night At The Opera
White vinyl LP with die cut sleeve
French promo issue – 1975

News Of The World
Green vinyl LP with die cut sleeve
French promo issue – 1977

Sample Of Magic
UK promo CD
1991

Bohemian Rhapsody
Yellow picture sleeve (French and Portuguese issues)
1975

Another One Bites The Dust
Portuguese picture sleeve
1980

Live Killers
Red/Green vinyl LP and insert
Japanese issue – 1979

Thank God It's Christmas
Brazilian LP
1985

Greatest Hits
Venezuelan LP
1986

Headlong
French issue featuring clown cover
1991

Live
Japanese LP
1985

Love Kills
One-sided acetate

Westwood One
Live in London

OTHER RARE ITEMS

Jealousy/Don't Stop Me Now
Blue flexi disc released in Russia

A Kind Of Magic (LP)
Orange vinyl released in Australia
Blue vinyl released in Columbia
Red vinyl released in France
Orange vinyl released in New Zealand

A Night At The Opera
White vinyl released in Holland and France

A Day At The Races
Green & white vinyl released in Japan
Green vinyl released in France

Sheer Heart Attack
Red vinyl released in France

News Of The World
Red vinyl released in France

Live Killers
Green & red vinyl released in Japan

Live Magic
Red vinyl released in New Zealand

QUEEN PROMOS & SAMPLERS

Promotional releases are normally sent out to journalists and radio stations and are usually identical to the official releases except that they carry a sticker stating they are promotional items and 'not for resale'. Samplers are also issued which feature major tracks of forthcoming albums.

Keep Yourself Alive/What's Going There
Italian jukebox record featuring B-side by Deep Purple

Flash/Football Fight
US 12" promo

Staying Power/Backchat
US 12" promo featuring extended version of 'Staying Power'

Excerpts From **The Works**
UK promo flexi-disc
Tracks: Radio Ga Ga/I Want To Break Free.It's A Hard Life/Hammer To Fall

Man On The Prowl/Keep Passing The Open Windows
Promo copy of withdrawn single

One Year Of Love/Gimme The Prize
French pink vinyl promo

Under Pressure (live)/Medley: **We Will Rock You – Friends Will Be Friends – We Are The Champions**
Live Magic promo single released in UK, USA and France

I Want It All/Hang On In There
UK promo press pack

These Are The Days Of Our Lives/Bijou
UK promo

I Can't Live With You (remix)/**I Can't Live With You** (edit)
US promo

Greatest Hits II
UK promo box set containing *Hits II* CD, *Flix II* video and *Pix II* book

A Sample Of Magic
UK promo CD
Tracks: Queen Talks/The Show Must Go On/A Sample Of Magic: A Kind Of Magic-Under Pressure-Radio Ga Ga-I Want To Break Free-Breakthru-Friends Will Be Friends-Innuendo-One Vision

One Year Of Love/We Are The Champions/Barcelona
US promo

Stone Cold Crazy (remix)/**We Will Rock You/We Are The Champions/Stone Cold Crazy** (out-take)
US promo

Hammer To Fall/Bohemian Rhapsody
US promo

Too Much Love Will Kill You
One track DJ promo CD

Heaven For Everyone
One track promo CD

Don't Stop Me Now
French one track promo

Hammer To Fall (live in Rio)
US 7" and 12" promo

Digital Master Sampler
Tracks: Liar/Funny How Love Is/In The Lap Of The Gods…revisited/Lily Of The Valley/I'm In Love With My Car/'39/You Take My Breath Away/Spread Your Wings/Mustapha/Get Down, Make Love/Dragon Attack/The Hero/Staying Power/Keep Passing The Open Windows

Queen Rocks Volume One
6 track promo CD
Tracks: Tie Your Mother Down/Stone Cold Crazy/Under Pressure/We Will Rock You/Sheer Heart Attack/Get Down, Make Love

Queen Rocks Volume Three
8 track promo CD
Tracks: Bohemian Rhapsody/You're My Best Friend/I'm In Love With My Car/Seven Seas Of Rhye/I Want It All/Flash's Theme/Let Me Entertain You/The Hitman

Queen Rocks Volume Four
8 track promo CD

Tracks: One Vision/Killer Queen/Play The Game/We Will Rock You/We Are The Champions/Dragon Attack/Hammer To Fall/Headlong

The Interview Collection
(4 volume set)
Volume 1: Freddie Mercury
Volume 2: Brian May
Volume 3: John Deacon
Volume 4: Roger Taylor

QUEEN SONGS USED IN RADIO & TV ADS

A Kind Of Magic
M-Net Cable TV (South Africa, 1984)
Del Monte Orange Juice (Sweden, 1995)
Mobil 1 Motor Oil (Germany, Finland, UK, 1995)
Maisel's Weisse Beer (Germany, 1996)
The Adventures of Pinnochio (US film promo, 1996)

Another One Bites The Dust
New South Wales Police Force (Australia, 1995)

Barcelona
Ford Mondeo Motor Cars (Germany, Spain, and Ireland, 1993)

Bicycle Race (cover version with different lyrics)
Batavus Bikes (The Netherlands, 1993)

Bicycle Race (original version)
Bicycle Helmets Safety Awareness (Switzerland, 1995)
Kellogg's Honey Smacks (USA, 1995)

Crazy Little Thing Called Love
Prell Shampoo (US)

Don't Lose Your Head
Northamptonshire Police Force (UK, December 1986)

Don't Stop Me Now
Club Orange (Northern Ireland, 1987)

Cosmo Oil (Japan, 1987)
M-Net Cable TV (South Africa, 1996)
Noevia Cosmetics (Japan, 1996)
Road Safety Awareness (Northern Ireland, 1995)

Driven By You
Ford Motor Cars (Germany, Spain, UK, 1995)
K-Mart (US, 1995)

Friends Will Be Friends
Oranjeboom Beer (The Netherlands, 1994)
Activ Foundation (Australia, 1995)

I Want It All
Seat Toledo Motor Cars (Germany, Spain,
The Netherlands, 1990)
Toyota Motor Cars (UK, 1990)
Twix Chocolate Bars (Germany, UK, 1994)

I Want To Break Free
Shell Petrol (UK, 1994)
Toyota Motor Cars (Australia, 1994)

I Was Born To Love
Kirin Beverages (Japan, 1996)

The Great Pretender
Honda Accord Motor Cars (Japan, 1993)

We Are The Champions
Soccer World Cup (Europe, 1986)
Super League Sports (Australia, 1995)
Falcon Beer (Sweden, 1996)

We Will Rock You
Sun City Hotel Group (South Africa, 1993)
Domino's Pizza (Australia, US, 1994)
Esso Petrol (Canada, 1994)
Huffy Bikes (US)
Kronenburg Beer (Spain)
LA Gear Shoes (US)
Ocean Spray Cranberry Juice Beverages (US)
River 105 (US)
Spec's Florida CD Store (US)
The Flintstones (US film promo, 1994)

Soccer World Cup (Australia, 1994)
Rugby League State of Origin (Australia, 1994)
Kirin Beverages (Japan, 1995)

QUEEN SONGS USED IN MOVIES

A Kind Of Magic (different version)
Highlander (1986)

A Kind Of Magic (original version)
Highlander II (1990)

Another One Bites The Dust
Heartbreak Ridge (1986)
Sea Of Love (1989)

Arboria (Planet Of The Tree Men)
Flash Gordon (1980)

Battle Theme
Flash Gordon (1980)

Bohemian Rhapsody
National Lampoon's Loaded Weapon (1993)
Wayne's World (1992)

Crash Dive On Mingo City
Flash Gordon (1980)

Crazy Little Thing Called Love
Breaking The Rules
Mr Wrong
Son In Law

Don't Stop Me Now
Racers (1984)
Space Riders (1984)

Escape From The Swamp
Flash Gordon (1980)

Execution Of Flash
Flash Gordon (1980)

Flash
Flash Gordon (1980)

Flash's Theme
Flash Gordon (1980)

Flash's Theme Reprise (Victory Celebrations)
Flash Gordon (1980)

Flash To The Rescue
Flash Gordon (1980)

Fooling Around
Teachers (1984)

Football Fight
Flash Gordon (1980)

Hammer To Fall
Highlander (1986)

Hold On
Zabou (1986)

Innuendo
La Carne (1991)

In The Death Cell (Love Theme Reprise)
Flash Gordon (1980)

In The Space Capsule (The Love Theme)
Flash Gordon (1980)

Keep Yourself Alive
Encino Man (aka California Man) (1992)

Love Kills
Metropolis (1984)

Love Kills (Remix)
National Lampoon's Loaded Weapon
Buffy The Vampire Slayer (1992)

Man On Fire
Racers (1984)

Marriage Of Dale And Ming (And Flash
Approaching)
Flash Gordon (1980)

Ming's Theme (In The Court of Ming The Merciless)
Flash Gordon (1980)

New York, New York (Cover Version)
Highlander (1986)

No Turning Back
Biggles (1986)

One Vision
Iron Eagle (1986)

Play The Game
And The Band Played On (1993)

Stone Cold Crazy
Encino Man (aka California Man) (1992)

The Great Pretender
Night And The City (1993)

The Hero
Flash Gordon (1980)

The Kiss (Aura Resurrects Flash)
Flash Gordon (1980)

The Ring (Hypnotic Seduction of Dale)
Flash Gordon (1980)

The Wedding March
Flash Gordon (1980)

Tie Your Mother Down
Super Mario Brothers (1993)

Vultan's Theme (Attack Of The Hawkmen)
Flash Gordon (1980)

We Are The Champions
D2: The Mighty Ducks
Two Moon Junction

We Will Rock You
FM

You're My Best Friend
Peter's Friends (1992)

QUEEN SONGS USED
IN TV PROGRAMMES

Crazy Little Thing Called Love
America's Funniest Home Videos (US, March 1996)

The Show Must Go On
Another World (12 December 1996)

Another One Bites The Dust
Derrick
The Gladiators (UK)
Singled Out (March 1996)

Don't Stop Me Now
The Frank Skinner Show (UK, 1995)
You've Been Framed (UK, 1995)

A Kind Of Magic
The Smell of Reeves & Mortimer (UK, 1995)
You've Been Framed (UK, 1995)

Princes Of The Universe
Highlander (Worldwide, 1994 to date)

We Are The Champions
Married With Children (US, 24 December 1995)
Singled Out (1995)
The Simpsons (US)

We Will Rock You
Married With Children (US, 24 December 1995)

You're My Best Friend
Oprah Winfrey Show (US, February 1996)

Innuendo
Rock Sports (Australia 1995/6)

Bohemian Rhapsody
Scared Straight (US Documentary)
You've Been Framed (UK, 1995)
UK National Lottery (1994)

I'm In Love With My Car
Unter Uns (Germany, June 1995)

Under Pressure
Watchdog (UK, January 1996)

The Great Pretender
The Young And The Restless (December 1994)

Flash
You've Been Framed (UK, 1995)

I Want It All
You've Been Framed (UK, 1995)

I Want To Break Free
You've Been Framed (UK, 1995)

One Vision
Premier League Sports (UK, 1995)
You Don't Fool Me
Baywatch Nights (Germany, 1996)

Barcelona
The Olympic Games (UK, 1992)

MUSIC BOOKS

The following music books contain music and lyrics to all the songs featured on the respective albums as listed below. The only exception where not all the songs from the album were included was on the *Jazz* album when 'Mustapha' was excluded. We have nevertheless listed all the songs featured in each book with composer/composers in brackets. All were published by IMP in the UK around the release of the album, although it is likely that most are out of print. The year of publication is as for the album, and is listed in brackets after the album/book title.

QUEEN (1973)

Keep Yourself Alive (May)
Great King Rat (Mercury)
Liar (Mercury)
Modern Times Rock'n'Roll (Taylor)
Jesus (Mercury)
Doing All Right (May/Staffell)
My Fairy King (Mercury)
The Night Comes Down (May)
Son & Daughter (May)
Seven Seas Of Rhye (Mercury)

QUEEN II (1974)

Procession (May)
Father To Son (May)
White Queen (As It Began) (May)
Someday One Day (May)
The Loser In The End (Taylor)
Ogre Battle (Mercury)
The Fairy Fellers Masterstroke (Mercury)
Nevermore (Mercury)
The March Of The Black Queen (Mercury)
Funny How Love Is (Mercury)
Seven Seas Of Rhye (Mercury)

SHEER HEART ATTACK (1974)

Brighton Rock (May)
Killer Queen (Mercury)
Tenement Funster (Taylor)
Flick Of The Wrist (Mercury)
Lily Of The Valley (Mercury)
Now I'm Here (May)
In The Lap Of The Gods (Mercury)
Stone Cold Crazy (May/Mercury/Taylor/Deacon)
Dear Friends (May)
Misfire (Deacon)
Bring Back That Leroy Brown (Mercury)
She Makes Me (Stormtrooper In Stilletoes) (May)
In The Lap Of The Gods...revisited (Mercury)

A NIGHT AT THE OPERA (1975)

Death On Two Legs (Dedicated to...) (Mercury)
Lazing On A Sunday Afternoon (Mercury)
I'm In Love With My Car (Taylor)
You're My Best Friend (Deacon)
'39 (May)
Sweet Lady (May)
Seaside Rendezvous (Mercury)
The Prophet's Song (May)
Love Of My Life (Mercury)
Good Company (May)
Bohemian Rhapsody (Mercury)
God Save The Queen (Trad. Arr. May)

A DAY AT THE RACES (1976)

Tie Your Mother Down (May)
You Take My Breath Away (Mercury)
Long Away (May)
The Millionaire Waltz (Mercury)
You & I (Deacon)
Somebody To Love (Mercury)
White Man (May)
Good Old Fashioned Lover Boy (Mercury)
Drowse (Taylor)
Teo Torriatte (Let Us Cling Together) (May)

NEWS OF THE WORLD (1977)

We Will Rock You (May)
We Are The Champions (Mercury)
Sheer Heart Attack (Taylor)

All Dead, All Dead (May)
Spread Your Wings (Deacon)
Fight From The Inside (Taylor)
Get Down, Make Love (Mercury)
Sleeping On The Sidewalk (May)
Who Needs You (Deacon)
It's Late (May)
My Melancholy Blues (Mercury)

JAZZ (1978)
Fat Bottomed Girls (May)
Jealousy (Mercury)
Bicycle Race (Mercury)
If You Can't Beat Them (Deacon)
Let Me Entertain You (Mercury)
Dead On Time (May)
In Only Seven Days (Deacon)
Dreamer's Ball (May)
Fun It (Taylor)
Leaving Home Ain't Easy (May)
Don't Stop Me Now (Mercury)
More Of That Jazz (Taylor)

THE GAME (1980)
Play The Game (Mercury)
Dragon Attack (May)
Another One Bites The Dust (Deacon)
Need Your Loving Tonight (Deacon)
Crazy Little Thing Called Love (Mercury)
Rock It (Prime Jive) (Taylor)
Don't Try Suicide (Mercury)
Sail Away Sweet Sister (To The Sister I Never Had)
(May)
Coming Soon (Taylor)
Save Me (May)

FLASH GORDON (1980)
Flash's Theme (May)
In The Space Capsule (The Love Theme) (Taylor)
Ming's Theme (In The Court Of Ming The Merciless)
(Mercury)
The Ring (Hypnotic Seduction Of Dale) (Mercury)
Football Fight (Mercury)
In The Death Cell (Love Theme Reprise) (Taylor)
Execution Of Flash (Deacon)

The Kiss (Aura Resurrects Flash) (Mercury)
Arboria (Planet Of The Tree Men) (Deacon)
Escape From The Swamp (Taylor)
Flash To The Rescue (May)
Vultan's Theme (Attack Of The Hawkmen)
(Mercury)
Battle Theme (May)
The Wedding March (May)
Marriage Of Dale And Ming (and Flash Approaching)
(May/Taylor)
Crash Dive On Mingo City (May)
Flash's Theme Reprise (May)
The Hero (May)

GREATEST HITS (1981)
Bohemian Rhapsody (Mercury)
Killer Queen (Mercury)
Bicycle Race (Mercury)
Don't Stop Me Now (Mercury)
Crazy Little Thing Called Love (Mercury)
Now I'm Here (May)
Play The Game (Mercury)
Seven Seas Of Rhye (Mercury)
We Are The Champions (Mercury)
Another One Bites The Dust (Deacon)
Fat Bottomed Girls (May)
You're My Best Friend (Deacon)
Save Me (May)
Somebody To Love (Mercury)
Good Old Fashioned Lover Boy (Mercury)
Flash (May)
We Will Rock You (May)

HOT SPACE (1982)
Staying Power (Mercury)
Dancer (May)
Back Chat (Deacon)
Body Language (Mercury)
Action This Day (Taylor)
Put Out The Fire (May)
Life Is Real (Song For Lennon) (Mercury)
Calling All Girls (Taylor)
Las Palabras de Amor (The Words Of Love) (May)
Cool Cat (Deacon/Mercury)
Under Pressure (Queen/Bowie)

THE WORKS (1984)

Radio Ga Ga (Taylor)

Tear It Up (May)

It's A Hard Life (Mercury)

Man On The Prowl (Mercury)

Machines (or Back To Humans) (Taylor/May)

I Want To Break Free (Deacon)

Keep Passing The Open Windows (Mercury)

Hammer To Fall (May)

Is This The World We Created...? (Mercury/May)

THE COMPLETE WORKS (1985)

All the songs listed above.

A KIND OF MAGIC (1986)

One Vision (Queen)

A Kind Of Magic (Taylor)

One Year Of Love (Deacon)

Pain Is So Close To Pleasure (Mercury/Deacon)

Friends Will Be Friends (Mercury/Deacon)

Who Wants To Live Forever (May)

Gimme The Prize (Kurgans Theme) (May)

Don't Lose Your Head (Taylor)

Princes Of The Universe (Mercury)

THE COMPLETE WORKS (UPDATED) (1987)

All the songs listed above.

THE MIRACLE (1989)

Party (Queen)

Khashoggi's Ship (Queen)

The Miracle (Queen)

I Want It All (Queen)

The Invisible Man (Queen)

Breakthru (Queen)

Rain Must Fall (Queen)

Scandal (Queen)

My Baby Does Me (Queen)

Was It All Worth It (Queen)

INNUENDO (1991)

Innuendo (Queen)

I'm Going Slightly Mad (Queen)

Headlong (Queen)

I Can't Live With You (Queen)

Don't Try So Hard (Queen)

Ride The Wild Wind (Queen)

All God's People (Queen & Mike Moran)

These Are The Day's Of Our Lives (Queen)

Delilah (Queen)

The Hitman (Queen)

Bijou (Queen)

The Show Must Go On (Queen)

GREATEST HITS II (1991)

A Kind Of Magic (Taylor)

Under Pressure (Queen/Bowie)

Radio Ga Ga (Taylor)

I Want It All (Queen)

I Want To Break Free (Deacon)

Innuendo (Queen)

It's A Hard Life (Mercury)

Breakthru (Queen)

One Vision (Queen)

Who Wants To Live Forever (May)

Headlong (Queen)

The Miracle (Queen)

I'm Going Slightly Mad (Queen)

The Invisible Man (Queen)

Hammer To Fall (May)

Friends Will Be Friends (Mercury/Deacon)

The Show Must Go On (Queen)

MADE IN HEAVEN (1995)

It's A Beautiful Day (Queen)

Made In Heaven (Mercury)

Let Me Live (Queen)

Mother Love (Mercury/May)

My Life Has Been Saved (Queen)

I Was Born To Love You (Mercury)

Heaven For Everyone (Taylor)

Too Much Love Will Kill You (May/Musker/Lamers)

You Don't Fool Me (Queen)

A Winter's Tale (Queen)

It's A Beautiful Day (Reprise) (Queen)

SHEET MUSIC

The following titles were available in sheet music and published in the UK by IMP, although it is likely that most are now out of print. The year of publication is listed in brackets after the song title.

KILLER QUEEN (1974)

NOW I'M HERE (1975)

BOHEMIAN RHAPSODY (1975 & 1991)

YOU'RE MY BEST FRIEND (1976)

SOMEBODY TO LOVE (1976 & 1993)

TIE YOUR MOTHER DOWN (1977)

GOOD OLD FASHIONED LOVER BOY (1977)

WE ARE THE CHAMPIONS (1977)

SPREAD YOUR WINGS (1978)

FAT BOTTOMED GIRLS (1978)

BICYCLE RACE (1978)

DON'T STOP ME NOW (1979)

LOVE OF MY LIFE (1979)

CRAZY LITTLE THING CALLED LOVE (1979)

SAVE ME (1980)

(Dave Hogan/Corbis)

PLAY THE GAME (1980)

ANOTHER ONE BITES THE DUST (1980)

FLASH (1980)

UNDER PRESSURE (1981)

BODY LANGUAGE (1982)

LAS PALABRAS DE AMOR (The Words Of Love) (1982)

BACK CHAT (1982)

RADIO GA GA (1984)

I WANT TO BREAK FREE (1984)

IT'S A HARD LIFE (1984)

HAMMER TO FALL (1984)

THANK GOD IT'S CHRISTMAS (1984)

ONE VISION (1985)

A KIND OF MAGIC (1986)

FRIENDS WILL BE FRIENDS (1986)

WHO WANTS TO LIVE FOREVER (1986)

I WANT IT ALL (1989)

BREAKTHRU (1989)

THE INVISIBLE MAN (1989)

SCANDAL (1989)

THE MIRACLE (1989)

INNUENDO (1991)

I'M GOING SLIGHTLY MAD (1991)

HEADLONG (1991)

THE SHOW MUST GO ON (1991)

HEAVEN FOR EVERYONE (1995)

A WINTER'S TALE (1995)

TOO MUCH LOVE WILL KILL YOU (1996)

LET ME LIVE (1996)

YOU DON'T FOOL ME (1996)

MUSIC TRIVIA

• 'Bohemian Rhapsody' has been covered by a diverse number of artists that include Elaine Paige, the London Symphony Orchestra, the Parachute Regiment Band, We've Got A Fuzzbox And We're Gonna Use It, the Allen Toussaint Orchestra and Frank Sidebottom.

• 'Bohemian Rhapsody' was the first Queen single to feature a picture sleeve.

• On it's release, one critic described 'Bohemian Rhapsody' as 'one of the most peculiar singles of the year'.

• 'Bohemian Rhapsody' spent nine weeks at number one and gave Queen their first platinum award.

• Kenny Everett played the song fourteen times during his weekend shows on Capital Radio, despite the fact that it was a preview copy and he had promised not to play it.

• EMI were dubious about 'Bohemian Rhapsody' fearing radio stations would not play a single that ran to six minutes.

• 'Bohemian Rhapsody' took close to three weeks to record, with the opera section needing seven days.

• On their first album *Queen*, the bass player was credited as Deacon John! The rest of the group used to call him that but on all subsequent albums he was John Deacon.

• 'Keep Yourself Alive' was rejected by the BBC Radio One Playlist an incredible five times.

• In late 1973 they supported Mott The Hoople on their UK tour.

• The original title of their second album *Queen II* was to be *Over The Top*.

• *Sheer Heart Attack* was recorded utilising four different studios.

• The 'Bohemian Rhapsody' video had a budget of just £4,500.

• Three of their albums took their titles from Marx Brothers films: *A Night At The Opera*, *A Day At The Races* and *News Of The World*.

• *A Day At The Races* had over 500,000 advance orders.

• A launch party for *Jazz* was held in New Orleans.

• Their 1981 eight-date South American stadium tour played to over half a million people, with a crowd of 251,000 watching the group at the Sao Paulo Morumbi Stadium.

• 'I Want To Break Free' was accompanied by a video pastiche of the soap opera *Coronation Street*.

• *Live Magic*, released in December, sold 400,000 copies by Christmas.

• 'Innuendo' was the groups first single to enter the British charts at number one. It was also the longest number one single, running at over six minutes, since 'Bohemian Rhapsody'.

• *Innuendo* was the first Queen album to be released on the Walt Disney Hollywood label in America.

• The 1986 'Magic' Tour played to over 1 million people in Europe and grossed well over £11 million.

• The proceeds of their 1986 Newcastle concert went to the Save The Children Fund.

• Over fifty-three different compilations released in 1986, in twenty-three countries, featured a Queen hit.

• 'I Want To Break Free' was adopted by Shell for their radio and television campaign.

• Roger Taylor was the first member of the group to release a solo single.

• Queen were one of the highlights of the Live Aid concert. The organiser, Bob Geldof, stated, 'It was the perfect stage for Freddie. He could ponce about in front of the whole world.'

• The first fan club convention was held in 1986 at Great Yarmouth.

• In 1976 Queen gave a concert at Cardiff Castle. They were supported by Rainbow.

• The charity Save The Children benefitted from a concert held in Newcastle in 1986.

• The video for 'We Are The Champions' was the first of Queen's promo videos where fan club members were asked to participate.

• Mike Stone engineered six of Queen's albums.

• The launch for *A Day At The Races* was held, appropriately, at Kemptown Park race course in 1976. The group also sponsored a race.

• Actress Jane Seymour appeared with Freddie at the Fashion Aid charity show in 1985.

• Elton John's 'Saturday Night's All Right For Fighting' was a regular in Queen's live set.

• The soundtrack album *Flash Gordon* won a BAFTA (British Academy of Film And Television Arts) Award.

• 'Somebody To Love' was the first of their videos to mix studio and live footage. 'One Vision' also used this technique.

• 'Misfire' was the first of John Deacon's solo compositions to appear on a Queen album.

• Brian May played the ukelele on 'Bring Back That Leroy Brown'.

• In 1973 Queen and 10cc both appeared on the same bill at the Top Rank Club in Liverpool.

• Mr Big supported Queen during their 1975 UK tour.

• The hot & spacy horns on 'Staying Power' were arranged by Arif Mardin.

• The Magnum album *Vigilante* was produced by Roger.

• TV presenter Michael Aspel presented the group their 25-year award for best single with 'Bohemian Rhapsody'.

• Status Quo supported Queen on all their UK dates in 1986.

• The inspiration for 'Bicycle Race' was the Tour de France.

• Freddie Mercury's favourite film was *Some Like It Hot*.

• Freddie once read the weather forecast, incorrectly, on the Kenny Everett radio show.

• Roger produced 'Love Don't Live Here Anymore' for Jimmy Nail.

• Roger played drums for Gary Numan on his *Dance* album.

• 'Save Me' was Queen's first video animation promo.

• 'Princes Of The Universe' is the theme song to the *Highlander* TV series.

• Freddie Mercury was awarded the Outstanding Contribution award, posthumously, at the annual Brits Ceremony in 1992. It was received by Roger and Brian.

• Abbey Road Studios were used to digitally remaster the Queen Digital Master Series.

• 'White Queen (As It Began)' was the first song to have a subtitle.

• 'Seven Seas Of Rhye' was the first Queen song to be issued in Sheet Music form.

• Pan's People, the legendary dancers from BBC TV's *Top Of The Pops*, danced to Queen's 'Somebody To Love'.

• Blackpool was the opening gig of their first headlining tour.

• The 'Calling All Girls' video was inspired by the film *THX 1138*.

• 'Kind Of Magic' was used by Mobil Oil on their TV advert.

• 'World Exclusive-We Want It All' was the newspaper headline at the start of the 'Scandal' video.

• Dutch artist Robbie Valentine supported Brian May during his European tour in 1993.

• 'Body Language' was remixed by Susan Rogers for the Hollywood records issue.

• *The Game* was the first of Queen's albums to reach number one in the Billboard Chart.

• *A Night At The Opera* was recently reissued by EMI as part of their centenary celebrations. It was released as part of The Vinyl Collection.

PART 3

THE PERFORMERS

(Corbis)

QUEEN CONCERT APPEARANCES

1970–1986

1970

27 June	UK: TRURO City Hall
12 July	UK: LONDON Imperial College
25 July	UK: TRURO PJ's Club
23 August	UK: LONDON Imperial College
4 September	UK: LONDON Swiss Cottage Private School
16 October	UK: LONDON College of Estates Management Hall
30 October	UK: ST HELENS College of Technology
31 October	UK: LIVERPOOL Cavern Club
14 November	UK: HERTFORD Ballspark College
5 December	UK: EGHAM Shoreditch College
18 December	UK: ST HELENS College of Technology
19 December	UK: ST HELENS Congregational Church Hall

1971

8 January	UK: LONDON Marquee Club
9 January	UK: EWELL Technical College
19 February	UK: LONDON Hornsey Town Hall
20 February	UK: LONDON Kingston Polytechnic
2 July	UK: SURREY College
11 July	UK: LONDON Imperial College
17 July	UK: PENZANCE The Garden
18 July	UK: LONDON Imperial College
19 July	UK: HAYLE Rugby Club
24 July	UK: WADEBRIDGE Young Farmers Club
29 July	UK: PENZANCE The Garden
31 July	UK: TRURO City Hall
2 August	UK: HAYLE Rugby Club
9 August	UK: ST AGENS Driftwood Spurs
12 August	UK: TRURO Tregye Hotel
14 August	UK: CULDROSE NCO's Mess, RAF Culdrose
17 August	UK: TRURO City Hall
21 August	UK: TRURO Tregye, Carnon Downs Festival
6 October	UK: LONDON Imperial College
9 December	UK: EPSOM Swimming Baths
31 December	UK: TWICKENHAM Rugby Club

1972

28 January	UK: BEDFORD College
10 March	UK: LONDON King's College Hospital Medical School
24 March	UK: LONDON Forest Hill Hospital
6 November	UK: LONDON Pheasantry Club
20 December	UK: LONDON Marquee Club

1973

9 April	UK: LONDON Marquee Club
13 July	UK: BASINGSTOKE Queen Mary College

Brian live on stage at the Rainbow, 31 March 1974 (© Jill Furmanovsky)

Queen in 1975 (Getty Images)

13 September	UK: LONDON Golders Green Hippodrome	4 March	UK: PAIGNTON Festival Hall
13 October	GERMANY: FRANKFURT Bagodesberg	8 March	UK: SUNDERLAND Locarno
14 October	LUXEMBOURG: Le Blow Up	9 March	UK: CAMBRIDGE Corn Exchange
20 October	UK: LONDON Paris Theatre	10 March	UK: CROYDON Greyhound
26 October	UK: LONDON Imperial College	12 March	UK: DAGENHAM Roundhouse
2 November	UK: LONDON Imperial College	14 March	UK: CHELTENHAM Town Hall
12 November	UK: LEEDS Town Hall	15 March	UK: GLASGOW University
13 November	UK: BLACKBURN St George's	16 March	UK: STIRLING University
15 November	UK: WORCESTER Gaumont	19 March	UK: CLEETHORPES Winter Gardens
16 November	UK: LANCASTER University	20 March	UK: MANCHESTER University
17 November	UK: LIVERPOOL Stadium	22 March	UK: CANVEY ISLAND Civic Centre
18 November	UK: HANLEY Victoria Hall	23 March	UK: CROMER Links Pavilion
19 November	UK: WOLVERHAMPTON Civic	24 March	UK: COLCHESTER Woods Leisure Centre
20 November	UK: OXFORD New Theatre		
21 November	UK: PRESTON Guildhall	26 March	UK: ISLE OF MAN Douglas Palace Lido
22 November	UK: NEWCASTLE City Hall		
23 November	UK: GLASGOW Apollo	28 March	UK: ABERYSTWYTH University
25 November	UK: EDINBURGH Caley Cinema	29 March	UK: PENZANCE The Gardens
26 November	UK: MANCHESTER Opera House	30 March	UK: TAUNTON Century Ballroom
27 November	UK: BIRMINGHAM Town Hall	31 March	UK: LONDON Rainbow Theatre
28 November	UK: SWANSEA Brangwyn Hall	2 April	UK: BIRMINGHAM Barbarellas
29 November	UK: BRISTOL Colston Hall	16 April	USA: DENVER Regis College
30 November	UK: BOURNEMOUTH Winter Gardens	17 April	USA: KANSAS CITY Memorial Hall
1 December	UK: SOUTHEND Kursaal	18 April	USA: ST LOUIS Keil Auditorium
2 December	UK: CHATHAM Central	19 April	USA: OKLAHOMA CITY Fairgrounds Appliance Building
6 December	UK: CHELTENHAM College		
7 December	UK: LONDON Shaftesbury Hall	20 April	USA: MEMPHIS Mid South Coliseum
8 December	UK: LIVERPOOL University	21 April	USA: NEW ORLEANS St Bernard Civic
14 December	UK: LONDON Hammersmith Odeon (two shows)	26 April	USA: BOSTON Orpheum Theater
		27 April	USA: PROVIDENCE Palace Theater
15 December	UK: LEICESTER University	28 April	USA: PORTLAND Exposition Hall
21 December	UK: TAUNTON County Hall	1 May	USA: HARRISBURG Farm Arena
22 December	UK: PETERBOROUGH Town Hall	2 May	USA: AILENTOWN Agricultural Hall
28 December	UK: LIVERPOOL Top Rank	3 May	USA: WILKES BARRE Kings College
		4 May	USA: WATERBURY Palace Theater

1974

		7 May	USA: NEW YORK Uris Theater
		8 May	USA: NEW YORK Uris Theater
		9 May	USA: NEW YORK Uris Theater
		10 May	USA: NEW YORK Uris Theater
		11 May	USA: NEW YORK Uris Theater
2 February	AUSTRALIA: MELBOURNE Sunbury Music Festival	12 May	USA: NEW YORK Uris Theater
		30 October	UK: MANCHESTER Palace Theatre
1 March	UK: BLACKPOOL Winter Gardens	31 October	UK: HANLEY Victoria Hall
2 March	UK: AYLESBURY Friars	1 November	UK: LIVERPOOL Empire
3 March	UK: PLYMOUTH Guildhall	2 November	UK: LEEDS University

3 November	UK: COVENTRY Theatre	16 February	USA: NEW YORK Avery Fisher Hall (two shows)
5 November	UK: SHEFFIELD City Hall	17 February	USA: TRENTON War Memorial
6 November	UK: BRADFORD St George's Hall	19 February	USA: LEWISTON Armory
7 November	UK: NEWCASTLE City Hall	21 February	USA: PASSAIC Capitol Theater
8 November	UK: GLASGOW Apollo Theatre	22 February	USA: HARRISBURG Farm Arena
9 November	UK: LANCASTER University	23 February	USA: PHILADELPHIA Erlinger Theater (two shows)
10 November	UK: PRESTON Guildhall	24 February	USA: WASHINGTON Kennedy Center
12 November	UK: BRISTOL Colston Hall	5 March	USA: LA CROSSE Mary E Sawyer Auditorium
13 November	UK: BOURNEMOUTH Winter Gardens	6 March	USA: MADISON
14 November	UK: SOUTHAMPTON Gaumont	7 March	USA: MILWAUKEE Uptown Ballroom
15 November	UK: SWANSEA Brangwyn Hall	8 March	USA: CHICAGO Aragon Ballroom
16 November	UK: BIRMINGHAM Town Hall	9 March	USA: ST LOUIS Keil Auditorium
18 November	UK: OXFORD New Theatre	10 March	USA: FORT WAYNE Coliseum
19 November	UK: LONDON Rainbow	12 March	USA: ATLANTA Municipal Auditorium
20 November	UK: LONDON Rainbow	13 March	USA: CHARLESTOWN Civic Auditorium
23 November	SWEDEN: GOTHENBERG	15 March	USA: MIAMI Marina
25 November	FINLAND: HELSINKI Helsingi Kulttuuritalo	18 March	USA: NEW ORLEANS St Bernard Civic Auditorium
1 December	BELGIUM: BRUSSELLS 140 Theatre	20 March	USA: SAN ANTONIO Municipal Hall
2 December	GERMANY: MUNICH	23 March	USA: DALLAS McFarlin Auditorium
4 December	GERMANY: FRANKFURT	25 March	USA: TULSA Municipal Theater
5 December	GERMANY: HAMBURG	29 March	USA: LOS ANGELES Santa Monica Civic Auditorium (two shows)
6 December	GERMANY: COLOGNE	30 March	USA: SAN FRANCISCO Winterland
7 December	GERMANY: SINGEN	2 April	CANADA: EDMONTON Kindmens Fieldhouse
8 December	HOLLAND: THE HAGUE Congress Gebouw	3 April	CANADA: CALGARY
10 December	SPAIN: BARCELONA	6 April	USA: SEATTLE
		19 April	JAPAN: TOKYO Budokan

1975

5 February	USA: COLUMBUS Agora	22 April	JAPAN: NAGOYA Aichi Taiikukan
7 February	USA: DAYTON Palace Theater	23 April	JAPAN: KOBE Nokusai Taikan
8 February	USA: CLEVELAND Music Hall (two shows)	25 April	JAPAN: FUKUOKA Kyden Taikukan
9 February	USA: SOUTH BEND Morris Civic Auditorium	28 April	JAPAN: OKAYAMA Taikukan
10 February	USA: DETROIT Ford Auditorium	29 April	JAPAN: SHIZUOKA Yamaha Tsumagoi Hall
11 February	USA: TOLEDO Student Union Auditorium	30 April	JAPAN: YOKOHAMA Bunkan Taiikukan
14 February	USA: WATERBURY Palace Theater	1 May	JAPAN: TOKYO Budokan
15 February	USA: BOSTON Orpheum Theater (two shows)	14 November	UK: LIVERPOOL Empire
		15 November	UK: LIVERPOOL Empire
		16 November	UK: COVENTRY Theatre
		17 November	UK: BRISTOL Colston Hall

18 November	UK: BRISTOL Colston Hall
19 November	UK: CARDIFF Capitol
21 November	UK: TAUNTON Odeon
23 November	UK: BOURNEMOUTH Winter Gardens
24 November	UK: SOUTHAMPTON Gaumont
26 November	UK: MANCHESTER Free Trade Hall (two Shows)
29 November	UK: LONDON Hammersmith Odeon
30 November	UK: LONDON Hammersmith Odeon
1 December	UK: LONDON Hammersmith Odeon
2 December	UK: LONDON Hammersmith Odeon
7 December	UK: WOLVERHAMPTON Civic Hall
8 December	UK: PRESTON Guildhall
9 December	UK: BIRMINGHAM Odeon
10 December	UK: BIRMINGHAM Odeon
11 December	UK: NEWCASTLE City Hall
13 December	UK: DUNDEE Caird Hall
14 December	UK: ABERDEEN Capitol
15 December	UK: GLASGOW Apollo
16 December	UK: GLASGOW Apollo
24 December	UK: LONDON Hammersmith Odeon

1976

27 January	USA: WATERBURY Palace Theatre
29 January	USA: BOSTON Music Hall
30 January	USA: BOSTON Music Hall
31 January	USA: PHILADELPHIA Tower Theater
1 February	USA: PHILADELPHIA Tower Theater
2 February	USA: PHILADELPHIA Tower Theater
5 February	USA: NEW YORK Beacon Theater
6 February	USA: NEW YORK Beacon Theater
7 February	USA: NEW YORK Beacon Theater
8 February	USA: NEW YORK Beacon Theater
11 February	USA: DETROIT Masonic Temple
12 February	USA: DETROIT Masonic Temple
13 February	USA: CINCINNATI Riverfront Coliseum
14 February	USA: CLEVELAND Public Hall
15 February	USA: TOLEDO Sports Arena
18 February	USA: SAGINAW Civic Theater
19 February	USA: COLUMBUS Veterans Memorial Auditorium
20 February	USA: PITTSBURG Syrian Mosque

22 February	USA: CHICAGO Auditorium Theater
23 February	USA: CHICAGO Auditorium Theater
26 February	USA: ST LOUIS Keil Auditorium
27 February	USA: INDIANAPOLIS Convention Center
28 February	USA: MADISON Dane County Coliseum
29 February	USA: FORT WAYNE Coliseum
1 March	USA: MILWAUKEE Auditorium
3 March	USA: MINNEAPOLIS St Paul's Auditorium
7 March	USA: BERKELEY Berkeley Community
9 March	USA: LOS ANGELES Santa Monica Civic Auditorium (two shows)
10 March	USA: LOS ANGELES Santa Monica Civic Auditorium
11 March	USA: LOS ANGELES Santa Monica Civic Auditorium
12 March	USA: LOS ANGELES Santa Monica Civic Auditorium
13 March	USA: SAN DIEGO Sports Arena
22 March	JAPAN: TOKYO Budokan
23 March	JAPAN: NAGOYA Aichi Ken Gymnasium
24 March	JAPAN: HAMEJI Kosei Kaikan
26 March	JAPAN: FUKUOKA Kyden Gymnasium (two shows)
29 March	JAPAN: OSAKA Kosei Nenkin Kaikan (two shows)
31 March	JAPAN: TOYKO Budokan
1 April	JAPAN: TOYKO Budokan
2 April	JAPAN: SENDAI Miyagi-Ken Sports Centre
4 April	JAPAN: TOKYO Nichidai Kodo
11 April	AUSTRALIA: PERTH Entertainments Centre
14 April	AUSTRALIA: ADELAIDE Apollo Stadium
15 April	AUSTRALIA: ADELAIDE Apollo Stadium
17 April	AUSTRALIA: SYDNEY Horden Pavilion
18 April	AUSTRALIA: SYDNEY Horden Pavilion
19 April	AUSTRALIA: MELBOURNE Festival Hall
20 April	AUSTRALIA: MELBOURNE Festival Hall
22 April	AUSTRALIA: BRISBANE Festival Hall

1 September	UK: EDINBURGH Playhouse Theatre	25 January	CANADA: OTTAWA Central Canadian Exhibition
2 September	UK: EDINBURGH Playhouse Theatre	26 January	CANADA: MONTREAL Forum
10 September	UK: CARDIFF Castle	28 January	USA: CHICAGO Stadium
18 September	UK: LONDON Hyde Park	30 January	USA: TOLEDO St John's Arena
		1 February	CANADA: TORONTO Maple Leaf Gardens

1977

		3 February	USA: SPRINGFIELD Civic Center
13 January	USA: MILWAUKEE Auditorium	4 February	USA: MARYLAND College Park, University of Maryland
14 January	USA: MADISON Dance County Coliseum	5 February	USA: NEW YORK Madison Square Garden
15 January	USA: COLUMBUS Gardens	6 February	USA: NASSAU Coliseum
16 January	USA: INDIANAPOLIS Convention Center	8 February	USA: SYRACUSE War Memorial Auditorium
18 January	USA: DETROIT Cobo Hall	9 February	USA: BOSTON Gardens
20 January	USA: SAGINAW Civic Center	10 February	USA: PROVIDENCE Civic Center
21 January	USA: LOUISVILLE Elliot Hall of Music	11 February	USA: PHILADELPHIA Civic Center
22 January	USA: KALAMAZOO Wings Stadium	19 February	USA: MIAMI Sportatorium
23 January	USA: CLEVELAND Richfield Coliseum	20 February	USA: LAKELAND Civic Center

Queen accepting one of their many awards (Duncan Raban/All-Action Pictures)

21 February	USA: ATLANTA Fox Theater
22 February	USA: BIRMINGHAM Auditorium
24 February	USA: ST LOUIS Keil Auditorium
25 February	USA: NORMAN Lloyd Noble Center
26 February	USA: DALLAS Moody Coliseum
27 February	USA: HOUSTON Sam Houston
1 March	USA: PHOENIX Coliseum
3 March	USA: LOS ANGELES Forum
4 March	USA: LOS ANGELES Forum
5 March	USA: SAN DIEGO Sports Arena
6 March	USA: SAN FRANCISCO Winterland
11 March	CANADA: VANCOUVER PNE Coliseum
12 March	USA: PORTLAND Paramount
13 March	USA: SEATTLE Arena
16 March	CANADA: CALGARY Jubilee Auditorium
17 March	CANADA: CALGARY Jubilee Auditorium
18 March	CANADA: EDMONTON Northlands Arena
8 May	SWEDEN: STOCKHOLM Ice Stadium
10 May	SWEDEN: GOTHENBERG Scandinavium
12 May	DENMARK: COPENHAGEN Broendby Hall
13 May	GERMANY: HAMBURG Congresscentrum
14 May	GERMANY: FRANKFURT Jahrunderhalle
16 May	GERMANY: DUSSELDORF Philipshalle
17 May	HOLLAND: ROTTERDAM Ahoy Hall
19 May	SWITZERLAND: BASLE Sporthalle
23 May	UK: BRISTOL Hippodrome
24 May	UK: BRISTOL Hippodrome
26 May	UK: SOUTHAMPTON Gaumont
27 May	UK: SOUTHAMPTON Gaumont
29 May	UK: STAFFORD Bingley Hall
30 May	UK: GLASGOW Apollo
31 May	UK: GLASGOW Apollo
2 June	UK: LIVERPOOL Empire Theatre
3 June	UK: LIVERPOOL Empire Theatre
6 June	UK: LONDON Earls Court
7 June	UK: LONDON Earls Court
6 October	UK: LONDON New London Theatre Centre

11 November	USA: PORTLAND Cumberland County Civic Center
12 November	USA: BOSTON Gardens
13 November	USA: SPRINGFIELD Civic Center
15 November	USA: PROVIDENCE Civic Center
16 November	USA: NEW HAVEN Memorial Coliseum
18 November	USA: DETROIT Cobo Hall
19 November	USA: DETROIT Cobo Hall
21 November	CANADA: TORONTO Maple Leaf Garden
23 November	USA: PHILADELPHIA The Spectrum
24 November	USA: PHILADELPHIA The Spectrum
25 November	USA: NORFOLK Scope Arena
27 November	USA: CLEVELAND Richfield Coliseum
29 November	USA: WASHINGTON DC Capitol Theater
1 December	USA: NEW YORK Madison Square Garden
2 December	USA: NEW YORK Madison Square Garden
4 December	USA: DAYTON University Arena
5 December	USA: CHICAGO Stadium
8 December	USA: ATLANTA The Omni
10 December	USA: FORT WORTH Tarrant County Convention Center
11 December	USA: HOUSTON The Summit
15 December	USA: LAS VEGAS Aladdin Center
16 December	USA: SAN DIEGO Sports Arena
17 December	USA: OAKLAND County Coliseum
20 December	USA: LONG BEACH Long Beach Arena
21 December	USA: LONG BEACH Long Beach Arena
22 December	USA: LOS ANGELES Forum

1978

12 April	SWEDEN: STOCKHOLM Ice Stadium
13 April	DENMARK: COPENHAGEN Falkoner Theatre
14 April	GERMANY: HAMBURG Ernst Merckhalle
16 April	BELGIUM: BRUSSELS Forest Nationale

17 April	BELGIUM: BRUSSELS Forest Nationale	4 November	USA: LAKELAND Civic Center
19 April	HOLLAND: ROTTERDAM Ahoy Hall	6 November	USA: WASHINGTON DC Capitol Center
20 April	HOLLAND: ROTTERDAM Ahoy Hall	7 November	USA: NEW HAVEN Coliseum
21 April	BELGIUM: BRUSSELS Forest Nationale	9 November	USA: DETROIT Cobo Arena
23 April	FRANCE: PARIS Pavilion	10 November	USA: DETROIT Cobo Arena
24 April	FRANCE: PARIS Pavilion	11 November	USA: KALAMAZOO Wings Stadium
26 April	GERMANY: DORTMUND Westfallenhalle	13 November	USA: BOSTON Gardens
28 April	GERMANY: BERLIN Deutschlandhalle	14 November	USA: PROVIDENCE Rhode Island Civic Center
30 April	SWITZERLAND: ZURICH Hallenstadion	16 November	USA: NEW YORK Madison Square Garden
2 May	AUSTRIA: VIENNA Stadhalle		
3 May	GERMANY: MUNICH Olympianhalle	17 November	USA: NEW YORK Madison Square Garden
6 May	UK: STAFFORD Bingley Hall	19 November	USA: NASSAU Coliseum
7 May	UK: STAFFORD Bingley Hall	20 November	USA: PHILADELPHIA Spectrum
11 May	UK: LONDON Empire Pool	22 November	USA: NASHVILLE Auditorium
12 May	UK: LONDON Empire Pool	23 November	USA: ST LOUIS Checkerdome
13 May	UK: LONDON Empire Pool	25 November	USA: CLEVELAND Richfield Coliseum
28 October	USA: DALLAS Convention Center	26 November	USA: CINCINNATI Riverfront Coliseum
29 October	USA: MEMPHIS Mid South Coliseum	28 November	USA: BUFFALO War Memorial Auditorium
31 October	USA: NEW ORLEANS Civic Auditorium		
3 November	USA: MIAMI Sportorium		

Queen live on stage in Rotterdam during their 'News of the World' concert tour 1977-8
(Fin Costello/Redferns)

30 November	CANADA: OTTAWA Central Canadian Exhibition Centre
1 December	CANADA: MONTREAL Forum
3 December	CANADA: TORONTO Maple Leaf Garden
4 December	CANADA: TORONTO Maple Leaf Garden
6 December	USA: MADISON Dane County Coliseum
7 December	USA: CHICAGO Stadium
8 December	USA: KANSAS CITY Kemper Arena
12 December	USA: SEATTLE Coliseum
13 December	USA: PORTLAND Coliseum
14 December	CANADA: VANCOUVER PNE Coliseum
16 December	USA: OAKLAND Coliseum
18 December	USA: LOS ANGELES Forum
19 December	USA: LOS ANGELES Forum
20 December	USA: LOS ANGELES Forum

1979

17 January	GERMANY: HAMBURG Ernst Merckhalle
18 January	GERMANY: KIEL Ostee Hall
20 January	GERMANY: BREMMEN Stadhalle
21 January	GERMANY: DORTMUND Westfallenhalle
23 January	GERMANY: HANNOVER Messesportspalace
24 January	GERMANY: BERLIN Deutschlandhalle
26 January	BELGIUM: BRUSSELS Forest Nationale
27 January	BELGIUM: BRUSSELS Forest Nationale
29 January	HOLLAND: ROTTERDAM Ahoy Hall
30 January	HOLLAND: ROTTERDAM Ahoy Hall
1 February	GERMANY: COLOGNE Sportshalle
2 February	GERMANY: FRANKFURT Festhalle
4 February	SWITZERLAND: ZURICH Hallenstadium
6 February	YUGOSLAVIA: ZAGREB Dom Sportova
7 February	YUGOSLAVIA: LJUBLJANA Tivoli Halle
10 February	GERMANY: MUNICH Basketball Halle
11 February	GERMANY: MUNICH Basketball Halle

13 February	GERMANY: STUTTGART Sporthalle Boeblingen
15 February	GERMANY: SAARBRUKEN Saalandhalle
17 February	FRANCE: LYONS Palaise De Sport
19 February	SPAIN: BARCELONA Palacio De Deportef
20 February	SPAIN: BARCELONA Palacio De Deportef
21 February	SPAIN: BARCELONA Palacio De Deportef
23 February	SPAIN: MADRID Pabellon De Real Madrid
25 February	FRANCE: POITIERS Les Arenas
27 February	FRANCE: PARIS Pavilion De Paris
28 February	FRANCE: PARIS Pavilion De Paris
1 March	FRANCE: PARIS Pavilion De Paris
13 April	JAPAN: TOKYO Budokan
14 April	JAPAN: TOKYO Budokan
19 April	JAPAN: OSAKA Festival Hall
20 April	JAPAN: OSAKA Festival Hall
21 April	JAPAN: KANAZAWA Practica Ethics Comm. Hall
23 April	JAPAN: TOKYO Budokan
24 April	JAPAN: TOYKO Budokan
25 April	JAPAN: TOYKO Budokan
27 April	JAPAN: KOBE Central International Display
28 April	JAPAN: NAGOYA International Display
30 April	JAPAN: FUKUOKA Kyuden Athletic Association
1 May	JAPAN: FUKUOKA Kyuden Athletic Association
2 May	JAPAN: YAMAGUCHI Prefectural Athletic Association
5 May	JAPAN: SAPPORO Makomani Ice Arena
6 May	JAPAN: SAPPORO Makomani Ice Arena
18 August	GERMANY: SAARBRUKEN Ludwigsparkstadion
22 November	EIRE: DUBLIN RDS Simmons Hall
24 November	UK: BIRMINGHAM National Exhibition Centre
26 November	UK: MANCHESTER Apollo Theatre
27 November	UK: MANCHESTER Apollo Theatre
30 November	UK: GLASGOW Apollo Theatre

1 December	UK: GLASGOW Apollo Theatre	24 August	USA: PITTSBURG Civic Center
3 December	UK: NEWCASTLE City Hall	26 August	USA: PROVIDENCE Civic Center
4 December	UK: NEWCASTLE City Hall	27 August	USA: PORTLAND Spectrum
6 December	UK: LIVERPOOL Empire Theatre	29 August	CANADA: MONTREAL Forum
7 December	UK: LIVERPOOL Empire Theatre	30 August	CANADA: TORONTO CNE
9 December	UK: BRISTOL Hippodrome	31 August	USA: ROCHESTER Convention Center
10 December	UK: BRIGHTON Centre	10 September	USA: MILWAUKEE Mecca
11 December	UK: BRIGHTON Centre	11 September	USA: INDIANAPOLIS Market Square Arena
13 December	UK: LONDON Lyceum Ballroom		
14 December	UK: LONDON Rainbow Theatre	13 September	USA: OMAHA Civic
17 December	UK: LONDON Purley Tiffany's	14 September	USA: MINNEAPOLIS St Paul Civic
19 December	UK: LONDON Tottenham Mayfair	16 September	USA: KANSAS CITY Kemper Arena
20 December	UK: LONDON Lewisham Odeon	17 September	USA: ST LOUIS Checkerdrome
22 December	UK: LONDON Alexandra Palace	19 September	USA: CHICAGO Horizon
26 December	UK: LONDON Hammersmith Odeon	20 September	USA: DETROIT Joe Louis Arena
		21 September	USA: CLEVELAND Coliseum
		23 September	USA: NEW HAVEN Veterans Memorial Coliseum

1980

		24 September	USA: SYRACUSE War Memorial
		26 September	USA: BOSTON Boston Gardens
30 June	CANADA: VANCOUVER PNE Coliseum	28 September	USA: NEW YORK Madison Square Garden
1 July	USA: SEATTLE Coliseum		
2 July	USA: PORTLAND Coliseum	29 September	USA: NEW YORK Madison Square Garden
5 July	USA: SAN DIEGO Sports Arena		
6 July	USA: PHOENIX Compton Terrace	30 September	USA: NEW YORK Madison Square Garden
8 July	USA: LOS ANGELES Forum		
9 July	USA: LOS ANGELES Forum	1 October	USA: NEW YORK Madison Square Garden
11 July	USA: LOS ANGELES Forum		
12 July	USA: LOS ANGELES Forum	23 November	SWITZERLAND: ZURICH Hallenstadion
13 July	USA: OAKLAND Coliseum	25 November	FRANCE: PARIS Le Bourget La Retonde
14 July	USA: OAKLAND Coliseum		
5 August	USA: MEMPHIS Mid South Coliseum	26 November	GERMANY: COLOGNE Sportshalle
6 August	USA: BATON ROUGE Riverside Centroplex	27 November	HOLLAND: LEIDEN Groenoordhal
		29 November	GERMANY: ESSEN Grudhalle
8 August	USA: OKLAHOMA City Myriad	30 November	GERMANY: BERLIN Deutchlandhalle
9 August	USA: DALLAS Reunion	1 December	GERMANY: BREMEN Stadhalle
10 August	USA: HOUSTON Summit	5 December	UK: BIRMINGHAM NEC
12 August	USA: ATLANTA The Omni	6 December	UK: BIRMINGHAM NEC
13 August	USA: CHARLOTTE Coliseum	8 December	UK: LONDON Wembley Arena
14 August	USA: GREENSBORO Coliseum	9 December	UK: LONDON Wembley Arena
16 August	USA: CHARLESTON Civic Center	10 December	UK: LONDON Wembley Arena
17 August	USA: CINCINNATI River Front Coliseum	12 December	BELGIUM: BRUSSELS Forest Nationale
20 August	USA: HARTFORD Civic Center		
22 August	USA: PHILADELPHIA Spectrum	13 December	BELGIUM: BRUSSELS Forest Nationale
23 August	USA: BALTIMORE Civic Center		

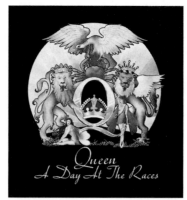

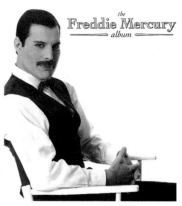

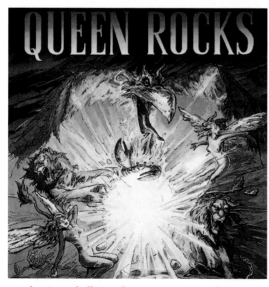

A selection of album sleeves (courtesy of Queen Productions)

14 December	GERMANY: FRANKFURT Festhalle
16 December	GERMANY: STRASBOURG Hall Rheus
18 December	GERMANY: MUNICH Olympiahalle

1981

12 February	JAPAN: TOKYO Budokan
13 February	JAPAN: TOKYO Budokan
16 February	JAPAN: TOKYO Budokan
17 February	JAPAN: TOKYO Budokan
18 February	JAPAN: TOKYO Budokan
28 February	ARGENTINA: BUENOS AIRES Velez Sarfield
1 March	ARGENTINA: BUENOS AIRES Velez Sarfield
4 March	ARGENTINA: MAR DEL PLATA Estadio Municipal
6 March	ARGENTINA: ROSARIO Alletico Rosario Central
8 March	ARGENTINA: BUENOS AIRES Velez Sarfield
20 March	BRAZIL: SAO PAULO Morumbi Stadium
21 March	BRAZIL: SAO PAULO Morumbi Stadium
25 September	VENEZUELA: CARACAS Poliedro De Caracas
26 September	VENEZUELA: CARACUS Poliedro De Caracas
27 September	VENEZUELA: CARACUS Poliedro De Caracas
9 October	MEXICO: MONTERREY Estadion Univeritano
16 October	MEXICO: PUEBLA Estadion Cuahtermoc
17 October	MEXICO: PUEBLA Estadion Cuahtermoc
24 November	CANADA: MONTREAL Forum
25 November	CANADA: MONTREAL Forum

1982

9 April	SWEDEN: GOTHENBURG Scandinavian
10 April	SWEDEN: STOCKHOLM Isstadion
12 April	NORWAY: OSLO Drammenshallen
16 April	SWITZERLAND: ZURICH Hallenstadion
17 April	SWITZERLAND: ZURICH Hallenstadion
19 April	FRANCE: PARIS Palais De Sport
20 April	FRANCE: LYON Palais De Sport
22 April	BELGIUM: BRUSSELS Forest Nationale
23 April	BELGIUM: BRUSSELS Forest Nationale
24 April	HOLLAND: LEIDEN Groenoordhalle
25 April	HOLLAND: LEIDEN Groenoordhalle
28 April	GERMANY: FRANKFURT Festhalle
29 April	GERMANY: FRANKFURT Festhalle
1 May	GERMANY: DORTMUND Westfallenhalle
3 May	FRANCE: PARIS Palais De Sport
5 May	GERMANY: HANNOVER Eilenriedehalle
6 May	GERMANY: COLOGNE Sporthalle
7 May	GERMANY: COLOGNE Sporthalle
9 May	GERMANY: WURZBURG Carl-Diem Halle
10 May	GERMANY: STUTTGART Sporthalle
12 May	AUSTRIA: VIENNA Stadhalle
13 May	AUSTRIA: VIENNA Stadhalle
15 May	GERMANY: BERLIN Waldbuehne
16 May	GERMANY: HAMBURG Ersnt-Mercke Halle
18 May	GERMANY: KASSEL Eisspdorthalle
21 May	GERMANY: MUNICH Olympiahalle
29 May	UK: LEEDS Elland Road Football Stadium
1 June	UK: EDINBURGH Ingliston Showground
2 June	UK: EDINBURGH Ingliston Showground
5 June	UK: MILTON KEYNES Bowl
21 July	CANADA: MONTREAL Forum
23 July	USA: BOSTON Gardens
24 July	USA: PHILADELPHIA Spectrum
25 July	USA: WASHINGTON DC Capitol Center

27 July	USA: NEW YORK Madison Square Garden
28 July	USA: NEW YORK Madison Square Garden
31 July	USA: CLEVELAND Richfield Coliseum
2 August	CANADA: TORONTO Maple Leaf Gardens
3 August	CANADA: TORONTO Maple Leaf Gardens
5 August	USA: INDIANAPOLIS Market Square Arena
6 August	USA: DETROIT Joe Louis Arena
7 August	USA: CINCINATTI Riverfront Coliseum
9 August	USA: MEADOWLANDS Brendon Burn Coliseum
10 August	USA: NEW HAVEN Coliseum
13 August	USA: CHICAGO Poplar Creek
14 August	USA: CHICAGO Poplar Creek
15 August	USA: ST PAUL Civic Centre Arena
19 August	USA: BILOXI Civic Center
20 August	USA: HOUSTON Summit
21 August	USA: DALLAS Reunion
24 August	USA: ATLANTA Omni
25 August	USA: MEMPHIS Mid South Coliseum
27 August	USA: OKLAHOMA City Myriad
28 August	USA: KANSAS CITY Kemper Arena
30 August	USA: DENVER McNichols Arena
2 September	USA: PORTLAND Coliseum
3 September	USA: SEATTLE Coliseum
4 September	CANADA: VANCOUVER PNE Coliseum
7 September	USA: OAKLAND Coliseum
10 September	USA: TEMPE ASU Arena
11 September	USA: IRVINE Irvine Meadows
12 September	USA: IRVINE Irvine Meadows
14 September	USA: LOS ANGELES Forum
15 September	USA: LOS ANGELES Forum
19 October	JAPAN: FUKUOKA Kyuden Auditorium
20 October	JAPAN: FUKUOKA Kyuden Auditorium
24 October	JAPAN: OSAKA Hankyu Nishinomiyakyujo
26 October	JAPAN: NAGOYA Kosusai Tenjijo
29 October	JAPAN: SAPPORO Hokkaidoritso Sangyo Kyoshinakaijo
3 November	JAPAN: TOKYO Seibu Lions Stadium

1984

24 August	BELGIUM: BRUSSELS Forest Nationale
28 August	EIRE: DUBLIN RDS Simmons Hall
29 August	EIRE: DUBLIN RDS Simmons Hall
31 August	UK: BIRMINGHAM NEC
1 September	UK: BIRMINGHAM NEC
2 September	UK: BIRMINGHAM NEC
4 September	UK: LONDON Wembley Arena
5 Septembe	UK: LONDON Wembley Arena
7 September	UK: LONDON Wembley Arena
8 September	UK: LONDON Wembley Arena
12 September	GERMANY: DORTMUND Westallenhalle
14 September	ITALY: MILAN Sportspalace
15 September	ITALY: MILAN Sportspalace
16 September	GERMANY: MUNICH Olympic Hall
18 September	FRANCE: PARIS Omnisports
20 September	HOLLAND: LEIDEN Groenoordhalle
21 September	BELGIUM: BRUSSELS Forest Nationale
22 September	GERMANY: HANNOVER Europhalle
24 September	GERMANY: BERLIN Deutschlandhalle
26 September	GERMANY: FRANKFURT Festhalle
27 September	GERMANY: STUTTGART Schleyerhalle
29 September	AUSTRIA: VIENNA Stadhalle
30 September	AUSTRIA: VIENNA Stadhalle
5 October	BOPHUTHATSWANA: SUN CITY Super Bowl
10 October	BOPHUTHATSWANA: SUN CITY Super Bowl
13 October	BOPHUTHATSWANA: SUN CITY Super Bowl
14 October	BOPHUTHATSWANA: SUN CITY Super Bowl
18 October	BOPHUTHATSWANA: SUN CITY Super Bowl
19 October	BOPHUTHATSWANA: SUN CITY Super Bowl
20 October	BOPHUTHATSWANA: SUN CITY Super Bowl

1985

12 January	BRAZIL: RIO DE JANEIRO Rock In Rio Festival
19 January	BRAZIL: RIO DE JANEIRO Rock In Rio Festival
13 April	NEW ZEALAND: AUCKLAND Mount Smart Stadium
16 April	AUSTRALIA: MELBOURNE Sports & Entertainments Centre
17 April	AUSTRALIA: MELBOURNE Sports & Entertainments Centre
19 April	AUSTRALIA: MELBOURNE Sports & Entertainments Centre
20 April	AUSTRALIA: MELBOURNE Sports & Entertainments Centre
25 April	AUSTRALIA: SYDNEY Entertainments Centre
26 April	AUSTRALIA: SYDNEY Entertainments Centre
28 April	AUSTRALIA: SYDNEY Entertainments Centre
29 April	AUSTRALIA: SYDNEY Entertainments Centre
7 May	JAPAN: TOKYO Budokan
9 May	JAPAN: TOKYO Budokan
10 May	JAPAN: TOKYO Yogishi Swimming Pool
11 May	JAPAN: TOKYO Yogishi Swimming Pool
13 May	JAPAN: NAGOYA Aichi Auditorium
15 May	JAPAN: OSAKA Castle Hall
13 July	UK: LONDON Wembley Stadium (Live Aid)

1986

7 June	SWEDEN: STOCKHOLM Rasunda Fotbollstadion
11 June	HOLLAND: LEIDEN Groenoordhal
12 June	HOLLAND: LEIDEN Groenoordhal
14 June	FRANCE: PARIS Hippodrome de Vincennes
17 June	BELGIUM: BRUSSELS Forest Nationale
19 June	HOLLAND: LEIDEN Groenoordahal
21 June	GERMANY: MANNHEIM Maimarktgelande
26 June	GERMANY: BERLIN Waldbuehne
28 June	GERMANY: MUNICH Olympiahalle
29 June	GERMANY: MUNICH Olympiahalle
1 July	SWITZERLAND: ZURICH Hallenstadion
2 July	SWITZERLAND: ZURICH Hallenstadion
5 July	EIRE: DUBLIN Iane Castle
9 July	UK: NEWCASTLE St James' Park
11 July	UK: LONDON Wembley Stadium
12 July	UK: LONDON Wembley Stadium
16 July	UK: MANCHESTER Maine Road
19 July	GERMANY: COLOGNE Muengersdorfer Stadion
21 July	AUSTRIA: VIENNA Stadhalle
22 July	AUSTRIA: VIENNA Stadhalle
27 July	HUNGARY: BUDAPEST Nepstadion
30 July	FRANCE: FREJUS Amphitheatre
1 August	SPAIN: BARCELONA Monumental Plaza de Toros
3 August	SPAIN: MADRID Rayo Vallecano
5 August	SPAIN: MARBELLA Estadio Municipal
9 August	UK: STEVENAGE Knebworth Park (Queen's final performance)

Queen at a press launch for their 1982 album *Hot Space* (Ebet Robert/Redferns)

QUEEN TOUR NAMES

Throughout their career, many of the tours had a central theme or title, and below we have listed the titles along with the dates they apply to.

12 November - 14 December 1973
MOTT THE HOOPLE UK SUPPORT TOUR

1 March - 2 April 1974
QUEEN II UK TOUR

16 April - 12 May 1974
MOTT USA SPECIAL GUEST TOUR

30 October - 10 December 1974
SHEER HEART ATTACK UK/EUROPEAN TOUR

2 February - 6 April 1975
SHEER HEART ATTACK USA/CANADIAN TOUR

19 April - 1 May 1975
SHEER HEART ATTACK JAPANESE TOUR

14 November - 24 December 1975
A NIGHT AT THE OPERA UK TOUR

27 January - 13 March 1976
A NIGHT AT THE OPERA USA TOUR

22 March - 4 April 1976
A NIGHT AT THE OPERA JAPANESE TOUR

11 April - 22 April 1976
A NIGHT AT THE OPERA AUSTRALIAN TOUR

1 September - 18 September 1976
UK MINI TOUR

13 January - 18 March 1977
QUEEN LIZZY USA/CANADIAN TOUR

8 May - 7 June 1977
EUROPEAN SUMMER TOUR '77

11 November - 22 December 1977
NEWS OF THE WORLD USA/CANADIAN TOUR

12 April - 13 May 1978
NEWS OF THE WORLD EUROPEAN TOUR

28 October - 20 December 1978
JAZZ USA/CANADIAN TOUR

17 January - 1 March 1979
JAZZ EUROPEAN TOUR

13 April - 6 May 1979
JAZZ JAPANESE TOUR

22 November - 26 December 1979
THE CRAZY TOUR

30 June - 1 October 1980
THE GAME USA/CANADIAN TOUR

23 November - 18 December 1980
EUROPEAN GAME TOUR

12 February - 18 February 1981
JAPAN TOUR '81

28 February - 21 March 1981
SOUTH AMERICAN TOUR '81

25 September - 9 October 1981
GLUTTONS FOR PUNISHMENT TOUR

9 April - 5 June 1982
HOT SPACE EUROPEAN TOUR

21 July - 15 September 1982
HOT SPACE USA/CANADIAN TOUR

19 October - 3 November 1982
HOT SPACE JAPANESE TOUR

24 August - 20 October 1984
THE WORKS TOUR

13 April - 29 April 1985
NEW ZEALAND/AUSTRALIAN WORKS TOUR

7 May - 13 May 1985
JAPANESE WORKS TOUR

7 June - 9 August 1986
THE MAGIC TOUR

SOLO & MISCELLANEOUS CONCERTS

1987 – 1997

FREDDIE MERCURY

1987

1 October	SPAIN: IBIZA Ku Klub (with Montserrat Caballe)

1988

14 April	UK: LONDON Dominion Theatre: 'Give Time For AIDS' *Time* musical with Cliff Richard)
8 October	SPAIN: BARCELONA La Nit Festival (Freddie's final performance)

BRIAN MAY

1988

5 June	UK: LONDON Royal Albert Hall (Prince's Trust Concert, with John Deacon)

1991

19 October	SPAIN: SEVILLE Expo 92 Guitar Legends Concert

1992

1 November	ARGENTINA: BUENOS AIRES New York City Disco
3 November	CHILE: SANTIAGO Pista Atletica
5 November	URUGUAY: MONTEVIDEO Centenario Stadium
6 November	ARGENTINA: BUENOS AIRES Velez Sarsfield Stadium
9 November	BRAZIL: RIO DE JANEIRO Imperator Club

1993

23 February	USA: AUSTIN Erwin Center
25 February	USA: BIRMINGHAM Jefferson Civic Center
28 February	USA: ATLANTA Roxy Theater
2 March	USA: CLEVELAND The Agora
5 March	USA: BALTIMORE Hammerjacks
6 March	USA: NEW HAVEN New Haven Colisuem
8 March	USA: PORTLAND Cumberland Civic Center
9 March	USA: HARTFORD Civic Center
12 March	CANADA: HAMILTON Copps Coliseum
14 March	USA: NEW YORK Beacon Theater
16 March	USA: AUGUSTA Boston Garden
17 March	USA: BOSTON Boston Garden
20 March	USA: IOWA CITY Carver Hawkeye Arena
21 March	USA: FARGO Fargo Dome
27 March	CANADA: SASKATOON Saskatchewan Place
28 March	CANADA: EDMONTON Northlands Coliseum
30 March	CANADA: VANCOUVER BC Stadium
1 April	USA: PORTLAND Portland Coliseum
3 April	USA: SACRAMENTO Arco Arena
4 April	USA: RENO Lawlor Event Center
5 April	USA: LOS ANGELES *The Tonight Show*
6 April	USA: LOS ANGELES Palace Theater
22 May	ISRAEL: TEL AVIV Hayarkon Park
24 May	GREECE: ATHENS Olympic Stadium
26 May	TURKEY: ISTANBUL Inonu Stadium
29 May	GERMANY: COLOGNE Rock Am Ring
30 May	GERMANY: HANNOVER Gardsen Stadion
31 May	GERMANY: NUREMBERG Franke Stadion
2 June	FRANCE: PARIS Le Grand Rex Theatre
4 June	UK: EDINBURGH Playhouse
5 June	UK: WHITLEY BAY Ice Rink
6 June	UK: GLASGOW Barrowlands
8 June	UK: MANCHESTER Apollo
9 June	UK: SHEFFIELD City Hall
11 June	UK: CARDIFF Ice Rink
12 June	UK: BIRMINGHAM NEC
15 June	UK: LONDON Brixton Academy
16 June	UK: LONDON Hammersmith Odeon
19 June	UK: BOURNEMOUTH International Centre
21 June	HOLLAND: ROTTERDAM Ahoy Sport Paleis
22 June	GERMANY: KARLSRUHE Wildparkstadion
25 June	GERMANY: FRANKFURT Waldstadion
26 June	GERMANY: MUNICH Olympiastadion
27 June	HUNGARY: BUDAPEST Kis Stadion
29 June	ITALY: MODENA Stadio Bradioa
30 June	ITALY: MODENA Stadio Bradioa
2 July	ITALY: NAPLES Stadio Lamberti
5 July	SPAIN: BARCELONA Estadio Olympic
6 July	SPAIN: MADRID Estadio Vicente Calderon
8 July	FRANCE: NANCY Zenith-Carriere Soldly
9 July	FRANCE: LYON
11 July	BELGIUM: WERCHTER Stadium Site
13 July	FRANCE: PARIS Bercy
12 September	SWITZERLAND: WINTERTHURER Festival
4 October	CANADA: MONTREAL Metropolis
5 October	CANADA: TORONTO The Music Hall
7 October	USA: NEW HAVEN Palace Theater
8 October	USA: PROVIDENCE The Strand
10 October	USA: CHICAGO The Vic Theater
12 October	USA: DETROIT Royal Oak Theater
13 October	USA: MILWAUKEE Modjeska Theater
14 October	USA: MINNEAPOLIS World Theater
17 October	USA: DALLAS Majestic Theater
18 October	USA: HOUSTON Rockefellers West
4 November	JAPAN: TOKYO Kosei Nenkin Hall
5 November	JAPAN: TOKYO Kosei Nenkin Hall
7 November	JAPAN: HIROSHIMA Yubin Chokin Hall
8 November	JAPAN: OSAKA Kosei Nenkin Hall
10 November	JAPAN: SENDAI Denayoku Hall
11 November	JAPAN: KAWASAKI Kyoiku Bumka Kaikan
13 November	JAPAN: TOKYO BAY NHK Hall

Brian playing live at the Marquee Club, Wardour Street, London (Jim Jenkins)

20 November	GERMANY: MUNICH Terminal One
21 November	GERMANY: FRANKFURT Jahrhunderthalle
23 November	GERMANY: HAMBURG CCH1
24 November	GERMANY: HALLE Eissporthall
26 November	DENMARK: COPENHAGEN Tivoli Koncerthall (cancelled)
27 November	GERMANY: BERLIN Huxley's Neue Welt
29 November	FRANCE: PARIS Elysee Montmartre
30 November	GERMANY: DUSSELDORF Philipshalle
3 December	UK: LONDON Royal Albert Hall
4 December	UK: NOTTINGHAM Royal Centre
5 December	UK: BIRMINGHAM Aston Villa Centre
7 December	UK: BELFAST Ulster Hall
8 December	EIRE: DUBLIN Point
10 December	UK: LIVERPOOL Royal Court
11 December	UK: PLYMOUTH Pavilion
14 December	SPAIN: BARCELONA Zeleste
15 December	SPAIN: MADRID Aqualung
17 December	PORTUGAL: LISBON Cascais Pavilion
18 December	PORTUGAL: OPORTO Boavista

1994

26 June	UK: LONDON Wembley Arena ('Night of 100 Guitars')
17 December	UK: LONDON Shepherds Bush Empire (Fan Club Party)

The Brian May touring band were Brian on vocals and guitar; Cozy Powell on drums; Meil Murray on bass; Spike Edney on keyboards; Jamie Moses on guitar and vocals; Cathy Porter and Shelley Preston on backing vocals.

ROGER TAYLOR

1993

18 September	UK: MIDHURST Cowdray Park The Ruins Concert (with John Deacon)

1994

29 April	UK: LONDON Hammersmith Odeon (Mick Ronson Tribute Concert)
22 May	JAPAN: NARA *The Great Music Experience*
28 July	UK: GOSPORT Gosport Festival
15 September	UK: LONDON Shepherds Bush Empire
26 September	JAPAN: TOKYO Sun Plaza Hall
28 September	JAPAN: KAWASAKI Club Citta
29 September	JAPAN: OSAKA Kokusai Koryu Centre (cancelled due to typhoon)
30 September	JAPAN: NAGOYA Club Quattro
14 October	GERMANY: COLOGNE Presswerks
24 October	ITALY: MILAN
19 November	UK: LONDON Shepherds Bush Empire
20 November	UK: CAMBRIDGE Junction
22 November	UK: NOTTINGHAM Rock City
23 November	UK: NEWCASTLE Riverside
24 November	UK: LEEDS Irish Centre
26 November	UK: LIVERPOOL Royal Court
27 November	UK: SHEFFIELD Leadmill
29 November	UK: GLASGOW Garage
30 November	UK: BRISTOL Bierkeller
2 December	UK: TRURO City Hall
3 December	UK: MANCHESTER University Debating Hall
4 December	UK: WOLVERHAMPTON Civic Hall
8 December	FRANCE: PARIS

1 9 9 5

16 January	ITALY: MONFALCONE Hippodrome
17 January	ITALY: SCHIO Palazetto
18 January	ITALY: GENOVA Teatro Verdi
20 January	ITALY: CESNA Vidia
21 January	ITALY: FIRENZE Teatro Tenda
22 January	ITALY: ROME Palladium
24 January	MALTA: VALETTA Teatro Nazionale La Valetta
25 January	ITALY: PALERMO Teatro Metropolitan
26 January	ITALY: CATANIA Teatro Metropolitan

The Roger Taylor touring band were Roger on vocals, percussion and guitar; Jason Falloon on guitar and vocals; Stuart Bradley on bass; Joshua Macrae on drums; and Michel Crossley on keyboards.

THE CROSS

The Cross were Spike Edney (Keyboards), Josh Macrae (Drums), Clayton Moss (Guitar), Peter Noone (Bass), and Roger Taylor (Vocals).

1 9 8 7

6 November	UK: LONDON Thames Television Studios ('Meltdown')

1 9 8 8

19 February	UK: LEEDS University
20 February	UK: GLASGOW Queen Margaret Union
21 February	UK: LEICESTER Polytechnic
23 February	UK: SHEFFIELD Polytechnic
24 February	UK: NOTTINGHAM Rock City
26 February	UK: MANCHESTER University

27 February	UK: BRADFORD University
28 February	UK: NEWCASTLE Mayfair
1 March	UK: SOUTHAMPTON Mayfair
2 March	UK: CARDIFF University
4 March	UK: NORWICH University of East Anglia
5 March	UK: BIRMINGHAM Hummingbird
6 March	UK: LEEDS Polytechnic
7 March	UK: BRISTOL Studios
9 March	UK: GUILDFORD Civic Hall
10 March	UK: LONDON Town And Country Club
11 April	GERMANY: BREMEN Moderness
12 April	GERMANY: HAMBURG Markethalle
13 April	GERMANY: BERLIN Metropol
14 April	GERMANY: MUNICH Theaterfbrik
16 April	GERMANY: NUREMBERG E-werk-saal
17 April	GERMANY: FRANKFURT Music Hall
18 April	GERMANY: HANNOVER Capitol
19 April	GERMANY: STUGGART Club Music & Action
21 April	GERMANY: DUSSELDORF Capitol
22 April	GERMANY: MANNHEIM Tor 3
23 April	GERMANY: DORTMUND Westfallenhalle II
12 May	SWITZERLAND: MONTREUX Casino (Montreux Festival)
4 December	UK: LONDON Hammersmith Palais (Fan Club Party with Brian May and John Deacon guesting)

1 9 9 0

21 May	GERMANY: HANNOVER Capitol
22 May	GERMANY: BONN Biskuithalle
23 May	GERMANY: DORTMUND Tantastival Im Blickpunkt-Studio
24 May	GERMANY: GOETTINGEN Outpost
26 May	GERMANY: HAMBURG Docks
27 May	GERMANY: KIEL Max's Music Hall
28 May	GERMANY: BERLIN Metropol
29 May	HOLLAND: AMSTERDAM Milky Way
30 May	GERMANY: FRANKFURT Hugenottenhalle Neu Isenberg

1 June	SPAIN: IBIZA Ku Klub (Ibiza 92 Festival)
2 June	SPAIN: IBIZA Ku Klub (Ibiza 92 Festival)
3 June	GERMANY: ST WENDEL Open Air
4 June	GERMANY: NUREMBERG Serenadeenhof
5 June	GERMANY: TUTTLIMGEN Akntz
6 June	GERMANY: MANNHEIM Feuerwache
7 June	GERMANY: BIELEFELD PC69
8 June	GERMANY: STUGGART Theatrehaus
15 June	AUSTRIA: VIENNA Outdoor Festival
7 December	UK: LONDON Astoria (Fan Club Party – Brian May guesting)

1991

3 October	FINLAND: HELSINKI Tavastia
5 October	NORWAY: HULTSFRED Hagadal
7 October	SWEDEN: GOTHENBURG Konserthuset
9 October	GERMANY: HANNOVER Music Hall
10 October	GERMANY: HEREFORD Rock Heaven
11 October	GERMANY: HAMBURG Docks
12 October	GERMANY: BREMEN Astoria
13 October	GERMANY: BERLIN Tempodrom
14 October	GERMANY: HOF Freiheitshalle
15 October	GERMANY: MUNICH Circus Krone
16 October	GERMANY: MEMMINGEN Stadhalle
18 October	SWITZERLAND: ZURICH Volkshaus
19 October	GERMANY: APPENWEIHER Schwartzwaldhalle
20 October	GERMANY: WEIRTHEIM Mainauberhalle
21 October	GERMANY: OFFENBACH Stadhalle
22 October	GERMANY: DUSSELDORF Phillpshalle
23 October	GERMANY: EERLANGEN Stadhalle
25 October	GERMANY: DIETENHEIM Festhalle
26 October	GERMANY: ERNDTERBRUCK Sporthalle Birkelbach
27 October	GERMANY: LUDWIGSBURG Forum

1992

30 July	UK: GOSPORT Gosport Festival
21 December	UK: LONDON Marquee Club (Fan Club Party with Roger Daltry and Tim Staffel guesting)
22 December	UK: LONDON Marquee Club (Fan Club Party with Brian and Tim Staffel guesting)

1993

29 July	UK: GOSPORT Gosport Festival

1994

17 December	UK: LONDON Shepherds Bush Empire (Fan Club Party without Roger)

MISCELLANEOUS CONCERTS

1992

20 April	UK: LONDON Wembley Stadium (The Freddie Mercury Tribute Concert)

1997

17 January	FRANCE: PARIS National Theatre De Chailot (with Elton John)

ARTISTS/GROUPS WHO
HAVE PLAYED SUPPORT
TO QUEEN

AFTER THE FIRE
THE ALARM
AIRRACE
ANGEL CHILD
THE B52'S
BANGLES
BELOUIS SOME
BIG COUNTRY
THE BLASTERS
BOW WOW WOW
BULLITT
CATE BROTHERS
CHEAP TRICK
THE COMMODORES
CRAFT
DAKOTA
KIKI DEE
THE EXPLOITED
ANDY FAIRWEATHER-LOW
FOUNTAINHEAD
RORY GALLAGHER
GENERAL PUBLIC
THE GO GO'S
MOLLY HATCHET
HEAD EAST
HEART
STEVE HILLAGE
HUSTLER
INXS
JOAN JETT & THE BLACKHEARTS
KANSAS
ALVIN LEE & TEN YEARS AFTER
LUCIFER
MAHOGANY RUSH
MANFRED MANN'S EARTH BAND
MARILLION
FRANKIE MILLER'S FULL HOUSE
MR BIG
GARY MOORE

NUTZ
CHRIS REA
RED BARON
THE ROYAL DRAGON GUARDS
BOB SEGAR
BILLY SQUIER
SOLUTION
STARIGHT EDGE
STATUS QUO
SUPERCHARGE
THE TEARDROP EXPLODES
THIN LIZZY
TOMBSTONE
VOYAGER
YESTERDAY AND TODAY
Z'ZI LABOR

ORIGINAL MATERIAL
QUEEN HAVE
PERFORMED LIVE

The following tracks were all performed by Queen during their fifteen years of touring. The songwriter and album on which the track originally appeared are listed beneath each song title.

A Kind Of Magic
(Roger Taylor) from *A Kind of Magic* 1986

Action This Day
(Roger Taylor) from *Hot Space* 1982

Another One Bites The Dust
(John Deacon) from *The Game* 1980

Back Chat
(John Deacon) from *Hot Space* 1982

Battle Theme
(Brian May) from *Flash Gordon* 1980

Bicycle Race
(Freddie Mercury) from *Jazz* 1978

Body Language
(Freddie Mercury) from *Hot Space* 1982

Bohemian Rhapsody
(Freddie Mercury) from *A Night At The Opera* 1975

Brighton Rock
(Brian May) from *Sheer Heart Attack* 1974

Bring Back That Leroy Brown
(Freddie Mercury) from *Sheer Heart Attack* 1974

Calling All Girls
(Roger Taylor) from *Hot Space* 1982

Crazy Little Thing Called Love
(Freddie Mercury) from *The Game* 1980

Death On Two Legs
(Freddie Mercury) from *A Night At The Opera*
1975

Doing All Right
(Brian May/Tim Staffel) from *Queen* 1973

Don't Stop Me Know
(Freddie Mercury) from *Jazz* 1978

Dragon Attack
(Brian May) from *The Game* 1980

Dreamer's Ball
(Brian May) from *Jazz* 1978

Fat Bottomed Girls
(Brian May) from *Jazz* 1978

Cloth access pass
(courtesy of Nicola
Demott)

Laminated backstage
access pass (courtesy
of Nicola Demott)

Father To Son
(Brian May) from *Queen II* 1974

Flash
(Brian May) from *Flash Gordon* 1980

Flick Of The Wrist
(Freddie Mercury) from *Sheer Heart Attack* 1974

Friends Will Be Friends
(Freddie Mercury & John Deacon) from *A Kind Of Magic*
1986

Get Down, Make Love
(Freddie Mercury) from *News Of The World* 1977

God Save The Queen
(Arr: Brian May) from *A Night At The Opera* 1975

Good Old Fashioned Lover Boy
(Freddie Mercury) from *A Day At The Races* 1976

Great King Rat
(Freddie Mercury) from *Queen* 1973

Hammer To Fall
(Brian May) from *The Works* 1984

Hangman
(unknown) possibly recorded but never released

The Hero
(Brian May) from *Flash Gordon* 1980

I Want To Break Free
(John Deacon) from *The Works* 1984

If You Can't Beat Them
(John Deacon) from *Jazz* 1978

Impromptu
(Queen) not on any studio album but on *Live At Wembley '86*

Improvisation
(Queen) not recorded and not on any album.

I'm In Love With My Car
(Roger Taylor) from *A Night At The Opera* 1975

In The Lap Of The Gods
(Freddie Mercury) from *Sheer Heart Attack* 1974

In The Lap Of The Gods...revisited
(Freddie Mercury) from *Sheer Heart Attack* 1974

Instrumental Inferno
(Queen) not recorded and not on any album

Is This The World We Created...?
(Freddie Mercury & Brian May) from *The Works* 1984

It's A Hard Life
(Freddie Mercury) from *The Works* 1984

It's Late
(Brian May) from *News Of The World* 1977

Keep Yourself Alive
(Brian May) from *Queen* 1973

Killer Queen
(Freddie Mercury) from *Sheer Heart Attack* 1974

Lazing On A Sunday Afternoon
(Freddie Mercury) from *A Night At The Opera* 1975

Let Me Entertain You
(Freddie Mercury) from *Jazz* 1978

Liar
(Freddie Mercury) from *Queen* 1973

Life Is Real
(Freddie Mercury) from *Hot Space* 1982

Love Of My Life
(Freddie Mercury) from *A Night At The Opera* 1975

Machines (Or Back To Humans)
(Brian May & Roger Taylor) from *The Works* 1984

The March Of The Black Queen
(Freddie Mercury) from *Queen II* 1974

The Millionaire Waltz
(Freddie Mercury) from *A Day At The Races* 1976

Modern Times Rock'n'Roll
(Roger Taylor) from *Queen II* 1974

Mustapha
(Freddie Mercury) from *Jazz* 1978

My Melanchony Blues
(Freddie Mercury) from *News Of The World* 1977

Need Your Loving Tonight
(John Deacon) from *The Game* 1980

Now I'm Here
(Brian May) from *Sheer Heart Attack* 1974

Ogre Battle
(Freddie Mercury) from *Queen II* 1974

One Vision
(Queen) from *A Kind Of Magic* 1986

Play The Game
(Freddie Mercury) from *The Game* 1980

Procession
(Brian May) from *Queen II* 1974

The Prophet's Song
(Brian May) from *A Night At The Opera* 1975

Put Out The Fire
(Brian May) from *Hot Space* 1982

Radio Ga Ga
(Roger Taylor) from *The Works* 1984

Rock In Rio Blues
(Queen) not recorded and not on any album

Rock It (Prime Jive)
(Roger Taylor) from *The Game* 1980

Save Me
(Brian May) from *The Game* 1980

See What A Fool I've Been
(Brian May) single B-side only, not on any album

Seven Seas Of Rhye
(Freddie Mercury) from *Queen II* 1974

Shag Out
(Unknown) part of *Hangman*, possibly recorded but never released

Sheer Heart Attack
(Roger Taylor) from *News Of The World* 1977

Somebody To Love
(Freddie Mercury) from *A Day At The Races* 1976

Son & Daughter
(Brian May) from *Queen* 1973

Spread Your Wings
(John Deacon) from *News Of The World* 1977

Staying Power
(Freddie Mercury) from *Hot Space* 1982

Access pass from 1978 (courtesy of Nicola Demott)

Stone Cold Crazy
(Queen) from *Sheer Heart Attack* 1974

Sweet Lady
(Brian May) from *A Night At The Opera* 1975

Tear It Up
(Brian May) from *The Works* 1984

Tie Your Mother Down
(Brian May) from *A Day At The Races* 1976

Teo Torriatte
(Brian May) from *A Day At The Races* 1976

'39
(Brian May) from *A Night At The Opera* 1975

Tokyo Blues
(Queen) not recorded and not on any album

Under Pressure
(Queen & David Bowie) from *Hot Space* 1982

We Are The Champions
(Freddie Mercury) from *News Of The World* 1977

We Will Rock You
(Brian May) from *News Of The World* 1977

White Man
(Brian May) from *A Day At The Races* 1976

White Queen (As It Began)
(Brian May) from *Queen II* 1974

Who Wants To Live Forever

(Brian May) from *A Kind Of Magic* 1986

You're My Best Friend

(John Deacon) from *A Night At The Opera* 1975

You Take My Breath Away

(Freddie Mercury) from *A Day At The Races* 1976

SONGS QUEEN HAVE PERFORMED LIVE BUT DID NOT WRITE

Bama Lama Bama Loo

Reached No.37 in July 1977 for Little Richard. Written by Penniman (Little Richard) and Collins.

Be Bop A Lula

Reached No.30 in July 1956 for Gene Vincent. Re-entered the charts on two more occasions. Written by G Vincent and T Davis.

Big Spender

Reached No.21 in October 1967 for Shirley Bassey. Written by C Coleman and D Fields.

Danny Boy

Written in 1913 by Fred Weatherly; original recording by Madame Schumann. Has become an Irish favourite.

Gimme Some Lovin'

Reached No.2 in November 1966 for Spencer Davis Group. Written by Steve Winwood, Muff Winwood and Spencer Davis.

Hello Mary Lou (Goodbye Heart)

Reached No.2 in June 1961 for Ricky Nelson. Written by Gene Pitney.

I'm A Man

Reached No.9 in January 1967 for Spencer Davis Group. Written by Steve Winwood and Jimmy Miller.

Imagine

Reached No.6 in November 1975 and No.1 in December 1980 for John Lennon. Written by John Lennon.

Immigrant Song

Recorded by Led Zeppelin for the *Led Zeppelin II* album in 1970. Not issued as a single. Written by Jimmy Page and Robert Plant.

Jailhouse Rock

Reached No.1 in January 1958 for Elvis Presley. Reissued in December 1971, September 1977, and February 1983. Written by Jerry Leiber and Mike Stoller.

Lucille

Reached No.10 in June 1957 for Little Richard. Written by Penniman (Little Richard) and Collins.

Mannish Boy

Reached No.51 in July 1988 for Muddy Waters. Written by Muddy Morganfield (Muddy Waters), E McDaniel and M London.

Mull Of Kintyre

Reached No.1 in 1977 for Wings. Written by Paul McCartney.

Not Fade Away

Reached No.3 in February 1964 for the Rolling Stones. Written by Buddy Holly.

Saturday Night's Alright For Fighting

Reached No.7 in July 1973 for Elton John. Written by Elton John and Bernie Taupin.

Shake, Rattle & Roll

Originally recorded by Big Joe Turner. Reached No.4 in December 1954 for Bill Haley And His Comets. Also covered by Elvis Presley, Buddy Holly, Carl Perkins, and Cliff Richard, amongst others. Written by Jessie (Charlie Calhoun) Stone.

Silent Night

Reached No.8 in December 1952 for Bing Crosby, No.47 in 1978 for The Dickies, and No.2 in 1988 for Bros. Originally a German hymn. Written by Joseph Mohr.

Stupid Cupid
Reached No.1 (B-side of Carolina Moon) in August 1958 for Connie Francis. Written by Sedaka and Greenfield.

Take Me Home
Essentially a Brian guitar ad-lib, it crops up on numerous bootleg compilations.

Tavaszi Szel Vizet Araszt
Hungarian folk song. Composer unknown.

Tutti Frutti
Reached No.29 in February 1957 for Little Richard. Also covered by Elvis Presley. Written by Lubin, LaBostrie and Penniman (Little Richard).

White Christmas
A hit for numerous artists between 1952 and 1985, most familiarly Bing Crosby - No.5 in December 1977. Reissued in December 1985 (No.69). Written by Irving Berlin.

Baby I Don't Care (You're So Square)
Originally recorded by Elvis Presley for his movie *Jailhouse Rock*. Reached No.12 in July 1961 for Buddy Holly. Written by Jerry Leiber and Mike Stoller.

ALBUM TRACKS QUEEN DID NOT PERFORM LIVE

QUEEN (1973)
My Fairy King
The Night Comes Down
Jesus

QUEEN II (1974)
Someday One Day
The Loser In The End
The Fairy Fellers Masterstroke
Nevermore
Funny How Love Is

SHEER HEART ATTACK (1974)
Tenement Funster
Lily Of The Valley
Dear Friends
Misfire
She Makes Me

A NIGHT AT THE OPERA (1975)
Seaside Rendezvous
Good Company

A DAY AT THE RACES (1976)
Long Away
You And I
Drowse

NEWS OF THE WORLD (1977)
All Dead, All Dead
Fight From The Inside
Sleeping On
The Sidewalk
Who Needs You

JAZZ (1978)
Jealousy
Dead On Time
In Only Seven Days
Fun It
Leaving Home Ain't Easy
More Of That Jazz

THE GAME (1980)
Don't Try Suicide
Sail Away Sweet Sister
Coming Soon

FLASH GORDON (Soundtrack 1980)
With the exception of 'Flash's Theme', 'The Battle Theme' and 'The Hero', no other material from the album was considered appropriate for inclusion in the live set – it was after all a movie soundtrack project.

HOT SPACE (1982)
Dancer
Las Parablas de Amor
Cool Cat

THE WORKS (1984)
Man On The Prowl
Machines
Keep Passing The Open Windows

A KIND OF MAGIC (1986)
One Year Of Love
Pain Is So Close To Pleasure
Gimme The Prize
Don't Lose Your Head
Princes Of The Universe

DATE OF DEBUT LIVE APPEARANCE IN EACH COUNTRY

ARGENTINA	28 February 1981
AUSTRIA	2 May 1978
AUSTRALIA	2 February 1974
BELGIUM	1 December 1974
BRAZIL	20 March 1981
CANADA	2 April 1975
DENMARK	12 May 1977
EIRE	22 November 1979
FINLAND	25 November 1974
FRANCE	23 April 1978
GERMANY	13 October 1973
HOLLAND	8 December 1974
HUNGARY	27 July 1986
ITALY	14 September 1984
JAPAN	19 April 1975
LUXEMBOURG	14 October 1973
MEXICO	9 October 1981
NEW ZEALAND	13 April 1985
NORWAY	12 April 1982
SOUTH AFRICA	5 October 1984
SPAIN	10 December 1974
SWEDEN	23 November 1974
SWITZERLAND	19 May 1977
UK	27 June 1970
USA	16 April 1974
VENEZUELA	25 September 1981
YUGOSLAVIA	6 February 1979

TELEVISION APPEARANCES

1973

13 November	Old Grey Whistle Test (BBC)

1974

21 February	Top Of The Pops (BBC)
14 March	Top Of The Pops (BBC)
28 March	Top Of The Pops (BBC)
17 October	Top Of The Pops (BBC)
31 October	Top Of The Pops (BBC)
14 November	Top Of The Pops (BBC)
28 November	Top Of The Pops (BBC)
25 December	45 (Granada)
26 December	Top Of The Pops (BBC)

1975

30 January	Top Of The Pops (BBC)
13 February	Top Of The Pops (BBC)
29 March	Los Angeles
18 April	Tokyo
24 December	Old Grey Whistle Test: Live Christmas Concert (BBC)

1976

20 March	Tokyo
10 April	Australia
14 December	Brian: Old Grey Whistle Test (BBC)
18 December	John: Multi Coloured Swap Shop (BBC)
21 December	ATV Today (ATV)
28 December	Old Grey Whistle Test: 75 Christmas Concert (BBC)

1977

16 June	Top Of The Pops (BBC)
30 June	Top Of The Pops (BBC)
21 July	Top Of The Pops (BBC)
10 September	Roger: Saturday Scene (ITV)
14 September	Roger: Marc (ITV)
24 September	Roger: Tiswas (ITV)
20 October	Britianna Award Ceremony (ITV)
– October	Roger: Italy
– October	Brian: Eire
– October	Brian: Ulster
29 October	Roger: Tiswas (ITV)
– November	Brian & Roger: Calendar Kids (Tyne Tees)
19 December	NBC Six O'Clock News (US)

1978

22 February	Brian: Pop Quest (Yorkshire TV)
6 May	Roger: Tiswas (ITV)
– May	Szene 78 (Germany)
31 October	Brian: Old Grey Whistle Test (BBC)

1979

10 February	Germany
10 April	Japan

18 April	Germany
21 November	Brian: Eire
24 November	Roger & John: Tiswas (ITV)
19 December	Tonight (BBC)

1980

18 February	Freddie: Kenny Everett Show (BBC)
25 November	France

1981

4 January	Kampuchea (ITV)
24 February	South America - Bandairantes TV
28 February	South America - Bandairantes TV
1 March	South America - Bandairantes TV
8 March	South America - Bandairantes TV
31 March	Roger: Old Grey Whistle Test (BBC)
30 April	Roger: Top Of The Pops (BBC)
– May	Roger: Dutch TV
– May	Roger: Germany
28 September	Brian & Roger & John: Venezuela TV

1982

28 May	Weekend (BBC): *Only live TV appearance of entire band*
10 June	Top Of The Pops (BBC)
24 June	Top Of The Pops (BBC)
– July	Brian: MTV
25 September	Saturday Nite Live (US)
– October	Roger: Pop Quiz (BBC)

1983

7 January	The Tube (C4) (Milton Keynes Concert)

7 August	John: Pop Quiz (BBC)
14 August	Roger: Pop Quiz (BBC)
20 August	Milton Keynes Concert (MTV)
19 November	Brian: Saturday Show (ITV)
24 December	Roger: Pop Quiz (BBC)

1984

– February	New York
9 February	Roger & John: Breakfast Time (BBC)
29 March	Roger & John: Japan
30 March	Roger & John: Seoul
2 April	Roger & John: Australia (Sydney)
5 April	Roger & John: Australia (Melbourne)
8 April	Roger & John: Los Angeles
19 June	Roger: Montreux Pop Festival (BBC)
23 June	John: Pop Quiz (BBC)
23 June	Roger: EarSay (C4)
23 August	Rock Around The Clock (BBC)
1 September	Brian & Roger: Saturday Starship (ITV)
24 December	Montreux Pop Festival (BBC)
24 December	Roger: Pop Quiz (BBC)

1985

12 January	Rock In Rio (Global TV, South America)
18 January	Friday People (BBC)
19 January	Rock In Rio (Global TV, South America)
15 April	Australia (Melbourne)
12 July	Good Morning Britain (ITV)
13 July	Live Aid (BBC)
17 July	Brian: Breakfast Time (BBC)

1986

12 April	Roger: Saturday Superstore (BBC)
– April	John: Dutch TV
17 June	Brian & Roger: Old Grey Whistle Test (BBC)

20 June	Freddie: Splash (ITV)
– June	Montreux Pop Festival (BBC)
5 July	Brian: EuroTube (C4)
9 July	Brian: Northern Life (Tyne Tees)
9 July	Brian: Look North (BBC)
14 July	Good Morning Britain (ITV)
29 July	Channel 4 News (C4)
2 August	RTE (Spain)
22 October	Brian: Good Morning Britain (ITV)
25 October	Queen: Real Magic (C4)

1987

2 January	Queen: Real Magic (C4)
– March	Freddie: Gegen Willi (Germany)
5 July	Roger: Network (C4)
17 July	Brian: Wogan (BBC)
21 July	Brian: Good Morning Britain (ITV)
29 September	Roger: Roxy (C4)
6 October	Roger: Roxy (C4)
17 October	Roger: No.73 (ITV)
12 November	Roger: Full Frontal (BBC)
5 December	Roger: Ibiza 92
17 December	Roger: Meltdown (ITV)

1988

1 February	Brian: Breakfast Time (BBC)
28 March	Roger: Breakfast Time (BBC)
2 June	Roger: Montreux Pop Festival (BBC)
5 June	Roger: Montreux Pop Festival (BBC)
16 June	Roger: Brainstorm (BBC)
23 June	Brian & John: Princes Trust 88 Rock Gala (C4)
21 October	Freddie: Off The Wall (ITV)
26 December	Freddie: Barcelona - A Musical Extravaganza (ITV)
31 December	Brian & Roger: Top Of The Pops 25th Anniversary (BBC)

1989

20 April	Brian: Daytime Live (BBC)
2 May	Brian & Roger: Good Morning Britain (ITV)
6 May	Ghost Train (ITV)
13 June	Brian: Good Morning Britain (ITV)
24 July	Brian: Pick Of The Week (ITV)
26 July	XPO (ITV)
30 August	Brian: Good Morning Britain (ITV)
1 October	Brian: Sunday Sunday (ITV)
23 October	Brian: Daytime Live (BBC)
26 December	Brian & John: Princes Trust 88 Rock Gala (C4)
31 December	Cilla's Goodbye To The Eighties (ITV)

1990

3 January	Magic Years (ITV)
5 January	Live In Budapest (ITV)
15 January	Techno (BBC)
18 January	Techno (BBC)
19 February	The Brits 1990 Awards Show (BBC)
7 May	Roger: Headbanger's Ball (MTV)
21 November	Brian: Thames Tonight (ITV)

1991

16 March	Brian: Comic Relief (BBC)
7 June	Brian: My Generation Special (VH1)
10 June	Brian: Torontos Much Music
- June	Toronto YTV + HTZ FM
17 August	Brian: Richard Digance Show (ITV)
25 November	Freddie Mercury – A Tribute (BBC)
27 November	Magic Years (ITV)
30 November	Queen: Real Magic (C4)
3 December	Brian & Roger: Good Morning Britain (ITV)

1992

5 January	Freddie Mercury – A Tribute (BBC)
11 January	Milton Keynes Live (C4)
12 February	Brian & Roger: Brit Awards 1992 (BBC)
29 March	Brian: Guitar Legends
30 March	Brian & Roger: MTV News
31 March	Brian & Roger: Good Morning Britain (ITV)
1 April	Brian & Roger: Good Morning Britain (ITV)
20 April	A Tribute To Freddie Mercury - AIDS Awareness (BBC)
2 May	Freddie Mercury - The Man & His Music (Super Channel)
7 September	Brian: Good Morning Britain (ITV)
10 September	Brian & Roger: MTV Awards
- September	Brian: Dutch TV
- September	Brian: Italy
2 October	Brian: This Morning (ITV)
16 October	Brian & Roger: MTV Awards Show (C4)
26 October	Brian: This Morning (ITV)
6 November	Brian: Argentina
19 November	Brian: Good Morning with Anne & Nick (BBC)
24 November	Brian: Good Morning Britain (ITV)
27 November	Brian: Good Morning Britain (ITV)
9 December	Brian: This Is Your Life (for Bert Weedon)
25 December	Freddie Mercury Tribute (BBC)

1993

23 January	Sound Of The Seventies (BBC)
17 February	Roger: The Brit Awards 93 (ITV)
5 April	Brian: The Tonight Show (NBC, USA)
20 April	Brian: In Conversation (for George Michael) (MTV)
4 June	Brian: GMTV Breakfast Show (ITV)
13 June	Brian: One To One (ITV)
13 June	Brian: The O Zone (BBC)
24 June	Brian: Top Of The Pops (BBC)
27 August	Brian: Pop Goes Summer (ITV)
28 August	Cue The Music (ITV)
25 September	Brian: Teratat (France)

1994

22 March	Roger: Czech Republic
11 May	Roger: News At Night (MTV)
12 May	Roger: News At Night (MTV)
22 May	Roger: The Great Music Experience (Japan)
26 May	Roger: Music Station (Japan)
30 May	Roger: The Great Music Experience (BBC)
25 June	Roger: Pop Quiz (BBC)
19 November	Brian: Videos Games & Movies (ITV)
19 November	Roger: German ZDF
25 November	Roger: This Morning (ITV)

1995

23 January	Roger: Maurizo Casteno Show (Italy)
17 April	Brian: Champion Children Awards Show (ITV)
24 October	Breakfast News (BBC)
4 December	The Queen Phenomenon (C4)
6 December	Live At Wembley (C4)

1996

20 February	Roger: The Brits 1996 Awards Show (ITV)
19 July	Brian: Top Of The Pops (with Rock Therapy) (BBC)

1997

– July	Brian: Top Ten (VH1)
– July	Roger: Top Ten (VH1)
– July	Brian: Queen Top Ten (VH1)
7 August	Brian: Airport (BBC)
15 August	Brian & Roger: Comet Awards (Germany)

14 September	Roger: An Audience with Elton John (ITV)
24 November	Brian: This Morning (ITV)
24 November	Brian & Roger: Sky News (Sky)
3 December	Brian: Review (VH1)
25 December	Brian: Queen Phenomenon introduced with a Christmas message (VH1)
28 December	Brian: The Rhythm of Life) (BBC)

1998

1 January	Brian & Roger: All Star Marathon (VH1)
9 January	Brian: Electric Circus (BBC)
10 January	Brian: Alive and Kicking (repeat of Electric Circus) (BBC)

RADIO APPEARANCES

1973

15 February	Sound Of The Seventies (BBC Radio 1)
13 August	Sound Of The Seventies (BBC Radio 1)
24 September	Sound Of The Seventies (BBC Radio 1)
20 October	In Concert (BBC Radio 1)
6 December	Sound Of The Seventies (BBC Radio 1)

1974

15 April	Sound Of The Seventies (BBC Radio 1)
4 November	Sound Of The Seventies (BBC Radio 1)

1975

– May	Roger: Maggie Norden Show (Capital)
– May	Freddie: Kenny Everett Show (Capital)
– December	Roger: Maggie Norden Show (Capital)
24 December	Live (BBC Radio 1)

1976

– January	Freddie: David Hamilton Show (Capital)
28 February	Live In Concert (BBC Radio 1)
21 August	Live In Concert (BBC Radio 1)
18 September	Live At Hyde Park (Capital)
9 October	BBC Radio 1
8 December	Roger: Dave Lee Travis (BBC Radio 1)
12 December	Freddie: Kenny Everett Be Bop Bonanza (Capital)
13 December	Roger: Newsbeat (BBC Radio 1)
13 December	Hullaballo (Capital)
18 December	Brian & Roger: Capital

1977

– March	Brian: Robin Valk (BRMB)
28 March	Brian: Capital
24 August	Roger: Newsbeat (BBC Radio 1)
– October	Freddie: Alan Freeman
16 November	Sound Of The Seventies (BBC Radio 1)
24 December	Queen Special Part 1 (BBC Radio 1)
29 December	Queen Special Part 2 (BBC Radio 1)

1979

26 June	Roger: Capital
27 June	Roger: Rock On (BBC Radio 1)
29 June	Roger: Roundtable (BBC Radio 1)
6 October	Freddie: Rock On (BBC Radio 1)

1980

18 January	Roger: Roundtable (BBC Radio 1)
17 April	Brian: Roundtable (BBC Radio 1)

1981

24 April	Roger: Roundtable (BBC Radio 1)

1982

– July	Mary Turner (US)
–	Brian: Guitar Greats (BBC Radio 1)

1984

25 March	Brian: Rock School (Capital)

1985

25 February	Brian: Capital (His own 2 hour show)
25 June	Freddie: Simon Bates (BBC Radio 1)

1986

4 March	Brian & Roger: Line One (US)
10 May	Roger: My Top Ten (BBC Radio 1)
25 October	Independent Radio Stations UK

1987

9 July	Brian: Newsbeat (BBC Radio 1)
1 October	Roger: Newsbeat (BBC Radio 1)

1988

13 May	Roger: Mike Smith (BBC Radio 1)
16 October	Night Rockin (BBC Radio 1)

1989

20 April	Brian: Simon Bates (BBC Radio 1)
29 May	Queen For An Hour (BBC Radio 1)
– June	Brian & Roger: US
24 November	Brian: US
27 December	75 Christmas Concert (BBC Radio 1)

1991

2 January	Brian: Simon Bates (BBC Radio 1)
21 January	Roger: Simon Bates (BBC Radio 1)
4 February	Brian & Roger: Rockline (US)
6 February	Brian: LA KLOS
28 May	Brian: Boston WBCN
29 May	Brian: Philadelphia WMMR
29 May	Brian: Providence WHJY
30 May	Brian: Atlanta WKLS
31 May	Brian: Dallas KTXQ
3 June	Brian: Seattle KXRY + KISW
4 June	Brian: San Francisco KRQR
4 June	Brian: San Jose KOME + KSJO
5 June	Brian: San Diego KGMG
25 November	Freddie: BBC Radio 1 Special
18 December	Brian: Simon Bates (BBC Radio 1)

1992

18 January	Brian: Guitar Legends (BBC Radio 1)
22 February	Brian: Guitar Legends (BBC Radio 1)
30 March	Brian & Roger: Simon Bates (BBC Radio 1)
31 March	Brian & Roger: Simon Bates (BBC Radio 1)
20 April	Freddie Mercury Tribute (BBC Radio 1)
28 May	Brian: Capital
26 August	Brian: Simon Bates (BBC Radio 1)
28 August	Brian: Capital
7 September	Brian: Capital
8 September	Brian: Simon Bates (BBC Radio 1)
4 October	Brian: Rockline (BBC Radio 1)
17 October	Brian: Johnny Walker (BBC Radio 1)
27 November	Brian: Independent Radio Stations UK

1993

14 June	Brian: Simon Bates (BBC Radio 1)
15 June	Brian: Tommy Vance (Virgin)
15 June	Brian: Capital
6 December	Brian: Capital

1994

22 February	Nicky Campbell (BBC Radio 1)
3 May	Roger: Newsbeat (BBC Radio 1)
14 May	Johnny Walker (BBC Radio 1)
26 June	Brian: Night Of 100 Guitars (BBC Radio 1)
7 September	Roger: Nicky Campbell (BBC Radio 1)
20 November	Roger: Virgin

1995

16 January–17 March	Brian: The Amazing Spiderman (BBC Radio 1: every weekday)
9 February	Roger: Newsbeat (BBC Radio 1)
23 October	Brian: BBC Radio 1
10 December	Queen: A Kind Of Magic (BBC Radio 1)

PART 4

COLLECTING QUEEN

(Andrew Putler/Redferns)

COLLECTING QUEEN

Queen, Elvis and the Beatles are probably the most collected and collectible entertainers in the history of popular music. Their songs and their personalities have captured the hearts of millions of fans throughout the world. Queen is probably more popular today than when Freddie was alive. Whenever a new product becomes available, devotees rush to purchase it because it reminds them of the years in which they were part of the Queen phenomenon.

MEMORABILIA FROM

1974 ONWARDS

It would take hundreds of pages to list all of the Queen-related items that have been created and sold. *A Record Collector* article by Greg Brooks is a tremendous source for memorabilia and collectibles. Not including records, the earliest Queen memorabilia became available in October 1974 through the then newly formed Queen Fan Club and offered members a number of exclusive items that included transfers featuring either the Queen name or picture, a black sticker with the Gold Crest and Queen name on, two different sized posters, one a 23″ x 16″ black and white shot of the band, and the other a 40″ x 28″ live colour shot. Queen headed writing paper in beige and brown was also made available at this time.

By the time the fan club became the 'Official International Queen Fan Club', its first official merchandise leaflet listed such items as a 'Queen At The Castle' T-Shirt and sweatshirt as well as a 'Queen At Hyde Park' T-Shirt. There were also 'Queen At The Castle' badges and a twenty-page full colour biography of the band. Further merchandise mailings introduced items specially designed including 'A Day At The Races' kite which featured a replica of the album cover art, and 'A Day At The Races' belt that was produced in navy blue with a pale blue printed design and adjustable buckle. There was also a lightweight 'fun jacket' made available which was white and featured a large 'Q' with race horses running out of it on the back, while the front carried the wording 'Queen – A Day At The Races', and came in three different sizes: small, medium, and large. Another popular item at the time was a pack of six postcards depicting the album cover of 'A Day At The Races' and the photo of the band that spread across the centre of the gatefold sleeve. By the time of the third merchandise mail-out, souvenir US tour programmes had been added, as well as the fan club's own *Queen Magazine* issued quarterly in the spring, summer, autumn, and winter. Not long after, the fan club took to selling the official tour merchandise such as T-shirts, sweatshirts, hooded tour sweatshirts, colour 2″ circular badges with the crest printed on a white background, and a full colour 38″ x 25″ poster featuring a photo of the band, as well as the European tour programmes.

A complete set of phonecards, one of the most collectible items of Queen memorabilia (courtesy of Steve and Sarah Moulding)

Since then, Queen-related memorabilia has increased with a wide range of items that have included: a selection of enamel badges featuring the Queen crest, a piano, Brian's 'Red Special' guitar and Roger's drums as well as a *Hot Space* badge. A selection of mugs have included a gold and silver Queen crest black mug; a *Magic* mug with the word 'Magic' appearing when hot liquid is added; a white *Innuendo* mug; and a *Made In Heaven* mug. Miscellaneous items have included a Queen crest CD clock; Queen logo CD clock; belt buckle and watch; a lion belt buckle; key rings; Queen crest pendant earrings; microphone design 'antique' gold cufflinks; *Made In Heaven* bevelled edged, deep etched mirror; Queen crest and band signatures bevelled, deep etched mirror; record bag; cotton tote bag; Queen flag; Freddie flag; *Innuendo* flag; tea towel; Parker rollerball pen; fibre tipped pens; counted cross stitch Queen logo kit; make it yourself counted cross stitch bookmark kit; fridge magnets; address book; calendars; Queen crest mouse mat; memo pad and holder; stationery sets; Freddie postcard set of seven different photographs; large picture prints of Freddie and Brian; fan club magazines and magazine binders.

The clothing merchandise is probably among the most popular, with printed T-Shirts and sweatshirts firmly the favourite and featuring extensive range of designs that have included: *A Day At The Races; The Miracle; Bohemian Rhapsody; A Kind Of Magic; Friends Will Be Friends*; A Magic Year; Live In New York; *Thank God It's Christmas; Innuendo* Man; Freddie in Q; International Fan Club; Brian Silhouette, Brian Tri Images; *The Great Pretender*; Brian's *Back To The Light; Somebody To Love; The Show Goes On; A Night At The Opera*; Freddie On Stage; *It's A Hard Life*; Queen Red Arrow; Queen At The Castle; Queen At Hyde Park; *The Works; Hot Space*; Queen Crest; *Going Slightly Mad*; 25th Anniversary; Roger Taylor *Happiness*; Back Stage Passes; *Sheer Heart Attack*; Heaven For Everyone; Freddie Statue Montreux; Freddie Mercury Tribute Concert; Freddie Mercury Photographic Exhibition; The Cross; The Cross *Life Changes*; The Cross *Cowboys And Indians*. Embroidered items have included Queen Crest sweatshirts in various colours; Queen crest denim shirt; black padded bomber jacket; red and blue ski hats; blue polo shirt; green melton jacket with or without suede sleeves; green waistcoat; denim jacket with leather trimmed collar; woollen scarf; black and white baseball cap; maroon scarf; a black tour jacket. A mixture of other merchandise has ranged from a *Flash Gordon* vest; washable foil-print T-shirts in various colours; *Made In Heaven* patch with gold lettering; Queen Crest tie; black cap; printed scarf in blue or red; *Made In Heaven* purple patch with gold lettering; navy and red waterproof coach jacket; *Made In Heaven* cotton shorts, navy tie with gold crest; *A Kind Of Magic* scarf; Queen baseball cap; tour jackets: *Innuendo* baseball cap; *Innuendo* Man black satin jacket; *Innuendo* patch; and Queen logo and crest bandanna.

Among the collectible magazines and programmes are A *Tribute To Freddie Mercury; Back To The Light – The Brian May Band* tour programme; *Beat Instrumental*, February 1975; *Fan Club Biography*, 1991; *Flash Gordon – The Official Poster Magazine; Freddie Mercury – A Pictorial Tribute; Guitar Heroes* magazine with Brian on cover, February 1983; International Musician and Recording World with Brian on cover, October 1981; *Live Aid Special* newspaper with Freddie on cover; *Queen Killers* magazine; *Rock n' Shows Collection* magazine, February 1993; Music Life Japanese magazine, 1977; Official Queen Calendars, 1994, 1995; *Official Fan Club Magazines*: autumn 1976, winter 1976, autumn 1977, winter 1977, spring 1978, summer 1978, autumn 1978, winter 1978, spring 1979, summer 1979, autumn 1979, spring 1980, Christmas 1982, spring 1983, summer 1983, autumn 1983, Christmas 1983, spring 1984, autumn 1984, winter 1984, spring 1985, autumn 1985, Christmas 1985, summer 1986, Christmas 1986, spring 1987, summer 1987, autumn 1987, spring 1988, summer 1988, autumn 1988, winter 1988, summer 1989, autumn 1989, Christmas 1989, spring 1990, summer 1990, autumn 1990, Christmas 1990, summer 1991, autumn 1991, November 1991 (Freddie Issue), winter/spring 1992,summer 1992, autumn 1992, winter 1992, spring 1993, summer 1993, winter 1993, spring 1994, summer 1994, autumn 1994, winter 1994, spring 1995, summer 1995, autumn 1995; *Queen – A Salute*, 1984.

QUEEN PHONE CARDS

Over the last five years, phonecard collecting has become one of the fastest-growing and biggest collecting phenomenons in the UK with Queen album cover phonecards placed firmly as one of the most popular. The first official Queen phonecard depicting the *Made In Heaven* album cover art was launched in 1992, and by 1997 a further five were made available that depicted *Innuendo; The Miracle; Live Magic; Live At Wembley 86* and *A Kind Of Magic*. The set of six were made available officially for the first time and were accompanied by their own colour folder and individually numbered up to the limited edition print number of 5000. The phonecards were made available only in the set of six and cost £60 per set (see under Leading Sellers of Queen Memorabilia).

LEADING SELLERS OF QUEEN MEMORABILIA

Official International Fan Club Merchandise:
Adrian Hopkins Promotions
31 Highfield Avenue
Oxford
England OX3 7LR

Phonecards:
P & J Promotions
Dept QRC
PO Box 23
Shoreham By Sea
Sussex BN43 5EG

OTHERS SELLERS OF QUEEN MEMORABILIA

This list is a guide to the secondhand record shops in and around London specialising in original vinyl issues, as well as other memorabilia such as posters, books, and other Queen related material.

LONDON – OXFORD STREET AREA

Sister Ray, Berwick Street
Very good selection of 7" and 12" singles, CDs, and other items. Best bet in London for collectors. Very knowledgeable about rare items, as is reflected in their prices, but also known for the occasional bargains.

Music and Video Exchange, Berwick Street
Good selection of Queen items although their best is at their Notting Hill Branch.

Reckless Records, Berwick Street
Worth visiting for the occasional rare item.

Mister CD, Berwick Street
Recommended for cheap and reasonable prices of regular CDs and the odd bootleg.

Selectadisc, Berwick Street
Recommended for the occasional reasonably priced second hand LP. Worth visiting.

Cheapo Cheapo Records, Rupert Street
A goldmine of cheaply priced seventies and eighties vinyl, books and videos. Very few obscure items. There is also a market stall right outside that has the occasional bargain.

Steve's Sounds, Little Newport Street
Recommended for cheaply priced CDs and books.

Vinyl Experience, Hanway Street
Queen items upstairs. Often stock 'wonderful' material – sometimes nothing. Their prices are ridiculously cheap so worth a browse.

Soho Records, Hanway Street
Recommended for good 1970s and 1980s vinyl with some Queen titles.

On The Beat, Hanway Street
Often have a good selection at okay prices. Entirely vinyl and books/magazines. Often closed for lunch!

Going For A Song, Charing Cross Road
Recommended for their cheaply priced CDs. Some Queen or related.

Market Stall on Goodge Place
Recommended for their cheaply priced CDs. Some Queen or related.

Virgin Megastore, Oxford Street, (next to Tottenham Court Road station, and also at Marble Arch station)
Recommended for new releases. Typical megastore.

HMV, Oxford Street (next to Bond Street station, also at Oxford Circus station, and Piccadilly Circus station)
Recommended for new releases. Typical megastore. Soundtracks downstairs (at Oxford Circus).

Tower Records (next to Piccadilly Circus station, also at High Street Kensington station and in Queensway shopping centre)
Good for albums, bad for singles, no vinyl.

LONDON – NOTTING HILL AREA

Music and Video Exchange, two branches on Notting Hill Gate – one with collectors' records upstairs where the selection is recommended, and two branches in Pembridge Road (near the Queen Productions Office) – one with bargain basement downstairs. Highly recommended for rare and obscure items in their bargain section.

Stalls on Kensington Market (Monday to Saturday)
Bootleg store in basement, another upstairs. Good range of posters and other items.

LONDON – CAMDEN TOWN AREA

Music and Video Exchange (another branch!)
Good bargain basement. Visit and browse recommended. Also visit the branch on Goldhawk Road, near Townhouse Studios.

Stalls on Camden Market (Thursday to Sunday)
Good bootleg and used record stall with wide selection of Queen 7" vinyl.

Stalls on Camden Lock Market (reported to be open seven days a week)
Two bootleg stalls.

Basement Shop in Stuckley Place (formerly 'Vinyl Crypt')
Has a good selection of bootlegs and official releases.

Beanos, Croydon (Telephone 0181 680 1202)
Supposedly the largest secondhand record shop in maybe the UK, certainly in Croydon. Recommended for their good selection of Queen and rarities.

Greenwich Market (Sundays)
Lots of stalls with records and CDs. Worth a visit.

OTHER AREAS OUTSIDE LONDON

Reddington's Rare Records
17 Cannon Street
Birmingham B2 5EN
Telephone 0121 643 2017

The Rock Box
Camberely
Surrey
Telephone 01276 26628

BOOKS ABOUT QUEEN

Queen – An Official Biography, Larry Pryce
(Star Books, 1976 – out of print)

Queen, George Tremlett
(Futura, 1976 – out of print)

Queen – The First Ten Years, Mike West
(Babylon, 1981 – withdrawn)
Queen – An Illustrated Biography, Judith Davis
(Proteus, 1981 – out of print)

Queen's Greatest Pix, Jacques Lowe
(Quartet, 1981 – out of print)

Gluttons For Punishment – The South America Tours 1981
(Peter Lubin, probably 1983 – out of print)

Queen – The First Twelve Years, Mike West
(Babylon, 1984 – out of print)

Queen – A Visual Documentary, Ken Dean
(Omnibus, 1986 – Updated 1991 & 1992)

Queen – A Magic Tour
(Sidgwick & Jackson, 1987)

Queen's Greatest Pix II, Richard Gray
(IMP, 1991)

Freddie Mercury – A Kind Of Magic, Ross Clarke
(Kingsfleet, 1991 – second edition 1992)

Queen – As It Began, Jacky Gunn & Jim Jenkins
(Pan, 1992)

Freddie Mercury – This Is The Real Life, David Evans & David Minns
(Brittania, 1992)

Queen In Their Own Words, Mick St Michael
(Omnibus, 1992)

These Are The Days Of Our Lives, Stephen Ryder
(Kingsfleet, 1992)

These Are The Days Of Our Lives (Updated Version), Stephen Ryder
(Castle Communications, 1993)

The Show Must Go On, Rick Sky
(Fontana, 1992)

The Freddie Mercury Tribute Concert
(IMP, 1993)

Queen Unseen, Peter Hogan & Michael Putlands
(UFO, 1993)

Queen And I – The Brian May Story, Laura Jackson
(Smith Gryphon, 1994)

The Complete Guide To The Music Of Queen, Peter K Hogan
(Omnibus 1994)

Queen, Mick St Michael
(Carlton Books, 1994)

Queen About Queen, A Rassadin
(Russian publication, 1994)

Mercury & Me, Jim Hutton
(Bloomsbury, 1994)

Rock Lives: The Ultimate Story – Freddie Mercury & Queen, Neville Marten & Jeffrey Hudson
(Castle Communications, 1995)

They Died Too Young – Freddie Mercury, Simon Boyce
(Parragon, 1995)

A Photographic Record 1969-1980, Mick Rock
(Century 22, 1995)

Queen – The Early Years, Mark Hodkinson
(Omnibus, 1995. Hardback)

Queen – The Full Picture, Denis O'Regan
(Bloomsbury, 1995)

Queen Live – A Concert Documentary, Greg Brooks
(Omnibus, 1995)

Freddie Mercury – More Of The Real Life, David Evans & David Minns
(Brittania, 1995)

Living On The Edge, David Bret
(Robson, 1996)

Freddie Mercury – The Definitive Biography, Lesley Ann Jones
(Hodder & Stoughton), 1997

Mercury – The King Of Queen, Laura Jackson
(Smith Gryphon, 1997)

The Great Pretender – The Hidden Life of Freddie Mercury , Januszcak Waldemar
(Harper Collins,1997)

Queen: The Secret Revealed – A Kind Of Magic, Melina Richmond
(Magic Publications, 1997)

BOOKS THAT MENTION QUEEN

The Guitar Greats, John Tobler & Stuart Grundy
(BBC Books, 1983 – out of print)

London's Rock Landmarks, Marcus Gray
(Omnibus, 1985)

Live Aid – The Concert, Peter Hillmore
(Sidgwick & Jackson, 1985)

In Session Tonight, Ken Garner
(BBC Books, 1993)

Rock Family Trees, Pete Frame
(Omnibus 1993)

The Grammys For The Record, Thomas O'Neil
(Penguin Books, 1993)

The King Edward VII Hospital Cookery Book, compiled by Marina Pearson
(Dovecote, 1993) (Includes breakfast recipe by Roger Taylor)

The Guinness Book Of Rock Stars, Dafydd Rees & Luke Crampton
(Guinness, 1989. Second edition, 1990. Third edition, 1994)

The Virgin Story Of Rock 'n' roll
(Virgin, 1995. Hardback)

Good Vibrations – A History Of Record Production, Mark Cunningham
(Castle Communications, 1996)

The Guinness Book Of Hit Singles, Paul Gambaccini, Tim Rice, Jonathan Rice
(GRR Publications, 1997)

The Guinness Book Of Hit Albums, Paul Gambacinni,
Tim Rice, Jonathan Rice
(GRR Publications, 1997)

Record Collector Rare Record Price Guide 1997/98
(Diamond Publishing Group, 1997)

FICTIONAL BOOKS RELATING TO QUEEN

Flash Gordon, Arthur Byron Cover
(New English Library, 1980 – out of print)

Highlander, Garry Douglas
(Grafton, 1986)

MISCELLANEOUS BOOKS

The Guitar – A Guide For Students And Teachers, edited
by Michael Stimpson. Chapter 10 by Brian May
(Oxford, 1988)

The Art Of Queen: The Eye
(Boxtree, 1997)

Secrets Of Queen: The Eye
(Boxtree, 1997)

The Novel Of Queen: The Eye, Paul Darrow
(Boxtree, 1997)

QUEEN CD-ROM GAME

In March 1998, Electronic Arts, a leading global interactive entertainment software company, released 'Queen: The Eye', the first action adventure game of its kind, inspired by the music and imagery of Queen. It was made available on PC CD-Rom as a five disc set exclusively through Electronic Arts in the UK and Europe in four different languages; English, German, French and Spanish, and combined cutting edge technology with over 120 minutes of Queen music as it had never been heard before.

The game was created by Destination Design on behalf of Queen Multimedia in partnership with EMI Music, and featured both original and remixed versions of many of Queen's best-known tracks, aligned to full motion-captured and real-time animation, combining state of the art technology with the spirit and music of Queen.

The unique game, Which took a twenty-two man team over two years to produce, set new standards of collaboration between interactive entertainment and world class music, and appealed particularly to core game players as well as Queen fans, and those interested in ground-breaking technology.

With over thirty creative characters, 'Queen: The Eye' is a superior action adventure role-playing game which stimulates the eyes, ears and mind of the player. Set in the not-too-distant future, the game takes place in a post apocalyptic era where the economies of the world have collapsed into a brutal global recession. The last surviving remnants of urban society are governed by the Eye, a piece of self-replicating biotechnology which strives to ensure that the very roots of creative thought and action are burned from the memory of humanity.

The player takes on the role of Dubroc, a hero in his own time, who must overcome numerous and complex obstacles in each of five major domains, whilst being stalked by the creature Death on Two Legs. The environments of the domains are The Arena, The Works, The Theatre, The Innuendo Zone and The Final Domain, and are inspired by the visual imagery and iconography associated with the key Queen albums. Each Domain has its secrets, cerebral puzzles and physical dangers, that test the player to the maximum, while Queen's music provides a rich audio landscape. The game incorporates fifty-four of the band's tracks as they have never before been heard, in CD-quality stereo with a total of 120 minutes of music, some specially remixed for the game.

The release of the game marked one of the few collaborations between musicians and computer entertainment publishers, and was the first to succeed in playing to the strengths of both media, bringing together a truly committed interactive games development team, the audio and visual experience of an innovative world class rock group, and EA's expertise as the world's leading software entertainment publisher and distributor. The product set new standards in computer gaming just as 'Bohemian Rhapsody' had set pioneering standards in music video production. 'Queen The Eye' was the first music game of it's kind in which the band again led the market in terms of innovation and setting new industry milestones.

(Mick Rock/Redferns)

PART 5
MISCELLANEA

.(Jim Jenkins)

AWARDS

In 1958 the RIAA (Recording Industry Association of America) began certifying million-sellers and awarding gold discs for albums that had sold òne million dollars' worth of albums in value (wholesale price). This was based on one third of the list price, a figure that represented much less than one million actual units sold. This qualifying figure was changed in 1975 to half a million and also represented singles. It was a long time before Britain followed and devised its own scheme. In the mid seventies the BPI (British Phonographic Institute) were given the task of the certification and award of platinum, gold and silver discs. Besides the BPI awards, many record companies would present their own in-house awards. These often went, not only to the artists, but also to producers, engineers and companies.

Below are the qualifying figures for awards from the BPI (as at December 1993):

SINGLES (up to December 1988)
Silver	250,000
Gold	500,000
Platinum	1,000,000

SINGLES (after January 1989)
Silver	200,000
Gold	400,000
Platinum	600,000

ALBUMS
Silver	60,000
Gold	100,000
Platinum	300,000

The following list, correct as at August 1997, gives details of the awards made in the UK and US. For the UK details are also given of the date the particular release was certified for the award:

UK Platinum Discs – Albums
Greatest Hits (January 1992) – 11 x Platinum
Greatest Hits II (June 1992) – 5 x Platinum
Made In Heaven (January 1996) – 3 x Platinum
A Night At The Opera (January 1976)
Innuendo (March 1991)
A Kind Of Magic (January 1987)
Live Magic (January 1987)
Sheer Heart Attack (January 1982)
The Miracle (May 1989)
The Works (May 1984)
The Freddie Mercury Album (October 1993) – 2 x
    Platinum

UK Gold Discs – Albums
A Day At The Races (January 1976)
Flash Gordon (January 1981)
Hot Space (January 1982)
Jazz (January 1978)
Live At Wembley '86 (June 1992)
Live Killers (January 1979)
News Of The World (January 1977)
Queen (January 1976)
Queen II (January 1975)

The Game (January 1980)
Back To The Light (October 1992)
Mr Bad Guy (May 1985)

UK Silver Discs – Albums
The Game (January 1980)
Barcelona (November 1988)

UK Platinum Discs – Singles
Bohemian Rhapsody (January 1976)
Bohemian Rhapsody/These Are The Days Of Our Lives
  (December 1991)

UK Gold Discs – Singles
Crazy Little Thing Called Love (December 1979)
We Are The Champions (November 1977)
Living On My Own (December 1993)

UK Silver Discs – Singles
Don't Stop Me Know (May 1979)
Fat Bottomed Girls/Bicycle Race (November
  1978)
Flash (January 1981)
Heaven For Everyone (November 1995)
I Want It All (May 1989)
I Want To Break Free (May 1984)
Innuendo (April 1991)
Killer Queen (November 1974)
Radio Ga Ga (February 1984)
We Are The Champions (October 1977)
Too Much Love Will Kill You (October 1992)

US Platinum Discs – Albums
News Of The World
Jazz
The Game
Greatest Hits
Classic Queen

US Gold Discs – Albums
Queen
Queen II
Sheer Heart Attack
A Night At The Opera
A Day At The Races

Live Killers
Flash Gordon
Hot Space
The Works
The Miracle
Innuendo
Live At Wembley

As well as the numerous platinum, gold and silver discs awarded by the BPI in the UK and the RIAA in America, Queen have also received many other awards. The following is a detailed list of their Grammy nominations, Brit, Ivor Novello, various music press and other miscellaneous awards.

Grammy Nominations
1976
Broadcast from the Hollywood Palladium on 19
  February 1977
Best Pop Vocal Performance By A Duo, Group Or
  Chorus: 'Bohemian Rhapsody'

1980
Broadcast from Radio City Music Hall, New York on 25
  February 1981
Best Rock Performance By A Duo Or With Vocal:
  'Another One Bites The Dust'

Ivor Novello Awards
1976
Held at the Dorchester Hotel, London on 24 May 1976
Best Selling British Record: 'Bohemian Rhapsody'

1987
Held at the Grosvenor House Hotel, London on 15 April
  1987
Outstanding Contribution To British Music

1992
Held at the Grosvenor House Hotel, London on 15 April
  1992
Best Selling A-Side: 'Bohemian Rhapsody'
Best Theme From A TV/Radio Commercial: 'Driven By
  You'

British Record Industry Britannia Awards
1977
Held At Wembley Conference Centre on 18 October 1977

Best British Pop Single: 'Bohemian Rhapsody' (This tied with Procol Harum's 'Whiter Shade Of Pale')

Brit Awards
1990
Held At The Dominion Theatre, London on 18 February 1990

Outstanding Contribution To British Music

1992
Held At The Hammersmith Odeon on 12 February 1992

Best British Single: 'Bohemian Rhapsody'

Outstanding Contribution To British Music Special Award (posthumously): Freddie Mercury

Record Mirror & Disc Annual Polls
1976
World's Best Group (1st)

Best Single (1st): 'Bohemian Rhapsody'

World's Best Singer (6th): Freddie Mercury

Best British Singer (5th): Freddie Mercury

Best British Songwriter (4th): Freddie Mercury

Best British Group (1st)

World's Best Songwriter (5th): Freddie Mercury

Best British Musician (4th): Brian May

World's Best Musician (4th) Brian May

Best Album (6th): *A Night At The Opera*

American Music Awards
1981
Held at the ABC-TV Studios in Burbank, California on 30 January

Favourite Single in the Pop/Rock Category: 'Another One Bites The Dust'

Nordoff-Robbins Music Therapy
28 June 1984
Silver Clef Award

MTV Awards
1992
Held at Pauley Pavilion, Los Angeles on 9 September

Best Video From A Film Category: 'Bohemian Rhapsody'

QUEEN RELATED SIGHTS

1. Birthplaces:

Brian:	Gloucester House Nursing Home, Hampton, Middlesex.
Roger:	West London and Kings Lynn Hospital, Kings Lynn, Norfolk.
John:	St Francis Hospital, London Road at Leicester.
Freddie:	Government Hospital, Zanzibar.

2. Schools:

Brian:	Cardinal Road Infants School, Feltham, Middlesex. Hanworth Road Primary School, Feltham, Middlesex. Hampton Grammar School, Hanworth Road, Hampton.
John:	Lindon Junior School, Evington, Leicestershire. Langmoor Junior School, Leicester. Gartree High School, Leicester. Oadby Beauchamp School, Oadby, Leicester.
Roger:	Gaywood Primary School, Kings Lynn, Norfolk. Bosvigo School, Truro, Cornwall. Truro Cathedral School, Truro, Cornwall. Truro Public School, Truro, Cornwall.

Freddie's door, decorated with fans' tributes (courtesy of Steve and Sarah Moulding)

Freddie: Zanzibar Missionary School.
St Peter's School, Panchgani, near
Bombay.
Zanzibar St Joseph's Convent
School
Isleworth School, Ridgeway Road,
Isleworth, Middlesex.

3. Colleges:

Brian: **Imperial College:**
– Main Buildings, Imperial College
Road, London SW7.
– Physics Department, Prince
Consort Road, London SW7.
– Astrophysics group (now moved),
Prince's Gardens, London SW7.
– Student Union Buildings, Prince
Consort Road, London SW7,

John: **Chelsea College (now part of
Kings College):**
– Main Buildings, Manresa Road,
London SW3 (now closed)
– Electronics Department – Pulton
Place (now disused – near Fulham
Broadway)

Roger: **London Hospital Medical College:**
– Main Buildings – Turner Street,
London E1
– Dental Institute – just off Turner
Street, London E1

**North East London Polytechnic
(now East London University):**
– Main Buildings, Barking
Campus,Longbridge Road,
Dagenham.
– Stratford Campus, Romford
Road, Stratford E15.

Freddie: **Ealing College (now part of West
London University):**
– Main Buildings, St Mary's Road,

Ealing, London W5 (junction with
Warwick Road).
– 'Freddie's Bar' – inside main
buildings.

4. London concert locations where Queen performed:

Hammersmith Odeon (now Labatt's Apollo), Queen
  Caroline Street W6
Rainbow (disused), Seven Sisters Road, Finsbury
  Park N4
Earls Court, Warwick Road SW5
Hyde Park, W2 (presumably the concert was near the
  Serpentine)
Lyceum Ballroom (disused), Catherine Street, WC2
  (near Aldwych)
Tiffany's Purley (name changed), 100ish Brighton Road,
  Purley
Tottenham Mayfair (name changed), next to library on
  High Road N17
Lewisham Odeon (demolished 1992) Loampit Vale SE13
Alexandra Palace, Alexandra Park, Wood Green N10
Pheasantry (now a restaurant), 152 Kings Road SW3
Wembley Arena and Stadium, Empire Way, Wembley
Brixton Academy, 211 Stockwell Road SW9
Royal Albert Hall, Kensington Gore SW7
Marquee (new one), 105 Charing Cross Road WC2 (old
  one at 90 Wardour Street W1 demolished in 1990)
Town And Country Club (name changed), 9 Highgate
  Road NW5
Hammersmith Palais, 242 Shepherds Bush Road W6
Astoria, 157 Charing Cross Road WC2
Dominion, Tottenham Court Road W1 (at Oxford Street
  end)
Empire, Shepherds Bush Green W12
Golders Green Hippodrome (disused), North End Road
  NW11

5. Studio locations where Queen recorded:

De Lane Lea (name changed), Engineers Way,
  Wembley, Middlesex
Trident (name changed), 17 St Anne's Court,
  London W1

Townhouse, Junction of Goldhawk Road/Godolphin Road, London W12

Sarm West, 8 Basing Street, London W11

Olympic, 117 Church Road, Barnes, London SW13

Maison Rouge, 2 Wansdown Place, London SW6

Lansdowne, Lansdowne House, Lansdowne Road, London W11

Sarm East, 9 Osborn Street, London E1

Roundhouse, 100 Chalk Farm Road, London NW1

Wessex, 106 Highbury New Park, London N5

Air, 214 Oxford Street, London W1

Advision, 23 Gosfield Street, London W1

Abbey Road, 3 Abbey Road, St Johns Wood, London NW8

Utopia, 7 Chalcot Road, London NW1

Metropolis, Chiswick High Road, London W4 (next to bus station)

Cosford Mill, (in the back garden of Roger's house)

Allerton Hill, (in the back garden of Brian's house)

Rockfield, Monmouth, South Wales

Manor, Kidlington, Nr Oxford

Real World (owned by Peter Gabriel), Box, Nr Bath

Mountain (owned by Queen), Rue de Theatre 8, Montreux, Switzerland

Musicland, Arabellastrabe, Munchen, Germany

Record Plant, Los Angeles, USA

Sterling, New York, USA

Mediteraneo, Ibiza, Spain

Super Bear, Nice, France

6. Previous London locations of fan club:

17 St Anne's Court W1

40 South Audley Street W1

5 Camden Street W8

13 Cornwall Terrace NW1

46 Pembridge Road W11

16A High Street, Barnes SW13

7. London locations of Queen Productions:

Fairfax House, Fulwood Place WC1 (registered office)

14 William Road NW1 (Warehouse)

46 Pembridge Road W11

8. Other places of interest in and around London:

Ferry Road, Barnes SW13 where the band had a flat in the early days.

36 Sinclair Road W14 where the band had a flat in the early days.

9 or 10ish Queens Gate SW7 where Brian used to live.

54 Suffolk Road, Barnes SW13 where Brian used to live.

100 Holland Road W14 were Freddie used to live.

75 Holland Road W14 where Freddie was rumoured to live.

18ish Stafford Terrace W8 where Freddie used to live.

Kensington Pub, Russell Gardens W8 was the favourite band pub in the early days.

St Osmunds Church, Castelnau, Barnes SW13 where Brian was married.

Carmelite Church, Kensington Church Street where John was married.

Kensington Registry Office, Old Town Hall, Kings Road SW3 where Roger was married.

Kensington Market, 49 Kensington High Street W8 where Roger and Freddie ran their market stall.

Cafe Royal, 68 Regent Street W1 where presentation of first ever silver disc for the *Queen II* album took place.

Roof Garden, 99 Kensington High Street, W8 (entrance Derry Street) where the 'Magic' tour party was held.

Xenon Club, 195 Piccadilly, W1 which was a favourite haunt of Freddie's.

Nomis Studios, Sinclair Road, W14 where band held rehearsals.

Shaw Theatre, 100 Euston Road, NW1 where 'Live Aid' rehearsals were held.

Royal Opera House – Floral Street/Bow Street, WC2 where 'Barcelona' launch was held.

Kempton Park, Staines Road, Sunbury where *A Day At The Races* album launch was held.

New London Theatre, Parker Street, WC2 where 'We Are The Champions' video was filmed.

Pinewood Studios, Ivor Heath, Buckinghamshire where 'Barcelona' video shoot took place.

Wimbledon Stadium, Plough Lane, SW19 where 'Bicycle Race' video shoot was filmed.

Elstree Studios, Shenley Road, Borehamwood where 'I Want It All' video was shot.

The building used at the start of 'A Kind Of Magic' video is situated underneath Charing Cross Station.

Metropolis Studios was used for the beginning of the 'Innuendo' video.

9. Other places of interest outside the UK:

Hilton Hotel, Tivolistrasse, Munich where Freddie wrote 'Crazy Little Thing Called Love'.

Sugar Shack Night Club, Munchen is mentioned in 'Dragon Attack'.

Ritz Hotel, Barcelona where Freddie met Montserrat.

Nepstadion, Budapest where the *Live In Budapest* video was filmed.

Highlander places of interest:

Eilean Donan Castle on the main A87 road to the Isle of Skye Ferry.

The village of Glenfinnan on the shores of Loch Shiel on the main A830 road west of Fort William, though it wasn't there in 1518!

Silvercup Building, New York.

THE MERCURY PHOENIX TRUST

When Freddie died of AIDS related causes in London on 24 November 1991, the remaining members of Queen and Jim Beach, their manager, took the decision to raise money and awareness for AIDS in his memory. The Mercury Phoenix Trust was founded to distribute the money raised by the Freddie Mercury Tribute Concert for AIDS Awareness, which took place on 20 April 1992.

Since 1992 Queen have been responsible for donating more than £4 million to the fight against the AIDS crisis to over 100 different charities in countries in Europe, Africa, Asia and America.

Collaboration has been realised with groups as far removed as the World Health Organisation to grass-root organisations run by voluntary workers in Uganda, Kenya, and India. The Trust is supporting the UK-based skin disease charity START, with special research into itchy folliculitis, and is working with the Royal Marsden Hospital in London on research into Kaposi's sarcoma. Medical supplies have been shipped to Mother Teresa's Sisters of Charity in Calcutta. Also the Trust works with various fan-based charities around the world in co-ordinating their local AIDS fund-raising activities.

The release of the George Michael/Lisa Stansfield/ Queen mini album Five Live was in 1993. This mini album, and the single 'Somebody To Love' were released worldwide in aid of the Trust. They reached the top ten in 31 countries worldwide and the single reached number one in the UK on 22 April.

In the UK the first National Street Collection commenced in November 1994. This street collection was fan-initiated and has now become an annual event.

With the release of *Made In Heaven*, the final Queen album featuring Freddie, in November 1995, the Trust benefited from a donation by Queen and their respective record companies of all profits from the album worldwide on World AIDS Day, 1 December 1995. November 1996 saw the launching of a Freddie Mercury Photographic Exhibition in aid of the Trust, which is still touring the world.

With initiatives such as these the Trust continues its fundraising activities and intends to keep AIDS awareness in the forefront, through the use of Freddie's name, magic and music.

THE FREDDIE MERCURY PHOTOGRAPHIC EXHIBITION

On the fifth anniversary of Freddie's death, and just two months after he would have reached the age of 50, London's Royal Albert Hall joined in paying tribute to the extraordinary life and talent of Freddie. On 22 November 1996 a free public exhibition opened called 'The Freddie Mercury Photographic Exhibition', which marked the first public showing of a collection of over 100 photographs telling Freddie's remarkable story.

Drawn from both private and public collections, the images dated from Freddie's childhood days in Zanzibar, through his career with Queen, to the very last photo he allowed to be taken. Compiled with the support of Freddie's family and many friends, the exhibition contained a number of photographs never previously seen in public.

As well as the photo images, the exhibition also displayed the original 3' 6" clay model by sculptor Irena Sedlecka of the Freddie Mercury statue prepared for the full nine foot version that was erected in Montreux in late 1996.

The exhibition was sponsored by EMI Music, and raised funds for the Mercury Phoenix Trust, the AIDS support organisation established in memory of Freddie which to date has contributed more than £4 million to AIDS work worldwide.

Following the display at the Royal Albert Hall, the exhibition transferred to the National Theatre in Paris, France for its opening on 17 January 1997 for a two-week season before moving to the Cologne Philharmonie in Germany where it was seen throughout the month of February.

The exhibition continues to tour the world

FAN CLUB INDEX

UK – Official International Queen Fan Club

The Old Bakehouse
16A Barnes High Street
London SW13 9LW
Telephone on (+44) 0181 392 2800 between
10.30am and 5pm, or fax on (+44) 0181 878 6900, or if calling outside these hours, an answering machine is in operation.

Annual membership fees for the fan club vary depending on where you live. For the United Kingdom and Irish Republic, the cost is £11. For USA it's $28, while Europe is £13, and the rest of the world is £15. Payment is accepted in UK personal cheques or postal orders; Sterling Eurocheques; American personal cheques; and International Money Orders (UK sterling or US dollars only). Funds should be made payable to 'Queen Fan Club'.

Personal callers visiting the fan club should note the following directions of how to get there...There are at least a hundred 'High Streets' in London, so don't look in the *A to Z*! The one where the fan club is situated is located in Barnes. The best way to get there is to go over Hammersmith Bridge, down a road named 'Castelnau', turn right into 'Church Road', which then becomes 'High Street'. The 9A bus from Hammersmith Bus Station will drop you right outside the fan club if you ask for the stop after Barnes Pond. The fan club building is at the back of an alleyway between two rows of shops. (Look out for the gate with a phoenix sign at the front of the alleyway.)

Other UK Fanzines and Fan Clubs (Not Official)

Princes Of The Universe

E-mail Neil French at ndpotu@aol.com for details of his quarterly fanzine with reviews, information and other goodies.

A Kind Of Magic

32 Lancaster Avenue
Horwich
Bolton
Lancashire BL6 6ND

E-mail Denise Silcock at AKindOfMagic@BTInternet.com for details of this fund-raising organisation established in 1992. It organises Freddie parties twice a year and a Red Ribbon Making Day in November. Publishes *Winged Messenger* magazine. It also runs a fan club called Mr Fahrenheit's, with monthly get-togethers.

Other European Fan Clubs (Not Official)

Dutch Queen Fan Club

Hannie and Anja
Bernweg 181
3137 ND Vlaardingen
Holland
Telephone on 010 474 9879 (Thursday 7.30pm to 9pm). Answering machine outside these hours, or E-mail queenfanclubholland@bigfoot.com

Annual membership fees are 41,50 Dutch Guilders payable by Eurocheque, International Money Order or by bank transfer to Postbank 2313172.

German Queen Fan Club

Postfach 1642
23836 Bad Oldesloe
Germany

Annual membership fees includes four 28-page magazines in German and costs DM 35 for Germany, while Europe is DM 40, and elsewhere is DM 50. For a sample magazine send two International Reply Coupons and a self-addressed A5 envelope. Membership also includes an answering machine news information line number.

French Queen Fan Club 'Noblesse Oblige'

Philippe Nagot
43 Rue du Chateau-Fiat
67500 Haguenau
France
Annual membership fees are 60 French Francs. More details are available from Philippe by sending an International Reply Coupon or by E-mail from Andy Fitzgerald.

Hungarian Queen Fan Club

Magdolna Munkasci
Hungarian Queen Fan Club
Petofi Csarnok
Varosliget
Budapest
Hungary

Italian Queen Fan Club 'We Will Rock You'

Via Roma 1
23010 Berbbenno di Valtellina (SONDRIO)
Italy

E-mail: pontix@mbox.vol.it
WWW: http://www.vol.it/wwry

Barcelona Queen Fan Club

Apartat de Correus 5154
08080 Barcelona
Catalonia
Spain

E-mail: si04438@els.url.ed
WWW: http://www.els.url.es/-si04438/queen

Brazil Queen Club Of Fans

Londrina
Parana
Brazil
Tel: (043) 334-4739

E-mail: dcodato@sercomtel.com.br

A selection of fan club magazines and pamphlet advertising the 1998 convention at Prestatyn Sands (courtesy of Tony Durrant)